Social Realism, Knowledge
Sociology of Education

Also available from Continuum

Education, Policy and Social Justice, James Avis

Language, Knowledge and Pedagogy, Frances Christie and J.R. Martin

Sociology of Educating 5th Edition, Roland Meighan, Clive Harber, Len Barton, Iram Siraj-Blatchford and Stephen Walker

Sociology of Knowledge and Education, Rob Moore

Subject Knowledge and Teacher Education, Viv Ellis

Towards the Sociology of Truth, Rob Moore

Social Realism, Knowledge and the Sociology of Education

Coalitions of the Mind

Edited by

Karl Maton
and
Rob Moore

continuum

Continuum International Publishing Group

The Tower Building
11 York Road
London SE1 7NX

80 Maiden Lane
Suite 704
New York NY 10038

www.continuumbooks.com

Chapters 1, 2, 3, 4, 5 were originally published by Taylor & Francis
Chapter 6 was originally published by SAGE

Every effort has been made to trace copyright holders and we apologize in advance for any unintentional omission. We would be pleased to insert the appropriate acknowledgement in any subsequent edition.

British Library Cataloguing-in-Publication Data
A catalogue record for this book is available from the British Library.

ISBN: 9781441138507

Library of Congress Cataloging-in-Publication Data
Social realism, knowledge and the sociology of education: coalitions of
the mind/edited by Karl Maton and Rob Moore.
    p. cm.
Includes bibliographical references.
ISBN: 978-1-4411-3850-7
1. Educational sociology. 2. Education–Curricula. 3. Constructivism
(Education) I. Maton, Karl. II. Moore, Rob, 1946- III. Title.

LC191.S6565 2010
306.43–dc22   2009014865

Typeset by Newgen Imaging Systems Pvt Ltd, Chennai, India

Contents

List of Contributors

John Beck is a Fellow of Homerton College, Cambridge University, and formerly senior lecturer in the Faculty of Education.

Karl Maton is Senior Lecturer in Sociology at the Faculty of Arts, University of Sydney, Australia.

Rob Moore is a Fellow of Homerton College, Cambridge University, and is senior lecturer in the Faculty of Education.

Johan Muller is Professor of Education and Director of the Graduate School of Humanities, University of Cape Town.

Leesa Wheelahan is a Senior Lecturer in the School of Vocational, Technology and Arts Education at Griffith University, Australia.

Michael Young is Professor of Education at the Institute of Education, University of London and in the Department of Education at the University of Bath.

Introduction

A Coalition of Minds

Karl Maton
University of Sydney

Rob Moore
Cambridge University

> . . . *thinking consists in making 'coalitions of the mind,' internalised from social networks, motivated by the energies of social interactions.*
>
> *(Collins, 2000, p. 7)*

This book offers a fresh way of thinking about education that provides knowledge about knowledge. It comprises key papers by leading authors of 'social realism' in the sociology of education, a broad school of thought achieving prominence across a range of national contexts, including Australia, France, Singapore, South Africa and the United Kingdom. This school offers an alternative to approaches that have dominated educational thinking in recent decades, such as constructivism, post-structuralism and postmodernism. Though the relativizing consequences of these approaches have been increasingly questioned from a variety of directions, social realism goes further than criticism. It offers constructive concepts and ideas for moving beyond entrenched positions in both theoretical understanding and empirical research. In doing so, this emerging approach provides a way out of an impasse that has debilitated sociological thinking about knowledge and education for decades.

This impasse reflects the peculiar difficulty the sociologies of knowledge and education have with the very idea of knowledge. The basis of this problem is a longstanding belief in these fields in an 'epistemological dilemma' (Alexander 1995), an assumption that the only choice is between positivist absolutism or constructivist relativism (see Chapter 1 of this volume). This constructs a false dichotomy between, on the one hand, the belief that knowledge must be decontextualized, value-free, detached and 'objective' and, on the other hand, the idea that knowledge is socially constructed within particular cultural and historical conditions (and necessarily entwined with issues of interest and power). Faced with this 'either/or', the sociologies of knowledge and education, since at least the early 1970s, have focused more on unmasking and debunking knowledge claims than on exploring the social grounds for objectivity in knowledge or the autonomy of knowledge-producing fields. Indeed, the very possibility of such objectivity or autonomy is often denied. As the chapters in this collection highlight, this false dichotomy has deleterious implications for understanding education, for policy and practice, and for social justice.

A major concern for the social realist school is to replace this 'either/or' with a refined and developed 'both/and'. This alternative view recognizes, *contra* positivism, the inescapably social character of knowledge but, *contra* constructivism, does not take this to inevitably entail relativism. In other words, rational objectivity in knowledge is acknowledged as itself a fact (we do actually have knowledge) but it is also recognized as a *social* phenomenon (it is something that people do in socio-historical contexts) and it is *fallible* rather than absolute or merely relative. This allows knowledge to be seen in itself, not merely as a reflection of either some essential truth or social power but as something in its own right, whose different forms have effects for intellectual and educational practices. This can seem an obvious point to make: knowledge is the very basis of education as a social field of practice; it is the production, recontextualization, teaching and learning of *knowledge* that makes education a distinct field. However, ironically, knowledge as an object is missing from approaches that have dominated the sociology of education. Having a *theory* of knowledge is not a necessary condition for having knowledge itself; as Ernest Gellner (1992a) argued, we *know* we have knowledge but we are not always quite sure how. Nonetheless, to understand education we need to understand knowledge. Social realism puts *knowledge as an object* centre-stage in thinking about education. This is not to fetishize or view knowledge as the *only* object but rather to recover and reclaim this crucial yet missing dimension of education. Doing so raises questions of the characteristics that enable knowledge to be created and developed over time, the modes of this creation and development, the forms this knowledge takes, and their effects for policies and practices. These form the principal concerns of the chapters brought together in this collection. So, what are the principal ideas associated with social realist approaches? Rather than précis arguments addressed in greater detail throughout the book, here we shall sketch some of the broad themes that underlie these chapters and their implications for knowledge and education.

Social Realism, Knowledge and Education

One way of understanding the shift in perspective that brings knowledge as an object into view is provided by a distinction Williams (2002) makes between 'truth' and 'truthfulness'. 'Truth' is based on the notion that some knowledge claims can be considered more epistemologically powerful than others. That is not to say such knowledge is unchanging, eternal Truth, but rather there are rational grounds for comparing the relative merits of knowledge claims in terms of their explanatory power. Williams describes 'truthfulness' as a 'reflex against deceptiveness' and a 'pervasive suspiciousness, a readiness against being fooled, an eagerness to see through appearances to the real structures and motives that lie behind them' (2002, p. 1). At its most general, such a reflex is part of the academic mindset – the desire to get beneath appearances. However, this commitment can become realized in ways that obscure the very thing being studied.

In the sociology of education the reflex to truthfulness has often been associated with debunking knowledge claims and the 'critical' deconstruction of the 'dominant' or 'hegemonic' curriculum. Typically, the aim is to reveal that 'official' knowledge is not what it claims to be but rather reflects the disguised interests and experiences of a dominant social group. As this aim has become itself dominant within educational research, the notion of 'truth' has become occluded by the desire to enact 'truthfulness'. Nonetheless, as Williams argues, truthfulness itself presupposes a deeper commitment to truth:

> If you do not really believe in the existence of truth, what is the passion for truthfulness a passion for? Or – as we might also put it – in pursuing truthfulness what are you supposedly being true to? This is not an abstract difficulty or just a paradox. It has consequences for real politics, and it signals a danger that our intellectual activities, particularly in the humanities, may tear themselves to pieces. (2002, p. 2)

In other words, a preoccupation with truthfulness that eclipses interest in truth undermines the very basis of that passion for truthfulness. This has been the fate of approaches dominant in the sociology of education over recent decades (see Chapters 3 and 6). From the radical social constructivism of the early 1970s, through waves of feminism and multiculturalism to post-structuralism and postmodernism, the passion for truthfulness has dominated at the expense of the passion for truth. As a result, knowledge as an object of study in its own right has been obscured. Ironically, the result is that truth and knowledge have become the dominated, silenced Others. The very basis of intellectual and educational practice is thus missing from the picture of education.

Knowledge as real

In contrast to previously dominant approaches, social realism does not construct truth and truthfulness as opposed, as an either/or, but rather embodies a passion for *both* truth *and* truthfulness. Social realist approaches aim to see through appearances to the real structures that lie behind them but acknowledge that these structures are more than the play of social power and vested interests. This position can be described as based on what critical realist philosophy terms 'ontological realism', 'epistemological relativism' and 'judgemental rationality' (e.g. Archer et al. 1998). First, the principle of *ontological realism* involves the recognition that knowledge is about something other than itself: there exists a reality beyond our symbolic realm. This 'otherness' of independently existing realities, both natural and social, provides an independent, external limit not on what we can believe (we can believe whatever we like, such as in fairies at the bottom of the garden) but rather on what we can *know*. We, as individuals, can believe in anything, but we collectively cannot in the same way *know* just anything. Secondly, *epistemological relativism* acknowledges that this knowledge is not necessarily universal, invariant, essential Truth – we can 'know' the world only in terms of socially produced knowledges which change over time and across socio-cultural contexts. Thus the nature of knowledge as an object, its forms and their modes of change, is crucial for understanding our subjective knowledge and what we can say we 'know' about the world. Lastly, epistemological relativism does not imply judgemental relativism, the view that we cannot judge between different knowledges. Rather, *judgemental rationality* holds that there are rational, intersubjective bases for determining the relative merits of competing knowledge claims. This is central to social realism in education: one of its key concerns is with how 'we', that is, humanity, come to produce knowledge. What makes this *social* realism is that in contrast to traditional epistemology as represented by positivism, for example, the concern is not with the logical properties of knowledge claims but with the collective procedures through which judgements are produced against the background constraints of the real.

Though drawing here on critical realist terms, the concerns of social realism in education are more substantive than philosophical – its focus lies with the properties of knowledge-producing fields of social practice and its problematic concerns the structured principles and procedures developed in those fields that provide the basis for rational objectivity in knowledge. Here the social realist position represents, as we stated earlier, an alternative to the 'epistemological dilemma' of choosing between positivist absolutism or constructivist relativism. This false dichotomy suggests one analyse either the formal and epistemological properties of knowledge or the play of power among actors in the social contexts of its production. Similarly, it suggests at the level of curriculum and pedagogy that the only important factor is either transmitting knowledge or valorizing the learner's experiences. One approach neglects the social in favour of focusing on the 'what' and 'how' of knowledge; the other neglects knowledge in favour of focusing on 'who' is speaking or learning (they exclusively address either the 'epistemic relation' or 'social relation' of knowledge, respectively; see Chapter 2). Instead, social realism views knowledge-producing fields as comprising *both* relational structures of concepts and methods for relating these to the empirical world *and* actors positioned in institutions within specific social and historical contexts. In contrast to hegemonic approaches in the sociology of education, this recognizes that knowledge involves more than social power; it also involves epistemic power.

This alternative vision is enabled by understanding that knowledge is *emergent from but irreducible to* the practices and contexts of its production and recontextualization, teaching and learning. As Moore puts it,

> [A] crucial distinction must be made between the production of knowledge and its emergent properties, i.e. knowledge is socially produced, but at the same time has the capacity to transcend the social conditions under which it is produced. (2000, p. 32)

This is to say that knowledge is *both* social *and* has emergent properties that transcend and 'react back' on social contexts and practices. Thus 'social realism' does not denote that only the social is real (and not the natural), as if opposed to a more encompassing form of realism. Rather, 'realism' can be understood as superseding 'constructivism' – as Young puts it in the sub-title of his book (2008), 'from social constructivism to social realism'. It signals a shift from viewing knowledge in terms of *construction* – especially when this implies we can construct the world as we see fit, free of the consequences of how the world will react back on that construction – towards a focus on its *production* within relatively autonomous fields of practice according to socially developed and applied procedures that may have both arbitrary *and* non-arbitrary bases. It thus highlights a concern with the *sociality* of knowledge in terms of how knowledge is created ('social') and emphasizes that knowledge is more than simply produced – its modalities help shape the world ('realism'). This capacity is given by its 'objective' nature, by which is not meant its 'certainty' but rather its nature as an object in its own right that has real effects. The different forms taken by structures of knowledge have different effects. Social realism offers a language for theorizing these different forms with a view to exploring these effects, such as for the capacity for intellectual fields to build powerful and cumulative knowledge over time (Chapters 2, 3 and 6), the professional role of the teacher and models of professional identity (Chapter 4), how different groups of pupils can access different forms of knowledge (Chapter 5) and inclusion in cultural debates (Chapters 7 and 8). Thus, concerns which at one level might seem to be rather abstract issues in the rarefied realms of epistemology or the theory of knowledge translate into practical issues in educational theory and practice.

The educational dilemma

The epistemological dilemma is not only damaging to our understanding of education, it also plays out in education with damaging results. As Freebody et al. (2008, p. 189) argue, over the past thirty years institutional changes in initial teacher training have been accompanied by more emphasis in teacher preparation and research on the processes of 'learning' (rather than 'learning *this*') or the social and cultural nature of 'the learner' (rather than 'the learner faced with *this*') – knowledge has been sidelined in favour of knowing or knowers. While this has moved educational thinking forward from its overly learner-decentred past, it has also propagated a radical scepticism towards knowledge. At the level of curriculum this scepticism is reflected in constructivist beliefs that the disciplinary basis of a subject-based curriculum is arbitrary and specialist expertise merely a power play. 'Knowledge' is often viewed as undifferentiated – 'generic' skills or interchangeable packets of information – and the basis of its selection and sequencing in a curriculum seen as arbitrary. At the level of pedagogy, this position can be heard in the view that how such knowledge is taught, learned and assessed is similarly arbitrary, that teaching is processual and divorced from the form of knowledge being taught, and that the authority of teachers is based solely on social position and unrelated to possessing knowledge. There is, from this view, little reason for the forms taken by curriculum or pedagogy beyond historical and cultural conventions – one can begin studying physics by learning quantum mechanics, howsoever one pleases, enabled by anyone sufficiently proficient at facilitating learning. Such knowledge-blindness is also realized in debates over information and communication technologies where the universality of 'learning' (understood generically) in everyday life is held to signal a need to dismantle formal educational institutions. When enacted as policy, these beliefs that there exist no differences between everyday and educational knowledge, and between different forms of educational knowledge, result in the deprofessionalization of teaching (see Chapter 4), withhold powerful knowledge from the very people who need it most (Chapter 5) and impoverish the wider cultural sphere (Chapters 7 and 8).

In contrast, while acknowledging the significance of convention and social power, social realism also highlights the differentiation of knowledge and the role this plays in shaping educational experiences and outcomes. This position has profound implications for education. First, if knowledge is not epiphenomenonal but real, differentiated and possessing emergent structural qualities, then it follows that curriculum and pedagogy should be structured to take account of those qualities, such as the sequencing of knowledge through a curriculum. Social realism acknowledges differences between the logics of intellectual production and educational reproduction – the practices found in a physics research laboratory are not the same as those found in a physics classroom. However, it does not thereby sever relations between the two. There may be good reasons for why some subjects are typically organized in curricula and taught differently to others. Absolutism would essentialize and fix these differences; relativism would dismiss them as merely arbitrary. Exploring their reasons and sifting the arbitrary (such as historical convention) from the non-arbitrary (the effects of an ontological imperative) is a key issue for ongoing and future social realist research.

Secondly, if there are rational grounds for judging knowledge claims that are more than arbitrary expressions of power, then it follows that some forms of knowledge are more epistemologically (or aesthetically) powerful than others and that curriculum and pedagogy should, again, be structured to take account of such hierarchies (which are not identical with social hierarchies). This would, for example, militate against forms of assessment that aim to avoid evaluating the content knowledge of learners.

Thirdly, if the above points hold, then in liberal democratic societies it follows that all citizens should be provided with equality of access to the most powerful forms of knowledge through the means that most reliably enable that access. This militates against pedagogic practices which aim to simply celebrate the experiences of students and which fall into (as Maton in Chapter 8 quotes Hoggart) 'that sloppy relativism which doesn't stretch *any* student because "they are all, in their own ways, doing wonderfully"' (1969, in 1982, p. 12). Of course, the means for enabling access to powerful forms of knowledge are likely to vary according to the different social backgrounds those citizens bring to education but they will also vary according to the forms of knowledge involved.

All this involves a recognition that intellectual and educational practices necessarily involve hierarchies, that hierarchies are not always and everywhere social and arbitrary, and that expertise is not antithetical to democracy and social justice. Popper (1983) argued that progress in productive intellectual fields is shown by the problems they create, and these general principles pose more problems than they resolve, but they are problems with which social realism is actively engaging, with a commitment to both truth and truthfulness.

Social realism for social justice

Knowing about knowledge is not just an epistemological or educational matter. The dichotomy of absolutism or relativism also has a political dimension; to repeat Williams: it 'has consequences for real politics' (2002, p. 2). The notion that knowledge is decontextualized and value-free is associated with conservative positions, and relativizing attempts to unmask the power behind knowledge are self-described as 'critical' and radical. Arguments for studying knowledge as an object or, worse, defending the notion of values in culture (see Chapters 7 and 8) are then often heard as the voice of reactionary conservatism. Again, social realism aims to move beyond this false dichotomy by offering a non-relativistic but socially progressive alternative.

Social realist authors are, of course, not alone in engaging with the troubling consequences of relativism, consequences that reach far beyond education. A number of books have brought this issue to a wider audience, such as Frank Furedi's (2004) *Where Have All the Intellectuals Gone?*, Francis

Wheen's (2004) *How Mumbo-Jumbo Conquered the World* and Benson and Stangroom's (2006) *Why Truth Matters.* Such interventions are energized by a desire to recover respect for the concept of truth and the principles of rational objectivity in both intellectual circles and the public sphere. Furedi, for example, proclaims:

> The prevailing level of education, culture and intellectual debate is important for the flourishing of a democratic ethos. Intellectuals in different guises play a crucial role in initiating dialogue and engaging the curiosity and passion of the public. Today that engagement is conspicuously feeble. Unsurprisingly, the cultural elites' cynicism towards knowledge and truth has been transmitted to the people through educational and cultural institutions and the media. Apathy and social disengagement are symptoms of a culture that tends to equate debate with the banal exchange of technical opinions. Because all of this really matters, a culture war against the philistines is long overdue. (2004, p. 24)

The polemical language and call to arms of such writers as Furedi may sometimes provoke their mislabelling as reactionary, but they call attention to the wider import of neglecting knowledge. In particular, they highlight a peculiar reversal whereby progressive forces historically claimed to have Reason and Truth on their side but have now rejected the authority of Reason and abandoned Truth to the forces of reaction. Both the broader argument of intellectuals in the public sphere and the more specific arguments represented in this volume reflect a mood captured by Lopez and Potter (2001, p. 4) when arguing that 'one can say that a new and different intellectual direction must come after postmodernism, simply because postmodernism is inadequate as an intellectual response to the times we live in'. Why it is inadequate is illustrated by Baggini with reference to the events of 11 September 2001 and their consequences:

> On that date, the 'real world' stamped its imprint on the collective consciousness of the West. It demonstrated that which had previously been argued by postmodernism's critics: that to deny the existence of objective reality and celebrate that denial is politically dangerous and intellectually lazy. (2002, p. 10)

In these terms, the problem of knowledge is urgent. In celebrating what Gellner (1992b) called the suicide of reason, too many intellectuals have been happy to cut away the branch upon which they perch, namely a belief in 'the value of truth' (Williams 2002, pp. 6–7). Without truth, truthfulness leads to outcomes that harm the very causes in whose name it is espoused. Fields such as the sociology of education (Chapters 3 and 6) and cultural studies (Chapters 2 and 8) have, as Williams warns, torn themselves to pieces, resulting in intellectual fragmentation, political toothlessness and deleterious educational outcomes. Social realism attempts to recover knowledge in the service of progress and social justice. The impulse underlying social realist work is towards both the creation of epistemologically more powerful forms of knowledge and establishing the means to enable them to be accessible to everyone.

A Coalition of Minds

We have referred to social realism as a 'school of thought', but it is more accurately described as a coalition of minds rather than a self-identifying or conscious group. There are differences of focus, emphasis, theoretical influence, affiliation and so on, among those who can be heuristically described as 'social realists'. Moreover, the term itself drifted into use as convenient shorthand – it was neither determined by committee nor deliberately defined. Social realism is, though, a genuine coalition in the sense of collaboration and constructive engagement. What unites these disparate authors is not only how seriously they take knowledge as an object but also their engagement in an unfolding dialogue that itself models the very thing they study. Durkheim stated:

> Collective representations are the product of an immense cooperation that extends not only through space but also through time; to make them, a multitude of different minds have associated, intermixed, and combined their ideas and feelings; long generations have accumulated their experience and knowledge. (1967, p. 15)

Durkheim's description encapsulates both a central concern of this book and the nature of the social realist enterprise: a key aspect of the process of knowledge production and development is its sociality, the way in which people are related in that process, whether through direct engagement or indirectly through participation in a shared intellectual field. Because constructivist and post-structuralist approaches see only power at play, they cannot fully understand the social nature of knowledge. The argument being developed in this book is *not* that knowledge is not social, but that these approaches cannot provide an adequate account of the character of its sociality. By overfocusing on the social (in terms of power relations) and neglecting knowledge they paradoxically neglect a crucial dimension of the social in knowledge and education. Durkheim's quote also highlights how the work of knowledge production is both highly personal and inescapably collective; or as Collins puts it,

> The intellectual alone, reading or writing: but he or she is not mentally alone. His or her ideas are loaded with social significance because they symbolize membership in existing and prospective coalitions in the intellectual network. (2000, pp. 51–2)

These quotes exemplify the way productive intellectual fields comprise a coalition of minds extending across time and space in which individuals engage in both internalized coalitions of the mind and direct interpersonal engagements. The papers collected together in this volume embody such an intellectual exchange, one that has developed over the past decade in the sociology of education. The book is thereby not only about the social nature of knowledge but also embodies that social nature.

Unlike 'post-' theories, social realism does not proclaim a radical break with the past or with other contemporary ideas. This coalition of minds extends backwards in time and across a range of current intellectual developments to embrace the ideas of a number of key figures from:

- sociology, especially the intellectual tradition inspired by Emile Durkheim (who has often been misread as a positivist rather than a realist), such as the work of Pierre Bourdieu and Randall Collins;
- philosophy, including Roy Bhaskar's critical realism, Ernest Gellner and Bernard Williams; and
- linguistics, especially the systemic functional linguistics of Michael Halliday and its development through the work of such luminaries of the 'Sydney School' as Jim Martin.

The most immediate influence on social realism, however, has been the sociology of Basil Bernstein. This influence is made explicit throughout the chapters of the book. It suffices to say here that, above all, his ideas serve as a principal starting point for social realist thinking and continue to provide a source of inspiration for its development. Bernstein's ideas provide a central thread through the book because, as many of the chapters highlight, they bring knowledge into view and provide the basis for a language with which to study this crucial object of study.

Intellectual coalitions, Collins suggests, are 'motivated by the energies of social interactions' (2000, p. 7). Social realism has similarly been motivated by a series of interpersonal associations among its protagonists. These initially coalesced at the end of the 1990s through discussions among, among others, John Beck, Karl Maton, Rob Moore and Joe Muller, and a series of publications, the titles of which illustrate their focus, such as *Reclaiming Knowledge* (Muller 2000), 'For knowledge' (Moore 2000) and 'Recovering pedagogic discourse' (Maton 2000). As these suggest, the initial focus was often on the structural features of knowledge, not to obscure pedagogy or negate agency but rather to bring these into the light so as to explore their implications for such issues as pedagogy and agency. These publications then led to further engagements; for example, Maton's analysis of the fragmenting effects for intellectual fields of basing knowledge claims on attributes of knowers (Chapter 2 of this volume) resonated with the work of Moore and Muller tracing such effects through the history of the sociology of education (Chapter 3), a paper that in turn prompted Michael Young to publish a response evaluating the gains and losses in the field enabled by such positions (2000b). Such exchanges also scrolled outwards into a wider space where new actors enter the conversation via publications, personal communications and face-to-face encounters at international symposia, constituting what Collins (2000) calls 'interaction ritual chains'. For example, what can be described as a 'second wave' of participants came together in July 2008 with such 'kindred spirits' as critical realist philosophers for an international symposium in Cambridge University, and in December 2008 a three-day interdisciplinary conference at the University of Sydney brought together social realist sociologists and systemic functional linguists to address *Disciplinarity, Knowledge and Language*. There is thus now a genuinely international and interdisciplinary network of networks engaging to varying degrees with the social realist problematic, including participants of the biennial *Bernstein International Symposium*, systemic linguists, critical realists and others.

The chapters collected here, many of which have been revised for this publication, are thus but illustrative of a wider intellectual enterprise that is evolving and expanding. They also highlight the different though overlapping forms of intellectual work in a productive field, including mapping, critique, concept-building and application. Chapter 1 by Moore and Young provides a mapping of orientations towards knowledge within policy and education debates, reconfiguring the conventional understanding of positions within these fields to reveal their underlying commonalities and differences and bringing to light positions obscured by the default settings of debates, in particular the neglected dimension of knowledge. Chapter 2 by Maton introduces new conceptual tools for analysing knowledge and understanding the nature and consequences of these orientations, in particular the effects of basing knowledge claims on membership of social categories of knowers, taking British cultural studies as an illustrative example. Chapter 3 by Moore and Muller brings these concerns together within an analysis of how these issues have played out in the sociology of education. Chapter 4 by Beck and Chapter 5 by Wheelahan extend the intellectual connections of social realist work outwards to Durkheim and to critical realism, and apply these expanded ideas to critique educational policies in the United Kingdom and Australia. Chapter 6 by Young and Muller returns to the concerns of Chapters 1 and 3 by tracing through the gains and losses of the sociology of education, bringing in more fully the later work of Basil Bernstein and critiquing its capacity for addressing disciplines beyond the natural sciences. Chapter 7 by Moore and Chapter 8 by Maton take up this challenge to address the arts and humanities. Moore focuses on a widely discussed instance of relativizing knowledge claims in the arts, while Maton develops Bernstein's model to explore the culture wars and the possibilities for knowledge-building in the arts and humanities.

As with any collection, other papers could have been selected (many of which are cited in the chapters), but this selection provides insights into the multifaceted, evolving and dialogic nature of the field, bringing together for the first time key papers that map, critique and conceptualize knowledge and which have been influential in shaping the ongoing and future social realist project. Like that of all productive intellectual fields, this story is unfinished. All these papers are characterized by a desire to forge a wider, more democratic and intellectually fruitful conversation – we hope that this collection, whatever your intellectual persuasion, motivates you to productively engage with this open coalition of open minds.

Chapter 1

Reconceptualizing Knowledge and the Curriculum in the Sociology of Education

Rob Moore
Cambridge University

Michael Young
University of London and University of Bath

Politicians tell us that we are (or soon will be) in a 'knowledge society' and that more and more jobs require people to be 'knowledge workers'. At the same time government policy documents have been remarkably silent about what this knowledge is (DfEE 1998, 1999). Is it more of the old disciplinary knowledge or is it a new kind of trans-disciplinary knowledge that is more transient and local (Gibbons et al. 1994; Muller 2000)? Answers to such questions should lie at the heart of the sociology of education, but also are strangely absent there as well (Chapters 2 and 3, this volume; Young 2000a, 2000b). In this chapter we wish to do two things. First we seek to clarify the nature of the problem and second, we shall propose a way ahead for the sociology of education. In developing our argument we will not only be examining the problem of knowledge in the curriculum, but also raising some concerns about how the sociology of education has tended to treat the issue of knowledge more generally. We will argue that contemporary trends in the sociology of education make it peculiarly ill equipped to meet the curriculum challenge posed by debates about the implications of globalization (Castells 1996, 1997, 1998) and the massification of post-compulsory education (Scott 2000) of the last decade.

We will begin by describing and contrasting what we see as the two dominant (and contending) sets of assumptions about knowledge and the curriculum that are reflected in contemporary curriculum policy: 'neo-conservative traditionalism' and 'technical-instrumentalism'. We then go on to examine the postmodernist critique of these assumptions that has been developed within the sociology of education (Hartley 1997; Moore 2000). Despite the critical stance of postmodernism, we will argue that all three positions exhibit some fundamental similarities. Each, in its own way, precludes a debate about knowledge as a category *in its own right*. It follows that what is lacking from current debates about the curriculum is precisely any *theory* of knowledge. It is here that the issue becomes most acute for the sociology of education. It is fair to say that postmodernist perspectives have become firmly entrenched, though not hegemonic, within the sociology of education (Hartley 1997) and, furthermore, that their proponents adopt a critical position vis-à-vis neo-conservatism and instrumentalism (Griffith 2000). In this respect they hold in a contemporary guise the place formerly held, within the sociology of education, by progressivism and certain kinds of Marxist critiques. Although on theoretical grounds postmodernists reject both the essentialist model of the child held by progressive educationists and the economic determinism of Marxism, they continue to emphasize the *experiential* basis of knowledge associated with progressivism and the view of academic knowledge as elitist and ideological that is found in many Marxist critiques. Furthermore, postmodernists have developed the relativism that is immanent in both Marxist and phenomenological theories of knowledge into a point of principle. Although in ideological terms, postmodernism is critical of both neo-conservative and technical-instrumental views of the curriculum, we shall show that in relation to their assumptions about knowledge, it is the *similarities* of the three approaches that are more significant than their differences. Furthermore, for reasons we will develop in this chapter, the relativizing of knowledge claims associated with postmodernist critiques vitiates their ability to mount any effective advocacy of realistic curriculum alternatives.

The implication of this argument is that there is a potential fourth position (the one that we intend to develop) that brings knowledge itself back into the debate about the curriculum without denying its fundamentally social and historical basis. However, such a position requires that the sociology of education develops a theory of knowledge that, while accepting that knowledge is always a social and historical product, avoids the slide into relativism and perspectivism with which this insight is associated in postmodernist writings (e.g. Usher & Edwards 1994).

The issues then are threefold. First, we believe there are important developments in related academic fields (especially in the sociology and philosophy of science) that can be drawn on in developing the fourth position we refer to above. Second, although what counts as school knowledge will always be a contested issue, it is important that this should be seen as something more than simply a power play between contending social interests. Account needs to be taken of how knowledge is developed (and acquired) within particular epistemic communities or 'cultures' (Collins 2000; Hoskyns 1993; Knorr-Cetina 1999). Third, as we shall show, the outcomes of disputes about knowledge are not mere academic issues. They directly affect learning opportunities for pupils in schools and have wider consequences through the principles by which knowledge is distributed in society.

The Current Debate

Recent curriculum policy has been driven by two competing imperatives or ideologies – one largely covert but embedded in the leading educational institutions themselves and the other more overt and increasingly dominant in government rhetoric. The first is what we refer to as 'neo-conservative traditionalism'. The idea of the curriculum as a given body of knowledge that it is the responsibility of the schools to transmit is as old as the institution of schooling itself. It is only articulated (e.g. Woodhead 2001) when it is felt that the traditional body of knowledge is being challenged. An example is in responses to proposals at various times in the last 20 years for the reform or even replacement of A levels which for neo-conservatives represent a 'Gold Standard' against which all other curricula must be evaluated. For them, real learning is still essentially the contemplative process that has its roots in the monastic tradition and the role of the curriculum and its attendant examinations is to engender respect for whatever are the canonical texts. It is therefore not just the specific texts (e.g. particular authors in the case of English) that are held to be of enduring value by neo-conservatives, but the relationship of deference to a given body of knowledge. In other words, what is important is the experience of submitting to the discipline of a subject and becoming the kind of person it is supposed to make you. In terms of the conventional knowledge-centred/child-centred and traditional/progressive dichotomies that have organized curriculum debates for so long, it must be stressed that neo-conservatism is not motivated primarily by epistemological concerns. Rather, it is inspired by the view that the traditional discipline of learning promotes proper respect for authority and protects traditional values (e.g. Scruton 1991).

The disregard by neo-conservatives of the importance of specific knowledge is associated with a peculiarly English form of anti-intellectualism (Wellens 1970) and a cult of amateurism and scepticism about expertise that still shapes the world view of the higher grades of the civil service and the top echelons of parts of industry and commerce. The endorsement of the idea of the 'civilised generalist' which is expressed in the English VIth Form curriculum that allows students to choose which collection of subjects to study has led to the inclusion of an increasing range of 'modern' subjects. English Literature, Modern (sic) Foreign Languages, geography and science were included in the nineteenth century and the social sciences later in the twentieth century (Young 1998). However, this diversification of the content of the VIth Form curriculum bears little relation to the transformations that have taken place in society or the actual development of knowledge itself. In the period of 50 years since A levels were launched, their basic structure has remained unchanged while whole new fields of knowledge have been created and the economy and society as a whole has changed out of all recognition. Furthermore, the numbers taking A levels have expanded tenfold as most jobs for 16 year olds disappeared by the 1980s and the numbers continuing as full-time students doubled.

Those who Raymond Williams (1961) called the 'industrial trainers', but who we refer to by the broader term 'technical-instrumentalists', have consistently challenged the neo-conservative view of education. For them the curriculum imperative is not educational in the traditional sense but supportive of what they see as the needs of the economy. Most recently this is expressed in terms of preparing for the global and more competitive knowledge-based economy of the future (DfEE 1998, 1999). From this perspective, education, the curriculum and even knowledge itself becomes a means to an end, not an end in itself. It is the curriculum's role in making a particular form of society that is stressed. Only secondarily is it seen as a maker of persons and then only to the extent that they exhibit the qualities of trainability and flexibility that it is assumed will be needed in the future 'knowledge society'.

What has changed, even as recently as in the last 10 years, is the scope of these instrumentalist views of the curriculum and knowledge. Prior to the 1970s they were largely confined to vocational education and training (hence Williams' term 'industrial trainers'); although they were also reflected in the assumption that the 20 per cent of each cohort who left school without any qualifications needed a more practically oriented, work-related curriculum. However, in the last decade, and particularly since the two reports by Lord Dearing on 16–19 qualifications (Dearing 1996) and higher education (NCIHE 1997), instrumentalism, under the guise of promoting the employability of all students, has been extended to the academic curriculum for 16–19 year olds and even to the apex of academic learning – the universities. All students are now encouraged to mix academic and vocational subjects (QCA 1999) and all subjects taught at university from Fine Art to Pure Mathematics have to incorporate key skills and show their students how to apply their knowledge (Bridges 2000). Subject specialists are increasingly expected to make explicit not only how their subject links with other subjects but also how it facilitates team work, communications or number skills. Technical-instrumentalism also imposes upon educational institutions a style of managerial regulation that is integrated with the broader apparatus of performance indicators, target setting and league tables (Beck 1999). While the formalities of academic freedom in deciding the university curriculum are retained, cash-starved institutions are unavoidably influenced by the incentives of funds linked to such government objectives as widening participation and promoting employability.

The tension between the two models has influenced the development of the curriculum for more than a century. However, it is since the early 1990s that technical-instrumentalism has provided the dominant rhetoric for change as well as contributing substantive elements of reform. Both models operate diagnostically by identifying deficiencies in existing educational arrangements. The traditionalists assert that the substantial expansion of post-compulsory education has only been possible by allowing the standards of excellence that were established in the past (the 'golden age') to fall. In contrast, the modernizers claim that the uneasy compromise between pressures to expand participation and maintain standards has resulted in a curriculum that fails to fulfil the skill and knowledge demands of the emerging economy. In both models, a view of the curriculum is related to a particular historical narrative of social change (Moore 2000).

With governments unable to resolve the tension between these two imperatives, it is not surprising that curriculum policy and its implementation is at best confused. Some schools and colleges are making a heroic effort to articulate a vision of a broader curriculum of the future while others adapt as best they can to the vagaries of student choice and the idiosyncrasies of HE admission tutors. Nor is it surprising that new divisions are emerging. In the most successful institutions students are encouraged to take four or even five subjects, at least in the first year of their post 16 studies, and degree programmes are being enhanced in leading universities. In contrast, students in less-privileged institutions tend to face the new forms of generic and, some would say, vacuous vocationalism.

Neither the neo-conservative nor the instrumentalist views have gone unchallenged by social theorists. However, our argument is that in failing to provide a way of discussing what must be central to any serious curriculum debate – the question of knowledge – the critiques from social theory fall into the same trap as the views they oppose. This is not as straightforward a point as it sounds as the critiques, increasingly from a postmodernist perspective, present themselves as treating the question of knowledge as central. They focus largely on the academic curriculum and claim that it relies on essentially arbitrary assumptions about knowledge and culture generally (Hartley 1997). It follows, from their perspective, that in asserting the givenness of what they claim to have demonstrated is arbitrary, the curriculum is responsible for the perpetuation of social inequalities.

Starting from the assumption that all knowledge is embedded in the interests of particular groups of knowers (see Maton 2000 and Chapter 3, this volume), postmodernist critiques appear to provide powerful support for the cultural demands of subordinate groups, whether these are ethnic, gender or (though increasingly less frequently) social class based. However, by arguing that knowledge is inseparable from how it is constructed, they cannot avoid the conclusion that all knowledge, whether based on professional expertise, research or the experience of particular groups, is of equal value. It follows that, when the standpoint and interests of those producing the knowledge have been identified, all that needs to be said has, in essence, been said. Debates between postmodernists and those they critique become little more than arguments about whose experience should underpin the curriculum and the purpose of social theory becomes the critical deconstruction of the dominant forms of knowledge associated with subjects and disciplines. If all standards and criteria are reducible to perspectives and standpoints, no grounds can be offered for teaching any one thing rather than any other (or, ultimately, for teaching anything at all!). It is not surprising that such theories, whatever their appeal to intellectuals, have made no contribution to curriculum policy. Worse, they have effectively marginalized the role of sociology in providing a theory for how we might think about knowledge in a 'knowledge society' and what the curriculum implications of such a theory might be.

Postmodernist ideas about knowledge have not only been the basis of critiques of traditionalist views of the curriculum, they have also been used to challenge the prevailing instrumentalism of current government policy and its rhetoric of performativity (Usher & Edwards 1994). However, because they have no theory of knowledge as such, they can do little more than expose the way that curriculum policies always mask power relations.

Further, by depending on an irreducible notion of experience ultimately removed from any social context, they neglect the uneven distribution of the experiences that learners need if they are to acquire and make use of curriculum knowledge.

The Problems with Postmodernist Critiques of Knowledge

Why do postmodernist accounts of knowledge and the curriculum neglect the very problem that they set out to address? One reason is that in their critique of neo-conservatism and instrumentalism, they polarize the alternatives as if each position they critique did not itself have within it a kernel of truth. The neo-conservative position may be flawed but it is not false. It reminds us that (a) education needs to be seen as an *end in itself* and not just as a means to an end (the instrumentalist position), and that (b) tradition, though capable of preserving vested interests, is also crucial in ensuring the maintenance and development of standards of learning in schools as well as being a condition for innovation and creating new knowledge. More generally, neo-conservatives remind us that the curriculum must, in Mathew Arnold's words, strive to 'make the best that has been thought and known in the world current everywhere' (1960, p. 70).

There are good reasons why we still want people to read Jane Austen's novels that are not weakened by the narrow community that she wrote about. Her novels are situated in time and context, but they are also timeless in the issues that they explore. One can make a slightly different kind of argument for keeping Newton's laws of motion and Mendeleev's Periodic Table on science syllabuses; both are examples of knowledge that remains powerful and transcends its origins in a particular social context. The problem with the neo-conservative position is that, like Arnold, it treats 'the best' as given and not the outcome, at any time, of wider social changes as well as internal debates within disciplines. Because neo-conservatives play down the social and historical nature of knowledge, they see no need for a theory about what should (and should not) be in the curriculum, whether it is particular novels or new subjects. For them the canon of English literature and the traditional school subjects are, self-evidently, just there; they define what a curriculum is. The result is that actual curriculum changes are invariably ad hoc and pragmatic.

In opposition to neo-conservatism, instrumentalism reminds us that the curriculum has always been, albeit selectively, related to the economic needs of the country and the future employability of students, despite claims to the contrary by liberal educators. It also reminds us that schools and colleges are never as insulated from the rest of society as they are portrayed in the subject-based curriculum. The issue which instrumentalism does not address is the conditions that are necessary if knowledge is to be produced or acquired and why economic realities can never be the only criteria for the curriculum. In contrast, social theories of knowledge, whether humanist, Marxist, or more recently postmodernist, all make explicit the social and historical character of knowledge and that knowledge is always, at least in part, 'some people's knowledge'. However, in making such features of knowledge explicit, these theories all too easily end up in claiming that knowledge is only some people's knowledge – no more and no less.

The second problem with postmodernist theories is that they imply that social theories of knowledge inevitably lead to relativism and the denial of any possibility that knowledge can be objective. Arguments about relativism have dominated and distorted debates about knowledge in the sociology of education since the 1970s (Chapter 3) in ways that have seriously impeded the development of a theory that might address the many urgent curriculum issues. Most social theories of knowledge have remained at too high a level of abstraction to have any clear curriculum implications and if not, as in the case of some forms of Marxism and feminism, they have made unsupportable claims about the links between knowledge and particular social interests. In this chapter we shall propose a social realist view of knowledge derived from Durkheim (1967) and developed more recently by Collins (2000) and Alexander (1995). In contrast to postmodernist theories these writers argue that it is the social nature of knowledge that in part provides the grounds for its objectivity and its claims to truth. In the final section of the chapter we shall discuss the implications for curriculum debates of such a social realist approach to knowledge and how it might take us beyond both the prevailing orthodoxies of neo-conservatism and instrumentalism as well as their postmodernist critics.

The Epistemological Dilemma

In developing an alternative to relativism, we begin by noting the peculiarity that anyone should hold such a position in the first place. In the academic community, objections to relativism are long established and widely known (Fay 1996; Gellner 1974, 1992a; Harre & Krausz 1996). Furthermore, at a common-sense level, it is inconceivable that advocates of relativism could actually live their personal lives as relativists. They may celebrate the uniqueness of individual standpoints in theory, but at the same time, in their everyday lives they cannot avoid making assumptions that transcend the uniqueness of particular standpoints. The question remains as to why, particularly in the sociology of education, has the appeal of relativism persisted.[1]

Relativism has taken different forms in the sociology of education. As a methodology it refers to the critical questioning that is a feature of the beginning of any enquiry. What distinguishes its use in the sociology of education is its role in questioning the form and content of the curriculum, the taken for granted assumptions that it makes about what counts as knowledge and therefore the society that supports those assumptions. However, relativism is never just a methodological strategy. Invariably theoretical claims are made about the social basis of knowledge as well as political claims about the consequences of particular theories of know-ledge in terms of wider questions of power and inequality. By arguing that all knowledge derives from partial and potentially self-interested stand-points relativism can be seen as a superficially powerful basis for challeng-ing what are assumed to be the repressive and dominant knowledge forms of the existing curriculum. Relativists attack the claims to objectivity of dominant forms of knowledge and by implication defend the 'voices' that are denied or hidden. It is this combination of the methodology and politics of relativism that goes some way to accounting for its appeal. However its actual political and educational significance outside the field of sociology of education has been minimal. This relates to the theoretical weaknesses of relativism especially in its most recent postmodern form. By polarizing dominant knowledge forms against 'silenced' others, postmod-ernism achieves its radical objective of not having to refer to any established traditions of academic debate; all academic theories, by definition exclude 'silent' others. However, in dismissing other theories rather than entering into a dialogue with them, postmodernism precludes the possibility of an alternative theory of knowledge, except one that reduces all knowledge to statements about knowers (see this volume, Chapters 2, 3 and 8). Debates about knowledge for postmodernists become forms of attack and defence between oppressors and oppressed (or rather those claiming to defend their interests). At the same time by privileging the exclusiveness of parti-cular experiences, they deny to oppressed communities the possibility of knowledge that goes beyond their experience and might play a part in enabling them to overcome their oppression.

This trend to dichotomize has, we would argue, a deeper basis in what is sometimes referred to as the 'linguistic turn' in social theory. Language is treated not as an aspect of social order or as a useful metaphor for characterizing aspects of social relations, but as the only way we have of representing social relations (Gellner 1992a). From such a dichotomizing perspective, dominant knowledge (such as that inscribed in the curriculum) requires the exclusion of the knowledge of 'others'. It follows that the only task of social analysis is to name the producers of the dominant knowledge (Moore 2000).[2]

A number of commentators have noted that in their critique of knowledge, postmodernists invariably characterize it as 'positivist' (Alexander 1995, chapter 3).[3] The typical version of positivism that is attacked is one that locates truth outside society and presents it as accessible through a 'neutral' language that is a direct representation of the external world. The postmodernist view of the inseparability of knowledge and knowers is then used to challenge the claims of the natural sciences that they can provide access to a truth that is outside society and history. The implications of this polarization between postmodernism and a positivist view of science is termed by Alexander as 'the epistemological dilemma', which he summarizes as follows:

> Either knowledge . . . is unrelated to the social position and intellectual interests of the knower, in which case general theory and universal knowledge are viable, or knowledge is affected by its relation to the knower, in which case relativistic and particularistic knowledge can be the only result. This is a true dilemma because it presents a choice between two equally unpalatable alternatives. [However] The alternative to positivist theory is not resigned relativism and the alternative to relativism is not positivist theory. Theoretical knowledge can never be anything other than the socially rooted efforts of historical agents. But this social character does not negate the possibility of developing either generalised categories or increasingly disciplined, impersonal and critical modes of evaluation. (Alexander 1995, p. 91)

We endorse Alexander's view that there is an alternative to this polarization and will explore it in some detail later. Next however, we turn to other problems of postmodernism as a critical social theory and in particular, its concept of knowledge.

Postmodernism reduces knowledge to a simple monolithic form that is then held to be hegemonic. However, as Collins argues in his encyclopaedic *Sociology of Philosophies* (Collins 2000), it is only rarely and under exceptional conditions that the certainty of knowledge is hegemonic in any intellectual field. He shows that intellectual fields are typically structured by competing traditions and positions and that the dominance of one is only ever partial and transient. Indeed, for Collins, the reality of competing traditions is one of the conditions for the objectivity of knowledge. In contrast, postmodernism polarizes present and absent meanings leading to an inevitably schematic and partial view of knowledge. The manner in which postmodernists typically equate science with positivism, despite the fact, at least in its cruder forms, positivism has never been widely accepted as a theory of science, is an example of this. Philosophers such as Toulmin, as well as sociologists, have shown that locating knowledge socially does not lead to the abandonment of truth and objectivity. It is in these developments that we can find a way out of Alexander's 'epistemological dilemma'.

Our argument so far has been that in reducing knowledge to particular standpoints, postmodernism follows a reductive logic that polarizes dominant knowledge against absent or silent voices that it excludes; it then goes on to treat this exclusion as mirroring the inequalities of power in the wider society. However, this reduction of knowledge to standpoints has a number of implications for the ability of sociology to contribute meaningfully to curriculum debates. Four such implications are worth listing:

1. *The genetic fallacy*
   If knowledge is reduced to the conditions of its production, it is denied any intrinsic autonomy either as a social institution in its own right or in terms of the application of independent truth criteria that might be applied to curriculum debates.
2. *Oversimplifying intellectual fields*
   If knowledge is reduced to the standpoint of a social group, the complexity of positions within any field at any point in time is neglected. Dominance and exclusion are at best very partial categories for curriculum analysis and inevitably neglect questions about why any knowledge is or is not included.
3. *Reducing knowledge to experience*
   Standpoint analysis reduces knowledge to what is known by different groups, the power relations between them and their different experiences. Thus we are left with a sociology of knowers, which says little about knowledge or the curriculum itself.
4. *Denying the possibility of categories which transcend experience*
   Equating knowledge with the experience of knowers means that research can lead only to non-generalizable findings and localized curricula.

It is not difficult to see the problems that are left for sociology as a basis for a critical theory if the logic of the postmodernist argument is accepted. It can be critical only in the limited sense of identifying possible interests behind claims to disinterestedness. We do not reject the possibility that claims to knowledge and objectivity may be linked to social interests (the history of educational testing is but one well-known example). The problems arise when knowledge is taken to be always and only identical with interest. If this is accepted, there are only interests and no good grounds for preferring one interest to another. It is a form of 'criticism in the head' or 'in the armchair' – a kind of academic radicalism of no consequence to anyone else. No wonder there have been suggestions, however misguided, to transfer resources for educational research away from academics. If all knowledge is from a standpoint and there are no standpoint-independent criteria for making judgements, appeals in terms of 'social justice' or the 'common good' become no more than other standpoints. Similarly peer reviews for preserving objectivity and standards become no more than a form of professional hegemony. The view taken in this chapter is that the objectivity of peer reviews has a social basis in the codes, traditions and debates of different intellectual fields that give it a degree of autonomy beyond the personal and professional interests of any particular group of academic peers. Postmodernism, as we have argued earlier, is trapped in its insistence that objectivity can only be supported by the untenable and a-social claims of positivism.

The educational dilemma

The problem faced by the sociology of education is twofold. First, at least in the last decades, most attempts to address the knowledge question have been by postmodernists with the consequences we have already described. Second, attempts to develop a sociology of education that gives knowledge its central place in the curriculum, easily slip back into the discredited neo-conservative traditionalist position discussed earlier in this chapter. This is what can be termed the 'educational dilemma' – either the curriculum is a given or it is entirely the result of power struggles between groups with competing claims for including and legitimising their knowledge and excluding that of others. This can be seen as a more specific example of the 'epistemological dilemma' (Alexander 1995) to which we referred earlier. It is in pointing to a way of resolving both dilemmas that we turn to what we have referred to as a 'social realist' approach to knowledge.

Towards a Social Realist Approach to Knowledge

The argument so far can be summarized as follows:

- First, relativism does not necessarily follow from a social theory of knowledge; on the contrary, a social theory can be the basis for claims to truth and objectivity by identifying the distinctive codes and practices through which they are produced.
- Secondly, a social theory must recognize that some knowledge is objective in ways that transcend the immediate conditions of its production (as in Euclid's geometry or Newton's physics).
- Thirdly, a social theory that seeks to link knowledge to social interests has to distinguish between two types of interest, the 'external' interests that reflect wider divisions in society and the 'internal' interests concerned with the production and acquisition of knowledge itself. Plagued by the assumption that it is always dealing with 'external' interests and their basis in the wider society, the sociology of knowledge has, until recently, given little attention to forms of 'internal' or as we shall suggest, cognitive interest (we will further develop this point later).
- Fourthly, in contrast to postmodernist theories, with their tendency to use dichotomous categories such as dominance and exclusion, a more adequate social theory must treat knowledge as rarely if ever, monolithic. This points to the importance of detailed historical and ethnographic studies that can make explicit the contested character of intellectual fields (Collins 2000; Toulmin 1996).

The political thrust of much recent social theory has assumed that (a) the social interests underpinning knowledge can be equated with wider inequalities of social class and more recently of gender and race and that (b) social interests are typically distorting and involve the introduction of bias in directions that need to be opposed. Our argument does not deny the possibility of social interests introducing bias and unequally distributed disadvantage. However it would not assume that this was inevitable in either the production or the acquisition of knowledge or that such 'external' interests were necessarily involved in defining what counts as knowledge in a particular intellectual field. With these provisos in mind this section of the chapter will describe the elements of the kind of a social realist theory of knowledge and the manner in which it might resolve the epistemological and educational dilemmas we have outlined. In the last section we will give an indication of its possible implications for current debates about the curriculum. In particular, we seek to provide an alternative to the reductionism and ultimately inconsequential social critiques of postmodernism. Essentially this means developing a knowledge-based model of the curriculum that is an alternative to neo-conservatism. Such a model would need to interrogate the knowledge structures and contents of the curriculum in a way that acknowledges their social basis and their capacity (or lack of capacity) to transcend it.

In their various forms, reductionist sociologies of knowledge produce critiques of knowledge by describing it in terms of interests and perspectives. Schmaus (1994) has pointed out that this assumes that cognitive goals do not enter into the explanation of actions and beliefs. 'Interest theories', he argues, are unable to recognize 'intellectual desires and motivations as being on a par with desires for power, prestige, money or sex'. He goes on to question the view that subscribing to a cognitive goal always reduces to belonging to a social group. He argues that knowledge relies on its own forms of collective social formation that are not just a reflection of some other social relations of power (Schmaus 1994). The crucial point is not necessarily to give cognitive interests primacy but to recognize that they are also *social* in character and have their own constitutive principles of autonomy from other social interests. As Schmaus says in relation to science (though the implications of his point are much wider):

[L]ike any other social institution, [it] is defined in terms of the norms and values that govern it. To the extent that science aims at the growth of knowledge, it is characterised by cognitive norms and values. Cognitive values specify the aims of science, while cognitive norms specify the means to achieve these goals. Both cognitive values and norms range widely. Cognitive values may include everything from a scientist's position regarding the ontological status of unobservable entities to the desire to solve a specific set of problems or to explain a particular set of facts. Cognitive norms may range from rules governing the forms of persuasive argument that can be brought in defence of one's theory in a journal article to procedures for manipulating 'inscription devices' in the laboratory. To say that such cognitive factors should play a role in the sociology of scientific knowledge is not to say that all scientific activity must be explained exclusively in terms of cognitive factors. There is no question that scientists can and have been influenced by many non-cognitive interests. However, it does not follow from this fact that cognitive goals must always be reduced to non-cognitive goals and interests. (Schmaus 1994, p. 263)

As Schmaus goes on to stress, he is not implying that there is only one social form that these cognitive values and norms can adopt; scientific communities can adopt a wide variety of forms. His crucial points are (a) the arbitrariness of excluding cognitive interests by adopting reductive sociological approaches, and (b) that cognitive interests are embedded within specific forms of social life or collectivities with their own distinctive 'associational codes' (Ward 1996). To assert that all knowledge is socially produced and historically located, as is agreed by virtually all schools of thought, no longer provides epistemological demarcation criteria for identifying what is 'social'. Only positivists and their postmodernist critics insist that for knowledge to be knowledge it must be outside history, though of course they then draw precisely opposite conclusions as to its actual possibility.

The exclusion of cognitive interests by standpoint and interest theories involves their 'replacement' (Mills 1998, p. 402) by other interests that the theories are prepared to acknowledge: for example, the sectional interests of power and domination. This replacement renders invisible the social form of the 'knowledge producing' or 'knowledge transmitting' communities as distinctive specialist collectivities; they are seen simply as homologues of some other social relationship (such as those between ruling and ruled classes, men and women, black and white, etc). This reduction masks the possibility of an asymmetry between cognitive and other interests whereby the social construction of knowledge is collectively realized through certain necessary practices and social relations that transcend other interests with values, norms and procedures of their own. However, from a social realist point of view, epistemological demarcation criteria are not to do with distinguishing the social from the non-social in knowledge claims. They are concerned with investigating the distinctive forms of social organization whereby powerful codes and procedures for the production and acquisition of knowledge have been developed that are increasingly global in scope (Ziman 2000). These codes and procedures are reflected in research traditions and curricula and inherit and are shaped by a legacy of divisions and inequalities that are becoming more acute, especially on a global scale. They exhibit an inertia and resistance to change, which are only partly cognitive in origin. However, they can in no meaningful sense be reducible to the interests of any particular social class, gender, national or ethnic group. It is precisely the relationship between these collective codes of knowledge production (research) and knowledge acquisition (teaching and learning) and changes in the societies in which they are located that should form a major focus of study for the sociology of education.

A social realist approach to knowledge can avoid Alexander's 'episte-mological dilemma' by arguing (in contrast to positivism and postmodern-ism) that the social character of knowledge is an indispensable basis for its objectivity rather than the condition that makes this objectivity impossi-ble (Collins 2000; Shapin 1994). More generally, the social realist view of knowledge has implications for our understanding of the idea of a 'knowl-edge society'. As we have argued, neither neo-conservative traditionalism, technical-instrumentalism nor postmodernism involve, in any proper sense of the term, *theories* of knowledge. Consequently, knowledge is precisely the central category that is missing from debates about the knowledge society and its educational implications.[4] In this chapter we have stressed (a) the intrinsically social and collective character of knowledge produc-tion, (b) the complexity of intellectual fields and the processes of knowl-edge production and transmission and (c) the asymmetry between cognitive and other interests that are involved in knowledge acquisition and produc-tion. Together, these issues bring the question of knowledge into focus in such a way that it becomes central to the future of knowledge societies and the relationship between the social organization of knowledge and social formation more generally (Moore 2000; Young 1998). This in no way denies that the production and transmission of knowledge is always entangled with a complex set of contending social interests and power relations. However, broad social trends that encompass both the emergence of what Castells (1998) calls a 'networked society' and the persistence and in some ways extension of structured inequalities always have to be seen in interaction with the social configurations of knowledge production itself (Ward 1996). It is only when the cognitive interests involved in the production and trans-mission of knowledge are given the importance that they warrant that a social theory of knowledge can avoid an all too often facile reductionism. The two goals of a social realist theory are (a) to properly reveal the manner in which external power relations might be affecting knowledge both in research and the curriculum and how and (b) to explore how the forms of social organization that arise from 'cognitive' interests may themselves shape the organization of society itself.

The curriculum implications of a social realist approach to knowledge

Following writers such as Ward (1996, 1997), Shapin (1994), Collins (2000) and Alexander (1995), we have argued that the objectivity of knowledge is in part located in the social networks, institutions and codes of practice built up by knowledge producers over time. It is these networks of social relations that, in crucial ways, guarantee truth claims and give the knowledge that is produced its emergent powers. The structure of these networks has changed in increasingly complex ways as part of the overall transformation of societies during the last two centuries and any attempt to depict these changes is in danger of oversimplification. What follows can be no more than a tentative and provisional way of suggesting how such changes may have effected the production and transmission of knowledge.

We note that with the massive expansion of knowledge in the nineteenth century, networks of knowledge production began to expand and cohere as disciplines, relatively insulated from each other (Collins 2000 chapters 10 and 12; Hoskyns 1993). We further note that this process was paralleled by the emergence of the subject-based school curriculum as a key context for the socialization of young people (Young 1998). What is less widely acknowledged is that the expanding public legitimacy and objectivity of knowledge was underpinned by what Ward (1996) refers to as 'codes of association'. These 'codes' were enshrined in institutions such as the university subject departments and specialist professional and academic organizations concerned with knowledge production and also in the school subject associations concerned with what counted as school knowledge and how it was assessed (Layton 1984). Despite significant expansion and diversification over the last century, these specialist forms of social organization remain the major social bases for guaranteeing the objectivity of knowledge and the standards achieved by an increasing proportion of each cohort of school students.

It is not surprising that the subjects and disciplines of the curriculum as the dominant form of the social organization of knowledge should have been contested. On the one hand they have been taken as a given and underpinned the neo-conservative defence of the traditional curriculum. On the other hand, their emergence and expansion was undoubtedly associated historically with profound inequalities in the access to education of different social classes that were in part a legacy of previous eras. It is this association between academic specialization and social inequality that has provided the basis for the radical attack on the subject-based curriculum. From the point of view argued in this chapter, such an attack is mistaken. There are no grounds for claiming that the historical association of the two patterns, curriculum specialization and inequality, has a causal explanation. On the other hand, the forms of social organization underpinning the production and transmission of specialist knowledge did not develop in a vacuum and the ahistorical view of knowledge associated with neo-conservatism is equally untenable. It is challenged, however, not for primarily epistemological reasons but by technical-instrumentalism that takes issue with its resistance to change linked to its uncritical deference to traditional authority. The neo-conservative model is increasingly seen as (a) too slow in the production of knowledge, (b) too inefficient and too elitist to ensure that the majority of the population gain the skills and qualifications they need and (c) too out of touch with the increasingly competitive global society in which we find ourselves (Gibbons et al. 1994, 2000). As a result the universities are under pressure to move away from a reliance on disciplines towards more 'connective' transdisciplinary models of knowledge production[5] and schools are expected to shift from a curriculum based on subjects to one based on modularity, the mixing of academic and vocational studies and generic skills (QCA 1999).

This conflict between the neo-conservatives and instrumentalists can be seen as one between different modes of knowledge production and curriculum organization along the following dimensions:

- from insulation to connectivity between disciplines and subjects and between knowledge and its application;
- from the separation of general and vocational knowledge and learning to their integration; and
- from specialization and linear sequencing as a curriculum principle to genericism and modularity from hierarchical to facilitative approaches to pedagogy.

Neo-conservatives tend to endorse the first of each of these options and take for granted that knowledge is best produced and transmitted through insulated, specialist, linear and hierarchical modes. At the same time they neglect the political and economic changes that are calling into question these principles as well as the inequalities of access and outcomes that are associated with them.[6] The technical-instrumentalists, on the other hand, support moves towards more connective, integrated, modular curricula and more facilitative approaches to pedagogy. Unlike the neo-conservatives, they are well aware of the changing global economy and its implications and they interpret knowledge and learning needs from what they hear from employers who call for a more skill-based curriculum (RSA 1998). However, unlike the neo-conservative model, their curriculum proposals have no social basis to draw on that is equivalent to the traditional networks and codes of practice such as the subject associations. As a result their curriculum proposals tend to provoke doubts about standards and whether real learning is taking place. From the social realist perspective argued for in this chapter, both are mistaken. Whereas the curriculum of the past (Young 1998, 1999) that is defended by neo-conservative traditionalism takes no account of the changing social context within which the curriculum is located, the new curriculum that is likely to emerge from the educational policy review 'Curriculum 2000' neglects the extent to which the capacity of any curriculum to be the basis for acquiring knowledge in any field depends on the social networks, trust and codes of practice which give it an objectivity and sense of standards. Whereas the old curriculum was undoubtedly elitist, its critics, both instrumentalists and postmodernists focus only on its elitism and resistance to change. They fail to recognize that the social organization of subjects and disciplines transcended its elitist origins as a basis for the acquisition and production of knowledge. Without networks and codes of practice, the emerging curriculum for 16–19 year olds will be little more than a pragmatic modification of the neo-conservative model. At its best the new curriculum continues to be underpinned by existing social networks of subject specialists associated with the old curriculum but which extend their activities to include the newer forms of assessment and modular programmes. The traditional groupings of subject specialists that have maintained standards have been extended in some cases by new types of specialist teacher networks. At its worst, elements of the new curriculum, as in such examples as vocational A levels and key skills, exemplify all the dangers of relying on the specification of learning outcomes which are not underpinned by any social network of expert practice.[7]

Postmodernist critiques point to the voices that are silenced in the new curriculum model as in the old. However, this is an example of the limitations of a dualist critique discussed earlier and does little more than demonstrate that some kind of silencing (or expressed less emotively, adaptation) will be a feature of any curriculum. The issues of what kind of adaptation of learners best promotes learning and what kind of learning is most important are not addressed. In re-emphasizing that both the emergent properties of knowledge as well as its wider social basis have to be taken into account, a social realist approach to knowledge offers a possible way forward for the sociology of the curriculum.

Conclusion

The social realist approach that we have argued for recognizes the social character of knowledge as intrinsic to its epistemological status because the logical reconstruction of truth is always a dialogue with others set within particular collective codes and values (Collins 2000). This has important implications, then, for avoiding the 'educational dilemma' posed by the alternatives of traditionalism and instrumentalism and their ('progressive') postmodern critics. For example, it provides the grounds for,

- avoiding both the ahistorical givenness of neo-conservative traditionalism and a reliance on such notions as relevance or the experience of the learner in decisions about the curriculum;
- maintaining an autonomy for the curriculum from the instrumentalism of economic or political demands;
- assessing curriculum proposals in terms of balancing such goals as overcoming social exclusion and widening participation of the 'cognitive interests' that are involved in knowledge production and transmission; and
- reorienting debates about standards and knowledge in the curriculum from attempts to specify learning outcomes and extend testing to the role of specialist communities, networks and codes of practice.

From a sociological point of view, these four implications of a social realist approach to knowledge take it beyond the alternatives posed by the two orthodoxies and their postmodern critics that we discussed earlier and brings knowledge back into curriculum debate as the historically located collective achievement of human creativity.

Endnotes

[1] The debates about relativism can be traced from the misplaced conclusions drawn from Kuhn's *The Structure of Scientific Revolutions* (1970) and the influence of forms of phenomenological idealism in the 1970s to the feminist and multicultural theories that have emerged since the 1980s (see Chapters 2 and 3, this volume).

[2] Robert Hughes (1993) gives examples of the way that authors can be dismissed by post-modernist writers as simply 'dead white males' without any intellectual engagement with what they are actually saying.

[3] An example of an educationalist who does this is Rhys Griffith (2000).

[4] As Knorr-Cetina (1999) comments, central to a knowledge society must be the 'epistemic cultures' that constitute it.

[5] Gibbons et al. (1994, 2000) coined the terms Mode 1 and Mode 2 to characterize this shift from the traditional disciplinary basis of knowledge production to the emerging 'transdisciplinary' approaches that involve university specialists forming partnerships with business and community interests. While suggestive of some

of the challenges that universities face in managing their research priorities, Gibbons' analysis avoids the epistemological issues that we are concerned with – as is made clear by Muller (2000).

[6] It is a common-sense recognition of the educational merits of the neo-conservative model that is expressed in what is referred to as 'academic drift' as students opt for traditional academic courses and employers, despite their official support for vocational qualifications, select their own employees on the basis of academic qualifications.

[7] An important sociological issue beyond the scope of this chapter is to account for the enormous and uncritical public and political support for the idea of generic key skills when all the evidence from vocational initiatives such as the Youth Training Scheme (YTS), the Certificate of Prevocational Education (CPVE) and General National Vocational Qualifications (GNVQs) suggests that such an approach is fundamentally flawed.

Chapter 2

Analysing Knowledge Claims and Practices: Languages of Legitimation

Karl Maton
University of Sydney

The medium is also a message.

Introduction

My principal purpose is to illustrate the significance of the structuring of knowledge for an understanding of intellectual and educational fields. At the same time I introduce a conceptual framework that both offers a social realist approach to education (see Chapter 1, this volume) and bridges a divide between what Basil Bernstein describes as analyses of 'relations to' and 'relations within' education (1990, pp. 165–80). According to Bernstein, the sociology of education has been overwhelmingly preoccupied with analyses of *relations to* education, such as the relations of class, race and gender to curricula and pedagogy. However, it has

> rarely turned its attention to the analysis of the intrinsic features constituting and distinguishing the specialized form of communication realized by the pedagogic discourse of education. (1990, p. 165)

This blindspot became increasingly salient after the 'new' sociology of education of the early 1970s. Previous research was dominated by a philosophy of education tradition which analysed academic subjects in terms of their development into 'indisputably logically cohesive disciplines' (Hirst 1967, p. 44). The new sociology of education critiqued this asocial and ahistorical approach as objectifying the internal structuring of educational knowledge and proposed a rejuvenated sociology of knowledge (Young 1971). However, as Bernstein argues, 'this programme, whatever else it produced, did not produce what it called for' (1990, p. 166). From

phenomenological studies of classroom interaction in the 1970s to preoc-
cupations with post-structuralism and 'voice' discourse in the 1990s, the
emphasis has tended towards the study of how knowledge works to reproduce external social relations of power rather than of the structure of
knowledge itself. While highlighting the coupling of power/knowledge,
such approaches have tended to reduce knowledge to power (see this
volume, Chapter 1).

Knowledge has, in other words, been taken for granted and treated as if
it were 'no more than a relay for power relations external to itself; a relay
whose form has no consequences for what is relayed' (Bernstein 1990,
p. 166). A proposed sociology of knowledge became realized as a sociology
without a theory of knowledge; in effect, the focus has been on the message
at the expense of the medium. My premise here is that, as Alexander
puts it, 'the sociology of knowledge can never substitute for the analysis
of knowledge' (1995, p. 129). My argument is that the medium of intellectual production and educational reproduction – the structuring of
knowledge – is itself also a message. This raises questions of how one
analyses and the significance of these relations within knowledge; that is,
what messages this medium might tell us and how we can register them.
This chapter illustrates one answer to these questions through an analysis
of the development of British cultural studies within higher education.

Integration through 'legitimation'

The form taken by this answer itself requires explanation. Analyses of the
sociology of education have described a schismatic development of oppositional and incommensurable approaches (Moore 1996a). One example
is a perceived tension within the field between the approaches of Basil
Bernstein and Pierre Bourdieu. Despite both arguing for a cumulative and
scientific sociology of education, the tendency is to compare and contrast
their work with a view to declaring a winner (e.g. Harker & May 1993).
Ironically, given Bourdieu's analysis of struggles for distinction (1984), they
have been largely kept distinct at least since the 1970s. In contrast, I aim
to overcome this false dichotomy, not at the philosophical level of a meta-
discourse on their relative merits, but by illustrating one dimension of a
conceptual framework that integrates insights from both their approaches.

The frameworks of Bourdieu and Bernstein offer a sociology of knowledge and a theory of knowledge, respectively. Bourdieu's 'field' theory
provides a means of describing intellectual and educational fields in terms

of relationally positioned struggles over status and resources; Bernstein's 'code' theory offers a means of conceptualizing the structuring of knowledge. Bourdieu's approach embraces questions of 'who', 'where', 'when' and 'how'; Bernstein's framework additionally captures the hitherto neglected issue of 'what' (1996, pp. 169–81). In short, Bourdieu highlights how intellectual and educational fields of practice structure knowledge, while Bernstein highlights the structuring significance of knowledge for those fields. Between them, their approaches conceive of knowledge as a structured and structuring structure.

Here I outline a potential means of embracing these insights by analysing knowledge-related practices as embodying claims made by actors on behalf of those practices. When actors make knowledge claims or engage in practices they are at the same time making a claim of legitimacy for those practices. Knowledge claims and practices can thus be understood as *languages of legitimation*: claims made by actors for carving out and maintaining intellectual and institutional spaces within education. These claims propose a ruler for participation within the field and proclaim criteria by which achievement within this field should be measured (cf. Bernstein 1990). Languages of legitimation thereby represent the basis for competing claims to limited status and material resources within education; they are strategic stances aimed at maximizing actors' positions within a relationally structured field of struggles (cf. Bourdieu 1988). At the same time, from a social realist perspective (see Chapter 1, this volume) the knowledge comprising these claims may be legitimate. That is, knowledge is not merely a reflection of power relations but also comprises more or less epistemologically powerful claims to truth. Social power and knowledge are intertwined but irreducible to one another; knowledge comprises both sociological and epistemological forms of power. Thus by conceiving of knowledge in terms of 'legitimation', an awareness of the structured and positioned nature of strategic position-takings within a field can be brought together with an emphasis upon the structuring and non-arbitrary nature of potentially legitimate knowledge claims; that is, embracing 'relations to' and 'relations within' analyses of knowledge, the knower and the known.

The chapter begins by briefly sketching the development of British cultural studies. By analysing the structuring principles underlying its language of legitimation, I outline a generative conceptualization of *legitimation codes*. This framework is then employed in analyses of relations to and relations within cultural studies. First, I analyse the relations of the social and institutional positions occupied by cultural studies to its legitimation code. Secondly, I outline the intrinsic dynamic generated by relations within the legitimation code, focusing on its ramifications for the field's trajectory. The latter analysis thus aims to show how an understanding of relations within knowledge sheds light on its location within social relations of power. Lastly, I briefly consider implications for the future direction of the sociology of knowledge and education.

British Cultural Studies in British Higher Education[1]

Institutional trajectory

For research into the institutionalization of cultural studies, I constructed a database of every course, option and module in cultural, media and communication studies offered in post-war British institutions of higher education, collected archival sources detailing the development of courses and collated information on the social profile of its student population. Analysis of this data reveals general patterns of institutionalization, two of which I shall focus on here: the sustained marginality and relative invisibility of cultural studies as a distinct, named area of study within British higher education.

Drawing on typologies of post-war British higher education institutions (e.g. King 1970; Tight 1996), cultural studies can be characterized as having occupied positions of relatively lower status within the institutional field throughout its emergence and development. Indeed, the first stirrings of interest in commercial or 'mass' culture as an educational issue arose outside universities. The earliest professional associations (such as the Society of Film Teachers 1950), journals (*The Film Teacher* 1952), conferences (National Union of Teachers 1960) and courses (Mainds 1965) in Britain were based in primary and secondary level education. Within this nascent educational formation the universities were considered solely in terms of the need for training schoolteachers and research on schooling (Harcourt 1964). When courses in cultural studies did emerge within higher education during the late 1950s, they were on the margins of the field, in extramural departments of adult education (Steele 1997), technical colleges (Hall 1964), colleges of art (Burton 1964) and teacher training colleges (Knight 1962). Similarly, the 'founding texts' of cultural studies (typically listed as Hoggart 1957; Williams 1958, 1961; Thompson 1963) were written by tutors of English in adult education.

During the 1960s several research centres in cultural studies emerged on the margins of existing university departments. The best-known example is the Centre for Contemporary Cultural Studies at Birmingham University

(CCCS), founded in 1964. Although the CCCS is now viewed as having been a site of intellectual pioneering, University of Birmingham (1964–74, 1975–89) and CCCS (1964–81) annual reports and my own interviews with participants show that its institutional standing was less impressive. The CCCS comprised limited staff (two and a half full-time equivalent staff supervised well over 220 postgraduate students in the period 1964–80) and endured low status in the eyes of actors within established disciplines (CCCS 1964–81; Hall 1990). The Centre survived financially through outside funding from the publishing company Penguin and sporadic projects commissioned by external bodies, such as UNESCO. At first Birmingham University offered only furniture and accommodation, the minimal nature of which is illustrated by directions given to prospective students in the late 1960s:

> The new Centre hut may be found by taking the main entrance to the Administration building; left along the corridor, first stairs down on the right; left at the bottom and left again into the back courtyard. The hut is at the far end of the outer courtyard, overlooking the parapet. (CCCS 1968, p. 4)

The main expansion of cultural studies as a taught academic subject occurred after the late 1970s, when it established a foothold within degree courses in colleges, the Open University (part-time distance learning) and former polytechnics, with a comparatively small presence in the longer established and higher status pre-1992 'older' universities. This institutional clustering has borne the brunt of educational expansion over the past 30 years and the social profile of the student body with which cultural studies is typically associated reflects this position. Bolstered by arguments that the less educated the pupil, the more susceptible they are to media influence (Newsom Report 1963), the study of mass culture often first entered curricula for the purposes of either cultivating critical discrimination among pupils deemed of lower ability or providing a liberal education enticing to non-traditional students thought to be unattracted by established disciplines (Hall & Whannel 1964). In addition, the status of the central intellectual figures of the field as social outsiders in higher education are oft-noted within the subject area (Turner 1990). Cultural studies has, in short, been associated with dominated social groups and low status institutions.

At the same time, cultural studies is often considered to have been a growth area within higher education since the 1980s (Milner 1994) and new journals, textbooks, conferences and courses which claim cultural studies among their central concerns have proliferated. However, in terms of numbers of departments, degree courses and students, cultural studies as a *named* area of study remains a relatively small-scale phenomenon. If it has found a place in the sun, this has largely been within other academic subjects, rather than in its own right. The institutional history of cultural studies is one of origins in the interstices of the curriculum and infiltration via existing subject areas. Its emergence within British higher education was within courses of 'liberal studies', 'social studies', 'general studies' and 'complementary studies' (Kitses 1964); the CCCS was established within an English department; and today much of what is commonly referred to as 'cultural studies' teaching and research is conducted within departments and courses and by actors with professional titles displaying a variety of nomenclature. Cultural studies is often visible more as an adjunct or adjective to more established disciplines (e.g. 'English and cultural studies', 'cultural geography') than as a distinct entity within higher education.

Even where it has found institutional spaces of its own, its position has been anything but certain. The first full degree course offered in Cultural Studies (at Portsmouth University, 1975) was closed down in 1999 and its teaching staff retired or dispersed despite a healthy student intake. Even the renowned CCCS was seriously threatened with closure at least twice and saved after a concerted campaign by international scholars proclaiming its *intellectual* significance (CCCS 1964–81).[2] Such institutional vulnerability has been reinforced by the scattered nature of the field. Courses and departments of cultural studies have typically been established as the result of individual initiatives (Mainds 1965) and professional subject associations have been until recently ad hoc, limited or short-lived; the first national organization embracing intellectual and institutional responsibilities (the Media, Communication and Cultural Studies Association) had its first annual conference in 2000.

This marginal institutional presence has been reflected in the status of the subject area. Cultural studies has long been the subject of attacks from both within and without higher education. From inception, it has been depicted as unacademic, politically pernicious and undermining academic standards (Watson 1977), a famous example being the eagerness with which the 'Sokal Hoax', perpetrated in the American journal *Social Text*, was taken up in Britain (Osborne 1997). In summary, cultural studies as a specialized academic subject has generally emerged and developed within the dominated pole of the field of British higher education institutions.

Language of legitimation: the voice of cultural studies

As outlined above, I shall explore how British cultural studies has been legitimated by its proponents rather than describing specific instances of enacted curricula or recounting its intellectual history. Focusing on its main period of institutionalization, since the late 1970s, two keys themes of this language of legitimation coalesce around questions of disciplinarity and notions of 'giving voice to'.

The vexed question of discipline

Proponents of cultural studies have often legitimated the subject area as 'multi-', 'cross-', 'inter-', 'post-', 'trans' or even 'anti-disciplinary' (Brantlinger 1990). Perceived signs of impending disciplinary status, such as the establishing of named degree courses, have evoked warnings that the defining oppositional status of the subject area is endangered (Hall 1992; Johnson 1983). Cultural studies has thus remained committed to breaking down academic boundaries, such as between: established disciplines; 'official' educational knowledge and everyday experience; 'high' and 'low' culture; inside and outside higher education; and the teacher and the taught. Such images of blurring, crossing and transgressing established borders or boundaries (intellectual, social, physical and so forth) feature regularly within its legitimating discourse. As 'undisciplined', cultural studies is also characterized by its advocates as free from disciplinary notions of a delimited object of study and specialized procedures of enquiry (Turner 1990). Although the subject area is nominally cultural studies, the definition of 'culture' and how it should be studied are often either explicitly eschewed or held open (Milner 1994). When defined, its object of study is typically boundless in scope – typified by such influential definitions as the study of 'a whole way of life' (following Williams 1961) – and specialized procedures are eschewed in favour of celebrating diversity in theories, methodologies and methods (McGuigan 1997). Indeed, that there is no defining 'cultural studies' approach is conventionally the opening remark of accounts of the subject area (Turner 1990). As a whole, its proclaimed objects of study and procedures of enquiry are thus *hypothetically* uncircumscribed.

Another central characteristic of cultural studies, related to this non-disciplinarity, is a proclaimed anti-canonical stance. Practitioners of cultural studies regularly announce its rebirth and their own originality and freshness, decentring its intellectual tradition (Wright 1998). The conventional account of its development is characterized by: a theoretical landscape of recurrent rupture and renewal (Hall 1971), illustrated by its enthusiasm for 'post-' theories, such as post-structuralism and postmodernism (McRobbie 1994); interventions on behalf of silenced voices declaring new beginnings (see below); and a rapid turnover of substantive areas of enquiry, related to the subject's preoccupation with the contemporary and new (Pickering 1997). Cultural studies is thus typically defined as developing by way of radical disjunctures, where progress is measured by the addition of new voices or 'theories of the break' rather than in terms of a cumulatively developing canon.

'Giving voice to'

Practitioners often identify cultural studies with a radical educational project committed to offering an oppositional pedagogy capable of empowering dominated social groups (Canaan & Epstein 1997). It has become associated with student-centred forms of teaching, more participatory forms of evaluation and social organization in education, and more open curricular structures, as well as pioneering innovative intellectual practices such as collaborative group work, collective authorship and publishing unfinished student research (McNeil 1997). The unifying thrust of these initiatives is the intention to 'give voice to' the knowledge and experience of those said to be silenced within official educational knowledge. This notion of 'giving voice to' members of marginalized social groups has become a central theme in the legitimation of cultural studies, associating its raison d'être with the dominated social positions of those whose interests it claims to be serving (Gray 1997). Correspondingly, the curricular history of cultural studies is conventionally schematized as centred upon the successive study of social class, race, gender and sexuality (Brantlinger 1990). In such accounts, key texts first focus upon giving voice to the experiences of working-class men (e.g. Willis 1977), turn to address the silenced voice of women (Women's Studies Group, CCCS 1978) and then of ethnic minorities (CCCS 1982), before more recently highlighting marginalized voices of sexuality (McRobbie 1997).

Cultural studies has thus been a key site within higher education for various interventions by feminism, race studies, queer theory and so forth. Common to these has been a critique of the ability of existing voices to represent a new voice, underpinned by (often implicit) notions of standpoint epistemology (Carby 1982); that is, an epistemological privileging of claims to specialized and unique insight based upon one's subjective experiences as a member of a specific, usually dominated, social category. Cultural studies is also legitimated as having been central to the development of anti-positivist and anti-foundationalist ideas, employing contextualist and perspectival epistemologies to celebrate difference and emphasize the multiplicity of truths and narratives against notions of objective truth and 'grand narratives'. These various theories share the contention that knowledge claims are reducible to the social characteristics of the group voicing them and a critique of notions of the possibility of a neutral voice expressing objective scientific truth. Cultural studies has thus tended to valorize the subjective over the objective, and primary experience over the detached viewpoint (Gray 1997). Studies of youth subcultures (Thornton & Gelder 1996) and of audiences (Morley 1992), for example, typically argue against an 'élitist' privileging of the detached observer and for beginning with participants' experiences, highlight the active construction of meanings 'from below', and explore subjectivity and identity. Similarly, the self-labelling of qualitative audience reception studies as 'ethnographic' – despite often involving limited contact time with the subjects of study, unnatural settings for this contact, and a focus upon only one aspect of their lives – highlights the guiding principle of giving voice to the viewpoint 'from below' (Murdock 1997).

Legitimation Codes

It is easy enough to proclaim one should view knowledge as 'a structured and structuring structure', but unless one can state what this structure comprises and how it differs from other possible structurings, then such a view remains limited to the metaphysical sphere. Thus before illustrating the structuring significance for the field of cultural studies of its language of legitimation, I shall first analyse the underlying principles structuring this language, necessitating an excursion into more theoretical discourse than hitherto. In accordance with my intention of embracing both approaches, I shall conceptualize languages of legitimation in terms of both relations within and relations to this knowledge formation. This distinction may be clarified by conceiving of knowledge as having two co-existing but analytically distinct sets of relations, highlighting that knowledge claims and practices are simultaneously claims to knowledge of the world and by authors, or oriented towards or about something and by somebody. These I shall term:

- the *epistemic relation*: between knowledge and its proclaimed object (that part of the world of which knowledge is claimed or towards which practices are oriented); and

- the *social relation*: between knowledge and its subject, author or actor (who is making the claim to knowledge or action).

In terms of languages of legitimation, this equates respectively to the questions of *what* can be legitimately described as, for example, 'cultural studies' and of *who* can legitimately claim to be producing legitimate 'cultural studies' knowledge. To analyse the answers cultural studies has given to these questions, I shall draw upon Bernstein's concepts of classification and framing (1975). The strength of *classification* (+/–C) refers to the relative strength of boundaries *between* categories or contexts (such as academic subjects in a curriculum); and the strength of *framing* (+/–F) refers to the locus of control *within* a category or context (stronger framing indicating stronger control from above, such as by a teacher).

The epistemic relation (ER) between cultural studies and its object of study is defined in its language of legitimation in terms of an espoused opposition to notions of disciplinarity, a relatively uncircumscribed object of study, open procedures of enquiry and teaching, and a commitment to problematizing categories, boundaries and hierarchies between and within forms of knowledge and objects of study. In other words, cultural studies can be described as attempting to *weaken* both classification and framing of the epistemic relation (–C, –F of ER, or simply ER–). In contrast, the social relation (SR) of this language of legitimation exhibits relatively *stronger* classification and framing (+C, +F of SR, or SR+). Here the emphasis is on 'giving voice to' the primary experience of specific knowers, where legitimate knowledge or 'truth' is defined by and restricted to the specific 'voice' said to have unique and privileged insight by virtue of who the speaker is. In other words, this language of legitimation places different strengths of boundaries around and control over the definitions of, on the one hand, what can be claimed knowledge of and how (ER–), and, on the other hand, who can claim knowledge (SR+).

Developing this distinction, one can outline a generative means of conceptualizing one dimension of *legitimation codes* or the structuring principles underlying knowledge claims and practices. Here I focus on 'specialization' or what makes someone or something different, special and worthy of distinction.[3] Varying independently the relative strengths of (classification and framing for) the epistemic and social relations generates four potential legitimation codes of specialization, as illustrated in Figure 2.1.

Here I shall focus on two legitimation codes: the *knowledge code* and the *knower code*. These refer to a distinction between legitimating knowledge by reference to procedures specialized to an object of study (knowledge code)

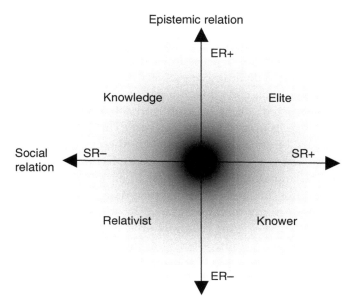

FIGURE 2.1   Legitimation codes of specialization

or personal characteristics of the author, actor or subject (knower code); that is, whether knowledge is specialized by its epistemic relation or its social relation. (The *elite code* refers to where legitimacy is based on both possessing specialist knowledge and being the right kind of knower; and the *relativist code* to where legitimate insight is ostensibly determined by neither specialist knowledge nor specific dispositions.) Table 2.1 presents the relative strengths of classifications and framings of the epistemic and social relations for knowledge and knower codes. I begin by defining a knowledge code, the opposing form of legitimation to that exhibited by cultural studies.

TABLE 2.1   Classification and framing of two legitimation codes

	Epistemic relation	**Social relation**
Knowledge code	(1) +C, +F	(2) –C, –F
Knower code	(3) –C, –F	(4) +C, +F

Note:

C = classification; F = framing. Plus (+)/minus (–) signs refer to stronger/weaker, respectively. Cell numbers refer to the order of discussion in the chapter.

In Figure 2.1 the above readings of C/F are condensed; e.g. cell number 1, ER(+C, +F) becomes ER+, and cell 2, SR(–C, –F) become SR–.

Knowledge codes

(1) Intellectual fields exhibiting knowledge codes are legitimated by reference to specialized procedures which are claimed to provide insight into a specified, discrete object of study (an explicitly realist epistemology).[4] This code thus emphasizes the difference between the field's constructed object of study and other objects, and between the knowledge its procedures are claimed to provide of this object and that provided by other intellectual fields – thereby exhibiting relatively *strong classification* of the epistemic relation. Its domain of study is thus not endless, and strong controls exist to ensure that the field's procedures are not 'misapplied' to inappropriate objects of study and its object of study is not 'misappropriated' by other fields using different procedures. There is thus relatively little personal discretion in the choice of objects of study, procedures and criteria – relatively *strong framing* – an adequate grasp of which serves as the basis of professional identity within the field.

(2) These disembodied sets of more or less consensual, relatively formal and explicit procedures and criteria are said to transcend differences among social categories of actors. In terms of their subjective characteristics, actors are neither strongly differentiated nor strongly controlled in their relation to legitimate knowledge claims. Everyone is said to be equally positioned in relation to the knowledge and practices of the field, and (it is claimed) anyone can produce knowledge provided they comply with these defining extra-personal practices. Knowledge codes thus exhibit relatively *weak classification* and *weak framing* of the social relation.

Knower codes

(3) Where knowledge codes legitimate intellectual fields according to specialized procedures for generating knowledge of a distinct object of study, knower codes base claims for fields on a privileged *subject* of study, the 'knower'. This specialized knower may claim unique knowledge of more than a delimited object of study; the knower's focus for truth claims may be hypothetically boundless, difficult to define, or encompass a host of disparate and seemingly unconnected objects of study. In other words, knower codes display relatively *weak classification* of the epistemic relation. The procedures of enquiry and criteria of validation prevalent within the field are thereby not deemed

appropriate/inappropriate according to a defined object of study, (hypothetically) enabling more personal discretion in the choice of topics, methods and criteria. The procedures are thus relatively tacit, and adjudication of competing knowledge claims on strictly 'intellectual' grounds is deemed problematic, if not directly renounced. In short, knower codes display relatively *weak framing* of the epistemic relation.

(4) Based on the unique insight of the knower, claims to knowledge by actors within the intellectual field are legitimated by reference to the knower's subjective or inter-subjective attributes and personal experiences (which serve as the basis for professional identity within the field). The aim is to 'give voice to' this experiential knowledge, with 'truth' being defined by the 'voice'. This unique knowledge is specialized to the privileged knower such that actors with different subjective characteristics are unable to make claims about this knowledge, and attempts to do so risk evoking censure from the field. The knower code thus exhibits relatively *strong classification* and *strong framing* of its social relation.

Summary

The knowledge code refers to languages of legitimation with relatively strong classification and framing of the epistemic relation and relatively weak classification and framing of the social relation (ER+, SR−); and the knower code refers to those languages of legitimation where these relative strengths are reversed (ER−, SR+; see Table 2.1). The key distinction between these two codes lies in which of the two relations specializes legitimacy within the field, that is, which is emphasized when actors claim a special status for the knowledge and practices of the field and thereby define its boundaries and limits. In the knowledge code such claims are validated, and the limits of the field defined, by specialized procedures claimed as exclusive to the field (the epistemic relation), and in the knower code by the privileged insight of the author (the social relation). In both cases it is the relation which is *strongly* classified and framed that provides the epistemological basis of truth claims, and the relation which is *weakly* classified and framed that comprises the (intellectual/social) resources drawn upon to make this truth claim. Those categories which are epistemological in the knowledge code are sociological in the knower code and a movement within an intellectual field from one code to the other effectively replaces epistemology with sociology.

Empirical realizations of legitimation codes

These two codes are not dichotomous ideal types. Rather, the two relations represent an analytical distinction between empirically co-existing and articulating dimensions of knowledge and practices. The strengths for the two relations are relative and represent continua. The four legitimation codes of Figure 2.1 are thus akin to naming directions created by points on a compass to help orientate oneself within a terrain. The lack of empirical examples given above is intentional, for their realizations as *languages* of legitimation are a function of the context – what lies North or South (or ER+/−) is relative to where one is standing. The structuring relations of power and control inhering within specific empirical contexts will condition which features of these codes are enabled and realized. The conceptualization does not, therefore, negate empirical analysis of the knowledge and practices of specific intellectual fields. Indeed, such conceptual development itself results from, highlights the necessity of, and (by defining the phenomena to be investigated) enables empirical investigation of specific realizations of knowledge in determinate conditions.

One must also distinguish between modelling academic practices and conceptualizing the principles underlying academic rhetoric regarding those practices. The above conceptualizations are inadequate as accounts of social practices in intellectual fields only inasmuch as self-characterizations are inadequate as descriptions of what practitioners actually do. That knowledge and knower codes may misrepresent the ongoing practices of actors does not prevent the very same actors from propagating these codes on their behalf. The inadequacy of these accounts as descriptions of intellectual and educational practice is thus not at issue here. My concern is with the underlying structuring principles of these accounts. Moreover, as I shall illustrate, understanding these principles of legitimation shows how the form taken by such strategic claims helps to shape the development of intellectual fields.

Analysing Relations to and Relations within Knower Codes

Using these concepts, the language of legitimation of British cultural studies since the late 1970s can be redescribed as one kind of knower code. This begins to address how relations within knowledge may be analysed; the questions remain, however, of the significance and value of such analyses and of whether this conceptualization is applicable in both 'relations to' and 'relations within' analyses. To address these issues, I shall briefly outline two illustrative analyses of the development of this knower code in terms of: (i) *relations to* its institutional positionings; and (ii) *relations within* this knowledge, focusing upon the ramifications of the knower code's intrinsic dynamic for the intellectual field's institutional trajectory within higher education. The aim is to illustrate how knowledge is both structured by and in turn structures intellectual fields. (I should highlight the crucial distinction between the *content* and purposes of a language of legitimation, such as advancing the claims of marginalized social groups, and its *structure*. What follows is *not* intended as a critique of the political and educational project of cultural studies; if anything, it may highlight that its means might not always serve its ends).

Analysing relations to knower codes

To analyse relations to knowledge requires focusing on its social and institutional positionings. Drawing upon Bourdieu (1984), one can characterize society (or 'social space') as structured according to, first, dominant (+) and dominated (−) poles or classes, and then, within each class, according to dominant and dominated class fractions (see Figure 2.2). For Bourdieu

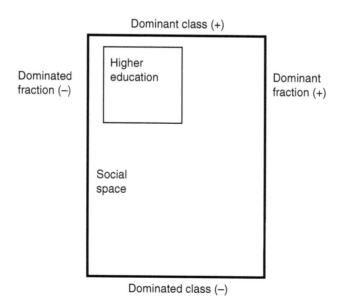

FIGURE 2.2 Social position of the field of higher education

(1988), higher education is located in the *dominated* fraction of the dominant class, its dominant social position being based upon cultural capital (knowledge and know-how) which is subordinate relative to economic capital. As outlined earlier, cultural studies emerged and developed within relatively low-status institutions associated with the teaching of socially and educationally marginalized social groups. It has thus occupied subordinate positions within the dominated fraction of the dominant class (higher education). According to Bourdieu's approach, intellectuals are prone to perceiving their dominated class fraction position as homologous to that of the dominated class in society as a whole: in Figure 2.2, the homologous relation of '+' and '−' between the axes of top-bottom and right-left. Cultural studies has occupied positions of multiple domination within higher education, making it a very plausible candidate for this kind of thinking, that is, regarding the hierarchical relations of the internal structure of the higher education field as applicable beyond this field to wider social relations, generating a perception of shared interests.

One finds this process reflected in the language of legitimation of cultural studies. Due to the sponsored mobility of a small number of scholarship boys (Hoggart 1957; Turner 1971), cultural studies began primarily with the working class as a dominant focus of enquiry. It also emerged out of attempts, via the involvement of its 'founding fathers' in the New Left and adult education, to forge alliances with the working class (Kenny 1995). The feminist intervention in cultural studies during the mid-1970s argued that the working class had served not only as a privileged empirical object of study but also as the epistemological basis of knowledge claims within the field; that is, that working-class membership operated as the specific social category upon which claims to privileged insight were made – a knower code of legitimation.[5] Social mobility through prolonged education, however, makes claims to membership of or shared interests with the working class increasingly hard to sustain. Thus one finds attempts within cultural studies to construct a theoretical basis for overcoming the distance between past social class origins and current social class position such as notions, drawing on Gramsci, of the 'organic intellectual' during the late 1970s. However, despite educational expansion, the proportion of working-class students within higher education remains relatively small, restricting the supply of potential organic intellectuals. In cases where actors are from other social class backgrounds, one then finds attempts to develop various theories of structural homology, such as the academic as 'intellectual proletarian'. This becomes the basis of what can be termed an *imaginary alliance* (between the 'intellectual' and 'proletarian'). Richard Johnson, for example, writes,

> My best practices, I imagine, seek out and ally with marginal positions, their agenda of study, and critical intellectual projects . . . I see the history of Cultural Studies . . . as a story of such alliances. (1997, p. 48)

Paradoxically for cultural studies, where this imaginary alliance is based on perceived similarities of social position it risks downplaying the role of *cultural* capital, the principal difference between the social positions of intellectuals and dominated classes. Conversely, social class tends to be suppressed as a marker of difference (between academic and non-academic members of the knower group) when membership or representation claims are based upon non-class characteristics, such as race, gender and sexuality. It is thus perhaps not entirely unrelated that social class has come to be eclipsed within cultural studies during the rise to prominence of these 'interventions'.

The idea of an imaginary alliance, however (like Bourdieu's notion of field on which it builds), is rather static. To address the development of academic subjects over time, it must be set in motion. In the case of cultural studies, the history of its knowledge structure comprises a *procession of the excluded*: the working class, women, ethnic minorities and so on. In other words, the field takes on the characteristics of a queue: once one group enters (usually within legitimating discourse rather than higher education institutions as staff or students), then another group appears to take its place outside the door demanding (or having demands made on its behalf for) entry. Until everyone and/or their experiences are included within higher education and/or knowledge, there is always scope for a new excluded group to emerge. This may explain the restless search for a new 'proletariat' (based on class, race, gender, sexuality) which characterizes cultural studies (Harris 1992).

In Bourdieu's approach, the relational practices ('position-takings' or 'stances') of actors within a specific field are viewed as being determined by their relational positions within that field. Positions and stances are 'methodologically inseparable' and 'must be analyzed together', but *'the space of positions tends to command the space of position-takings'* (Bourdieu & Wacquant 1992, p. 105, original emphasis). Basically, actors are held to be inclined towards conservative/subversive strategies, depending upon whether they occupy dominant / dominated positions, respectively, within the field. The discursive practices of cultural studies can thus be explained in terms of actors' strategies reflecting their institutional and social positions. In short, actors from dominated social positions (the working class, women, etc.) tend to occupy dominated institutional positions within higher education (colleges, polytechnics, etc.). By virtue of these positions of multiple domination, they are inclined to adopt subversive 'position-takings' in an attempt to maximize their position: against dominant notions of disciplinary specialization, cultural studies celebrates non-disciplinarity; against traditional pedagogy is set a radical educational project; against positivism, subjective experience is privileged and so forth. Thus, given the perceived dominance of knowledge codes within higher education during the development of cultural studies, a knower code provided the oppositional means for actors occupying dominated positions to attempt to subvert the hierarchy of the field. A form of this explanation can indeed be found within cultural studies itself; Epstein (1997), for example, emphasizes the subversive potential of marginal academic positions.

The whole story?

To conclude at this point, accounting for the legitimation code of cultural studies as reflecting its social positions within higher education, would be to have undertaken an (albeit simplistic) analysis of 'relations to': the relations of a language of legitimation to its social and institutional positions. As briefly illustrated above, such an analysis provides insights into questions of who, where, when, how and why. However, in this approach the form taken by knowledge is constructed as arbitrary and historically contingent and an analysis of its structural history viewed as irrelevant for an understanding of its development. Actors tend to adopt (subversive) practices which reflect their (dominated) relational position, regardless of the form taken by these practices. From this perspective it is perfectly feasible that if relativism had been dominant, cultural studies would now be associated with positivism. In other words, the *function* of languages of legitimation, as strategic 'position-takings', is abstracted from their *form*, which is described only in terms of being oppositionally defined to other possible position-takings. The point is to analyse actors' relational positions within the field, from which their practices can be 'read off'. The knowledge of intellectual fields is thereby viewed as a reflective epiphenomenon of the play of positions within the field. Such analyses thus have a blindspot: the question of 'what'.

This approach, then, provides only part of the story. I shall now illustrate how analysis of the intrinsic dynamic generated by this form of knower code offers a means of explaining the development of cultural studies without reducing its knowledge to an arbitrary reflection of external power relations. This highlights how relations *within* knowledge are significant both to the way knowledge itself develops and its institutional trajectory. Additionally, by using the same concepts of legitimation codes to consider the structuring of these position-takings, the aim will be to complement rather than displace the above approach.

Analysing relations within knower codes

The legitimation code represented by cultural studies is a particular kind of knower code, one based on a social category.[6] This social knower code comprises actors claiming to represent the interests of a social group outside academia, as in the notion of 'giving voice to'. Such knower codes base their legitimation upon the privileged insight of a *knower*, and work at maintaining strong boundaries around their definition of this knower – they celebrate difference where 'truth' is defined by the 'knower' or 'voice' – that is, they exhibit strong classification and framing of the social relation. Such discourses are legitimated on the basis of the inability of existing knowledge to articulate the voice of this previously silenced knower. However, once a knower code has succeeded in carving out an institutional or intellectual position within higher education, it is likely to become the most prone to the same legitimating strategy; it is difficult to deny new voices what one has claimed was denied to one's own. Such a strategy thus tends to evoke its own disrupter, a new voice – 'interruptions interrupted' as Brunsdon (1996, p. 179) characterizes feminist work in cultural studies – enabling a procession of the excluded.

If such developments are considered over time, then as each new voice is brought into the academic choir, the category of the new privileged knower becomes ever smaller, each being strongly bounded from one another, for each voice claims its own privileged and specialized knowledge inaccessible to other knowers. The range of knowers within the intellectual field as a whole thus proliferates and fragments, each client knower group having its own representative. For example, this may begin with 'the working class'; then, as the category of the working class fragments under the impact of the procession of the excluded (as the knower's ability to speak for other voices is critiqued), it may develop as follows:

class	– the working class
gender	– working-class men
race	– white, working-class men
sexuality	– white, heterosexual, working-class men
	– Oxbridge-educated, white heterosexual men of working-class origin in their late twenties currently living in Leicester
	– and so on, until you reach . . . me (in 1998).

Thus, while carving out a discursive space for itself, the knower critique of existing voices enables the possibility of its being critiqued in turn using the same legitimation code. Cultural studies itself has often illustrated the multiplicities of subjectivity and identity – the potential categories of new knowers are hypothetically endless. The procession of the excluded thus becomes, in terms of the privileged knower, an accretion of adjectives or 'hyphenation' effect. Thus, while the knower code can be understood as a Bourdieuan strategy of capital maximization, the dynamic of its *intrinsic* structure enables in turn the successive creation of new positions, leading to proliferation and fragmentation within the field.

With this proliferation of knowers, where new knowledge is defined according to the criteria of articulating each knower's specialized voice, and truth is defined as whatever may be said by this voice, then it is not *what* has been said before that matters, it is *who* has said it. It is thus likely that, with each addition of a new adjective or hyphen, existing work within the field will be overhauled – old songs will be sung by new voices in their own distinctive register. Rather than building upon previous knowledge, there is a tendency for new knowers to declare new beginnings, re-definitions and even complete ruptures with the past – an anti-canonical, iconoclastic and parricidal stance generating recurrent schismatic episodes. The intellectual field then gives the appearance of undergoing permanent cultural revolution, of perennially being at year zero. However, although the names and faces featured regularly change, the underlying form of the recurrent radical 'breaks' characterizing the field is the same: they are empirical realizations of knower code legitimation.

This process of proliferation and fragmentation also reduces the social bases for collective political action – the knower code emphasises *difference from* rather than *similarity with*, leading to ever smaller categories of knower. It is then perhaps unsurprising that professional associations within British cultural studies have often been precarious.[7] Furthermore, lacking an explicit and strongly defined notion of a specialized object of study and appropriate procedures opens up the intellectual field's knowledge and actors to being poached by other fields. Rather than design and develop a specialized and distinct course in and/or department of 'cultural studies', one can bolt an option or module in cultural studies on to existing courses or add a lecturer to an established department. Similarly, in research one can annex the field's name to use as an adjective: cultural geography, cultural history, cultural economics, even perhaps cultural physics. Thus, proliferation and fragmentation results in the paradoxical situation of an intellectual field appearing to be both blossoming and in decline, both everywhere and nowhere to be seen.

The social knower code also leaves intellectual fields vulnerable to criticism from outside higher education; after all, if it is only the specific knower who can know, then professional academics are dispensable (unless they research only themselves). Such an argument may seem facile, but is a realistic possibility. For example, telephone callers to a British radio programme on the issue of a referendum on European monetary union repeatedly asked the question: 'Why should we bother voting for and paying the salaries of politicians if they are only going to ask us to make decisions, that is *their* job, not ours.' That such attitudes have worrying political implications does not detract from the point that such knower codes are vulnerable to similar criticism. I would suggest that academics are currently less well positioned institutionally to rebuff such criticisms. The tendency of social knower codes to insist upon the multiplicity of truths and proclaim against the adjudication of competing knowledge claims renders them particularly vulnerable within the current educational environment, where policy-linked research funding and the market of student demand (characterized by credential inflation and, in Britain, rising student debts) are likely to induce increasingly utilitarian demands of subject areas.

One possible response to such calls to legitimate one's intellectual field (and thus oneself) is to highlight the significance of its object of study. As an instance of this strategy in reverse, one could relate Margaret Thatcher's declaration that 'society' does not exist to the targeting of the social sciences for funding cutbacks in Britain during the 1980s. Social knower codes, however, are not primarily based upon claims to provide specialized and theorized insight into a discrete foundational object. Instead they tend to emphasize the significance of their *subject* of study. While the marginalized position of a specific group of knowers may be highlighted, such a strategy tends to evoke its own disrupter and the vitality of this strategy varies inversely with its success – once a voice begins to be heard, claims to marginality begin to lose their force. In addition, with the proliferation and fragmentation of knowers, the question of whom the intellectual field is giving voice to becomes increasingly problematic. Knower codes may, therefore, problematize attempts to carve out spaces within high-status institutional positions by giving rise to a process of 'divide and be conquered'.

In summary, the intrinsic dynamic of social knower codes tends to proliferation and fragmentation. The resultant tendency towards a segmented and schismatic knowledge structure problematizes the ability of actors to establish or maintain discrete institutional spaces: they are vulnerable to utilitarian criticism from without, and to poaching of actors and knowledge from within the higher education field. In other words, relations within knowledge, through the dynamic they enable, may themselves contribute to the institutional and intellectual trajectories of an intellectual field. In practice, these tendencies may be unexercised (because of a lack of enabling conditions), exercised unrealized (due to countervailing pressures), or realized unperceived (see Bhaskar 1975); to reiterate, their status is a matter for empirical research.

Conclusion

I began this chapter by referring to Bernstein's argument that the sociology of education has tended to focus on 'relations to' rather than 'relations within' education. Studies of intellectual fields tend to treat knowledge as a neutral relay for external power relations and focus on the message relayed by this medium. By showing how relations within knowledge impact upon the basis of its positions within higher education, I demonstrated the significance of analyses of 'relations within' for a fuller understanding of the changing structuring of knowledge and education. In other words, this medium is *also* a message. My emphasis is deliberate – I am not claiming the medium is *the* message. I argue not that analyses of relations to knowledge should be displaced but rather complemented and the insights they afford retained. To this end I proposed conceiving knowledge in terms of legitimation and briefly illustrated how a conceptualization of the principles underlying languages of legitimation may be utilized within analyses of both relations to and relations within knowledge. By offering a means of integrating and building upon the insights of both approaches,

I also hope to contribute to breaking the habit of radical 'breaks' and reinvention characterizing the sociology of education (see Chapter 3, this volume).

My focus on legitimation has been related to the insights and blindspots of past studies of intellectual fields. Where the philosophy of education tended to construct knowledge as asocial, the sociology of knowledge has tended to neglect questions of epistemology – they have obscured the social relation and the epistemic relation of knowledge, respectively. In addition to showing the socially and historically located nature of knowledge – the role knowledge plays in legitimating social relations of power – one needs to hold out the possibility of the legitimate status of truth claims. The notion of legitimation offers a social realist approach that highlights both the sociological nature of knowledge, as comprising strategies by actors socially positioned within a field of struggle over forms of capital, and its epistemological nature as potentially legitimate knowledge claims. The development of intellectual fields comprises more than the will to power; there is also the will to truth. Both dimensions of knowledge must be accounted for by a realist sociology of knowledge which is to avoid the Scylla and Charybdis of reductionist relativism (the sociological fallacy) and asocial objectivism (the epistemological fallacy). To do so is to acknowledge that while the truth is no guarantee of belief, belief is no guarantee of the truth.

I focused on an explicit language of legitimation, but the framework elaborated above can obviously be applied to the study of educational knowledge and practices more generally.[8] All practices and knowledge claims are forms of legitimation. Conceiving of educational knowledge in terms of legitimation codes also enables one to see where debates which appear to differ at the level of ideas, actors and intellectual positions are recurrent forms of the same underlying principles (e.g. phenomenology, post-structuralism, postmodernism as anti-knowledge codes). This may facilitate a means of engaging with the underlying issues structuring such debates rather than their surface features, and so enable social science to move beyond such cyclical recurrences. In addition, the sociology of education often tends towards static synchrony, flattening out periods of time and neglecting the analysis of change. By focusing on how knower codes evolve highlights not only change over time but more importantly the dynamic underlying the development of intellectual fields.

Lastly, analysing the development of a social knower code indicates several issues of significance to the future direction of the sociology of education. The description of a segmented and schismatic intellectual field which appears to regularly begin from scratch, is resonant with the intellectual history of British sociology of education over the past 30 years. This is a pressing issue, which requires careful consideration (see Chapters 3 and 6, this volume). I would suggest, however, that an analysis of relations within the sociology of education may indicate that its marginal institutional and intellectual position is related to a tendency (similar to that outlined above) to substitute sociology for epistemology (Moore & Maton 2001). Knowledge, in this case, is studied indirectly, so to speak, out of the corner of one's eye. If so, there exists a need to establish knowledge as an *independent* object of study with its own specialized procedures in order to provide an adequate epistemological basis for the sociology of education. It is this end that the conceptualization of languages of legitimation aims to advance.

Endnotes

[1] This brief sketch is of *British cultural studies* within *British* higher education. The term 'British cultural studies' is commonly used to distinguish this tradition from those emanating from other national contexts. Subject areas related to cultural studies, such as media and communication studies, have divergent emphases, and institutional trajectories in other national contexts have differed (e.g. Blundell et al. 1993).

[2] This chapter was written in the late 1990s; the CCCS was finally closed down in 2002 (see further below).

[3] Other dimensions include Autonomy (Maton 2005) and Semantics (Maton 2009a).

[4] All languages of legitimation are realist about something, whether subjects or objects of study, or knowledge claims. For example, post-modernists tend to adopt an (albeit tacit) realist position on the status of their truth claims regarding the unavailability of 'truth'. The difference being drawn here is whether the realist epistemological basis is relatively explicit (knowledge code) or tacit (knower code).

[5] This knower code was retrospectively attributed to previous work in cultural studies during the mid-1970s. This period marked a decisive shift in the field's language of legitimation (see Chapter 8, this volume).

[6] Knower codes with a different basis may have a different intrinsic dynamic. On different kinds of knower codes, see Maton (2009b) and Chapter 8 of this volume.

[7] While threats to the CCCS prior to the mid-1970s were countered by international action, the Centre was closed down by the University of Birmingham in

2002, two years after the original publication of this chapter hypothesized the difficulty of maintaining an institutional presence.

[8] For examples of how the framework has subsequently developed, see Maton (2007, 2009c), Moore & Maton (2001), and Chapter 8 of this volume. For examples of research using the concepts, see Carvalho et al. (2009), Doherty (2008), Lamont & Maton (2008) and Shay (2008).

Chapter 3

'Voice Discourse' and the Problem of Knowledge and Identity

Rob Moore
Cambridge University

Johan Muller
University of Cape Town

Introduction

Our purpose in this chapter is to raise some issues about epistemological debates and approaches to knowledge in the sociology of education. Our starting point is the observation that since the phenomenologically inspired New Sociology of Education in the early 1970s to postmodernism today, approaches that question epistemological claims about the objectivity of knowledge (and the status of science, reason and rationality, more generally) have occupied an influential position in the field. In earlier times, this approach was often referred to as the 'sociology of knowledge' perspective. Yet then, as now it is precisely the idea of *knowledge* that is being challenged. Such approaches adopt, or at least favour or imply, a form of perspectivism which sees knowledge and truth claims as being relative to a culture, form of life or standpoint and, therefore, ultimately representing a particular perspective and social interest rather than independent, universalistic criteria. They complete this reduction by translating knowledge claims into statements about knowers. Knowledge is dissolved into knowing and priority is given to experience as specialized by category membership and identity (Chapter 2, this volume). For instance, a so-called 'dominant' or 'hegemonic' form of knowledge, represented in the school curriculum, is identified as 'bourgeois', 'male', or 'white' – as reflecting the perspectives, standpoints and interests of dominant social groups.

Today, the most common form of this approach is that which, drawing upon postmodernist and post-structuralist perspectives, adopts a discursive concern with the explication of 'voice'. Its major distinction is that between the dominant voice and those ('Others') silenced or marginalized by its hegemony. As Philip Wexler (1997, p. 9) has recently observed, 'The post-modern emphasis on discourse and identity remain overwhelmingly the dominant paradigm in school research, and with few exceptions, gives few signs of abating' (see also Delamont 1997). The main move is to attach knowledge to categories of knowers and to their experience and subjectivities. This privileges and specializes the subject in terms of its membership category as a subordinated voice. Knowledge forms and knowledge relations are translated as social standpoints and power relationships between groups. This is more a sociology of *knowers* and their relationships than of knowledge (Chapter 2, this volume). What we will term 'voice discourse' is our principle concern here.

Historically, this approach has also been associated with concerns to reform pedagogy in a progressive direction. At the time of the New Sociology of Education in the early 1970s, this move was expressed in the debate between 'new' sociologists such as Michael Young (1971, 1976) and the philosophical position associated with R. S. Peters and Paul Hirst. More recently, it has been associated with developments such as anti-sexist, multicultural and postcolonial education, and with postmodernist critiques of the 'Enlightenment Project' and 'grand narratives'. The crucial issue, for such approaches, is that social differentiation in education and the reproduction of social inequalities are associated with principles of exclusion structured in and through educational knowledge. Hence, the critique of knowledge and promotion of progressive pedagogy is understood as facilitating a move from social and educational exclusion to inclusion and the promotion of social justice.

This history can be summarized as follows: in the early 1970s, the New Sociology of Education produced a critique of insulated knowledge codes by adopting a 'sociology of knowledge' perspective that claimed to demystify their epistemological pretensions to cognitive superiority by revealing their class base and form. Knowledge relations were transcribed as class relations.[1] In the late 1970s, feminism challenged the masculinist bias of class analysis and turned attention to the gendered character of educational relations, rewriting knowledge relations in terms of patriarchy. This was in turn followed by a focus upon race. In the 1980s, the primary categories employed by gender and race approaches fragmented as various groups contested the vanguardist claims of the earlier proponents of those perspectives to be representing the interests of women or blacks in general. The category 'woman', for instance, fragmented into groups such as women of colour, non-heterosexual women, working-class women, third-world women and African women (Wolpe 1998). These fractions of gender and race were further extended by a range of sexualities and, to some degree (although never so successfully), by disabilities. Under this pressure of fragmentation, there was a rapid shift away from political universalism to a thoroughgoing celebration of difference and diversity; of decentred, hyphenated or iterative models of the self and, consequently, of identity politics. This poststructuralist celebration of diversity is associated with proclamations of inclusiveness that oppose the alleged exclusiveness of the dominant knowledge form that is revealed when its traditional claims to universalism and objectivity are shown for what they really are – the disguised standpoints and interests of dominant groups.

On this basis, epistemology and the sociology of knowledge are presented as antithetical. The sociology of knowledge undertakes to demystify episte-mological knowledge claims by revealing their social base and standpoint. At root, this sociology of knowledge debunks epistemology. The advocacy of progressive moral and political arguments becomes conflated with a particular set of (anti-) epistemological arguments (Maton, Chapter 2, this volume; Siegel 1997).

At this descriptive level, these developments are usually presented as marking a progressive advance whereby the assault upon the epistemolo-gical claims of the dominant or 'hegemonic' knowledge code (rewritten in its social form as 'power') enables a succession of previously marginalized, excluded and oppressed groups to enter the central stage, their histories to be recovered and their 'voices' joined freely and equally with those already there.[2] Within this advance, the voice of reason (revealed as that of the ruling class white heterosexual male) is reduced simply to one among many, of no special distinction. This is advanced through the multiplication of categories and their differences. Disparities of access and representation in education were (and are) rightly seen as issues that need addressing and remedying, and in this respect constitute a genuine politics. It is impor-tant to stress, here, that the issues are real issues and the work done on their behalf is real work. But the question is: is this politics best pursued in this way?

The tendency we are intending to critique, then, assumes an internal relation between:

(a) theories of knowledge (epistemological or sociological);
(b) forms of education (traditional or progressive); and
(c) social relations (between dominant and subordinated groups).

This establishes the political default settings whereby epistemologically grounded, knowledge-based forms of education are politically conservative, while 'integrated' (Bernstein 1977) or 'hybrid' (Muller & Taylor 1995) knowledge codes are progressive. On this basis, socially progressive causes are systematically detached from epistemologically powerful knowledge structures and from their procedures for generating and promoting truths of fact and value. For us, the crucial problem here is, these default settings have the effect of undermining the very argumentative force that progressive causes in fact require in order to press their claims.

The position of voice discourse and its cognate forms within the sociology of education has also profoundly affected theory and research within the field, with little attention being paid to structural level concerns with social stratification and a penchant for small-scale, qualitative ethnographic methods and 'culturalist' concerns with discursive positioning and identity (Hatcher 1998; Moore 1996a). We will argue that this perspective is not only politically self-defeating, but also intellectually incoherent – that, in fact, progressive claims implicitly presuppose precisely the kind of 'conservative' epistemology that they tend to reject and that, to be of value, the sociology of education should produce knowledge in the *strong* sense. This is important because the effects of the (anti-) epistemological thesis undermine the possibilities of producing precisely that kind of knowledge required to support the moral/political objectives. Indeed, the dubious epistemological assumptions may lead not only to an 'analytical nihilism that is contrary to (their) political project' (Ladwig 1995, p. 222), but also to pedagogic conclusions that are actively counterproductive and ultimately work, against the educational interests of precisely those groups they are meant to help (Dowling 1994; Stone 1981). We agree, thus, with Siegel that, '. . . it is imperative that defenders of radical pedagogy distinguish their embrace of particular moral/political theses from untenable, allegedly related, epistemological ones' (ibid., p. 34).

Episodic Return

It is not our purpose, however, to simply argue against 'voice discourse'. We have drawn attention to the way in which this position has assumed a number of forms over a fairly long period of time and it is also, of course, widespread in the social sciences and humanities (in literary studies and criticism, in particular). For reasons we give and develop in depth later, we see these facts as requiring attention in themselves. That 'voice discourse' has both endured in this fashion and is so widespread calls for explanation because, as an intellectual position, it lacks any sustainable credibility, and this has been the case for a long time! Hence, we will suggest that the issues here are not simply those of argument and critique but of the structuring of the intellectual field. In this respect 'voice discourse' must be described and understood as a position within the field. Its influence is difficult to explain intellectually because as an argument it is long discredited, but perhaps it can be accounted for sociologically.

Our reasons for adopting this approach to the position currently occupied by voice discourse are as follows. First, the refutations of the relativistic perspectivism of voice discourse are already well established and have been so for a long time (Harre & Krausz 1996). In part they were developed within the philosophy of science in the debates that arose in response to Kuhn's *The Structure of Scientific Revolutions* (1970), and the issue of incommensurability but can be found also, for instance, in debates over meaning and interpretation in radical ethnography.[3] It is fair to say that these arguments are so well established and convincing that perspectivism has no serious (or, at least, no seriously unqualified) support in those places where the issues have been debated longest and most rigorously. Hence, it is noteworthy that the position maintains such a strong allegiance within areas of the sociology of education. It may reveal something about the strongly insulated position of the field that it so often seems so indifferent to, or unaware of, developments elsewhere.

Second, given the centrality of science to these issues and to the way in which voice discourse defines itself and establishes its credentials through a critique of science and scientific rationality, the neglect of the past 30 years of debate in post-empiricist philosophy of science (see further below) can be seen as a positioning strategy rather than counting as an intellectually viable position. Symptomatic of this is the tendency for 'science' in this literature to be conflated with positivism and identified with absolutism rather than fallibilism (see Hammersley & Gomm 1997). As we shall argue, the force of the postmodern critique depends precisely upon restricting 'science' to this positivist and absolutist caricature.

Third, further evidence that we are dealing with a field position or position-taking strategy is in the peculiar tendency for it to repeat itself in different forms over an extended period of time, from the phenomenology of the New Sociology of Education in the early 1970s to today's post-structuralism and the uses made of Foucault and Derrida, as well as of postmodernists such as Lyotard.[4] Upon inspection, positions that are theoretically very different or even antithetical (phenomenological, structuralist, post-structuralist) are used in the same way at different times.

Placed in context, the discourse of voice appears as the repetition of a particular kind of intellectual episode that tends to recur, in ostensibly different forms, over the years (Moore 1996b). It represents a move to decentre or delegitimize what is held to be a dominant or hegemonic knowledge form and to promote some alternative linked with the alleged standpoint and interests of a marginalized or silenced group. We suggest that this episodic event must be understood sociologically in terms of the structuring of the intellectual field rather than intellectually in terms of its argument, or in terms of its moral or political stance. Hence, our critique of voice discourse will not only rehearse the arguments against, but also attempt to describe it.

Issues and Positions

Durkheim argued that everything must be described twice: first in its own terms as a 'practical' theory, then, again, in its social form. This distinction has been significantly refined and systematically developed by Bernstein in his discussion of discourses, knowledge structures and fields (1999). He makes a contrast between horizontal and vertical discourses, and knowledge structures, and we will argue that the discourse of voice has operated in the form of a 'horizontal' knowledge structure with a weak grammar, and the process we have described can be understood as the reproduction (through replication) of such a knowledge structure over time. It is useful to make a distinction here between 'issues' and 'positions'. The progressive description is at the level of issues – the issue of the working class, the woman issue, the black issue and so on. The issue, in each case, is different because the 'identity' is different. But from a sociological point of view, the *position* is the same. At the level of the issues, the rhetoric changes in each case, but their logics have a common and constant form: that of contesting a dominant knowledge claim by differentiating a subordinated category, and constructing its distinctive identity and interest by way of authorizing its own voice and authenticity of experience as knowledge (Delamont 1997). Hence, each instance (issue) can be rewritten in a common paradigmatic form (Moore 1996b). Our concern is to explore that form and explicate its structure; to rewrite the issue as the position.

Voice discourses identify a constituency or membership category and present themselves as the representation (representative) of that constituency, as its voice – the voice of 'woman', for example. We could say that this is a kind of anthropomorphism (in the generic rather than the gendered sense) which turns knowledge forms into 'characters'.[5] The realm of knowledge is *re*-presented as a cast of characters engaged in a drama of competing, antagonistic interests and struggles. Following Gellner (1974), the device can be seen as transforming the 'cold' world of secular rationalism in which knowledge is divorced from knowers (what Popper called 'epistemology without a knowing subject' [1983]), back into a 'warm' world of human characters. Whereas critical rationalism as an historically radical force systematically attempted to separate knower claims from knowledge claims (things are not true simply because the Chief, the Party or the Pope says so), this device sets out, once more, to privilege the knower, or the knower's imputed membership category, as the truth criterion. Perversely, postmodernism pursues a 'pre-modern' strategy of attempting to reinstate 'who knows' as the authority for 'what is known' (cf. Maton 2002). The fact that it celebrates the virtue of the oppressed against the calumny of the oppressor does not change the principle.

As the phonocentrism (Derrida 1976) of the term 'voice' implies, this discourse warrants itself through assertions of naturalistic authenticity. It counters 'hegemonic' epistemological knowledge claims with representations of the experience of exclusion attributed to those silenced by its dominance: it asserts the primacy of speech (experience) over writing (theory) – of the mundane over the esoteric or, in the terminology of Durkheim's path-breaking analysis in *The Elementary Forms of the Religious Life* (1967; originally 1915), the profane over the sacred.[6] However, and crucially, 'voices' imply hearers as well as speakers. The key question to be asked whenever we encounter the notion of 'voice' is not only who is speaking, but also who is hearing, or, more accurately, *reading*? Voices have to be read backwards. To say this is not inadvertently to mix metaphors; in reality, we only ever encounter 'voices' in texts. Voices are textual productions, or, to be precise, *recontextualizations* (Bernstein 1990). The rhetoric of voice discourse disguises the fact that 'voice' is entirely a product of texts (writing/theory) and is constituted by the principles whereby the text is written. The rhetoric that re-presents text as 'voice' suppresses precisely the syntax that generates the text and displaces its principle to the imaginary place occupied by the imaginary subject whose voice is invoked as author/authority. It is by reading 'voice' backwards (from 'speaker' to 'hearer') that we may be able to recover the specialized pedagogic device that, through constructing the 'imaginary subject' (Bernstein 1990) of voice (the 'speaker'), specializes and privileges the field position of the 'hearer' within the structuring of the field.

Every description of reality, every theoretical tendency, depicts the world in such a way that a certain community of members will recognize the description of the world as the world 'as it really is'. The question we now wish to address is: how does the discourse of voice constitute its description of the world? To answer the question requires determining the standpoint of that description as well as its positioning strategy, that is, determining how the standpoint is positively constructed (from where is the description made?) and, correlatively, in relation to what is it negatively characterized (against what is its distinctiveness constructed?).

Science and the Construction of the Dominant Discourse

We will begin by considering the *negative* construction, that is, the way in which this discourse represents itself and defines its distinctiveness in opposition to a position defined as dominant or hegemonic, and in relation to which it or those whose 'voices' it represents is marginalized or, hitherto, silenced. Discourses of voice all have the following as features of their positioning strategy:

- A description of the world from a standpoint that sees itself as subordinated; the standpoint of the voice is established by means of a critique of the dominant knowledge-form seen to be central to the construction of subordination.
- A description of the world in terms of social relations of domination/subordination is transcribed as an epistemic relation that is then treated as the constitutive principle of the social relation. For example, women are subordinated to men because the dominant forms of knowledge are male ('male' reason, 'male' science, 'male' history, etc.).

As Siegel (1997), has demonstrated, it is in the slide from the social/moral to the epistemic that this perspective not only becomes questionable, but also fatally undermines the moral and political grounds that inspire it in the first place. Inclusion, for instance, may be a morally defensible social virtue, but inclusiveness is not intrinsically an epistemic virtue: first, because there is no necessary relationship between inclusiveness and truth or exclusiveness and falsehood; and second, because epistemological inclusiveness ('anything goes') removes any effective basis for arguing for social inclusiveness because all arguments, including those against inclusion, are equally valid, dependent on the perspective of the belief holders (see Siegel, ibid., chapter 12).[7] It is through the negative construction that this position claims its radical distinctiveness. Furthermore, its major positive contentions, including its claims to originality, depend upon the viability of the way in which it constructs the dominant discourse to which it is opposed both morally and epistemologically.

We will begin by examining one current exemplar of the discourse of voice in education, that of Usher and Edwards (1994), and distil from it the discursive rules that typically reoccur across the range of positions within this field. The basic move is, as we have said, one that translates knowledge relations into social relations through a reductive critique of epistemology. The main argument purports to demolish the claims of the dominant form of knowledge. In this case, the issue we examine is the manner in which science is presented and how that presentation delegitimizes the epistemological claims made for science and, in so doing, opens the space for other 'voices'.

In their discussion of Lyotard, Usher and Edwards identify 'a number of familiar strands of the postmodern moment' (1994, p. 158), as it established itself against a sitting-duck version of modernism:

> [F]irst, the significance of the emergence of modern science with its empiricist epistemology and views of language as transparent and representational; second, the privileging of scientific knowledge over other forms of knowledge; third, given the privileged status of such knowledge, the importance, indeed the necessity, of imparting it to others, in other words, the centrality of education to modern science, as a condition for its ascendancy and an outcome of it; fourth, the oppressive consequences of those assumptions, in that the totalising of knowledge results in totalitarianism, the exclusion and silencing of difference. (Usher & Edwards 1994, p. 158)

This account succinctly displays both the central theses of the negative voice position and its cognates, and the crucial slippage between moral/political and epistemic arguments. First, 'modern science' is characterized exclusively in positivist terms and its massive social hegemony assumed, but nowhere demonstrated.[8] Second, this positivist characterization of 'modern science' is then further characterized as 'totalitarian' and held accountable for 'the exclusion and silencing of difference'. On this basis, sets of (defensible and desirable) moral/political claims relating to social justice and equality of treatment and respect are conflated with a set of (indefensible and undesirable) epistemic theses (Siegel 1997, p. 142).

To put our argument plainly and provocatively, this position is:

- misleading in its depiction of 'modern science' (see below);
- mistaken in its sociological view of the 'hegemonic' and 'totalizing' position of this epistemology within modern society;

- mistaken in its depiction of the position and status of such knowledge within education systems (particularly in the English case); and consequently,
- mistaken in its conclusions about its social consequences for the silencing and exclusion of subordinated groups.

On the final point, we must be very clear. We are not denying the facts of marginalization, exclusion and oppression; nor are we trivialising those conditions. Like Siegel, we support the progressive moral/political values and objectives but sociologically, we reject this idealist account of the causes of such material conditions and, philosophically, we reject its anti-intellectual implications.

Modern Science

We will now address in more depth the key issue of the characterization of 'modern science'. Usher and Edwards tell us that the 'dominant discourse of science . . . places science firmly outside of any context of social locatedness arguing that its knowledge is warranted precisely because it is outside' (1994, pp. 33–4).

> The ascendancy of scientific method as the means of establishing secure knowledge has resulted in a consistent failure to examine science as a social practice and as a historical and cultural product. Science has instead been seen as transcendent and decontextualized. Knowledge, as well as the knowing subject, therefore becomes context-free. Rationality is cast as universal and transcendental, operating across all historical and social contexts and practices but independent of them all. The result is an individualistic epistemology where the solitary individual confronts an independent reality of objects. (Usher & Edwards 1994, p. 36)

This account of science is representative of postmodernism, encountered within some feminisms (but not all: see, e.g. Scott [1994]) and, earlier, expressed in the anti-positivist interpretative sociological literature of the late 1960s and early 1970s that provided the context for the 'New Sociology of Education'.

An awkward problem with this type of description of the 'dominant discourse of science' arises immediately: it bears no significant relationship to any recognizable discourse of science today, in the recent past or even (with one exception) in the past century! It corresponds roughly only to logical positivism (see Bohman 1991, chapter 1). Even in relation to the empiricist tradition, the designation of 'dominant' ignores the massive counter influence of post-Kantian epistemology and its historicization from Schopenhauer through Hegel and Marx to Durkheim. Far from being dominant, this model of science is a very specific moment within empiricism and the modern empiricist tradition, itself a specifically Anglo-Saxon 'analytic' response to Kant (see West 1996).

What authorities do Usher and Edwards invoke to support their view? They refer in the main only to other postmodernist writers (Lyotard for instance) and hermeneutic precursors such as Gadamer.[9] There is a passing reference to Kuhn, but he vigorously rejected the idea that his work should be treated as relativist or irrationalist (Kuhn 1970). For most students of the philosophy of science, Popper put an end to positivism a long time ago, yet strangely, its image has been kept alive within a particular discourse in sociology as a kind of clanking modernist machine within the hermeneutic ghost of interpretative idealism. A number of commentators have noted this characteristic 'straw man' tactic by postmodernists (e.g. Norris 1997a,b), and its persistence and prevalence within this field over such a long time suggests that it should be seen as a discursive device, to be understood in terms of what it does rather than what it says. What it says, we contend, simply does not bear serious scrutiny.

It is not just the case that no serious scientists today would argue that science does have the form attributed to it by the postmodernists (see, e.g. the scientists contributing to 'Special Section: making sense of science' in *History of the Human Sciences*, 8(2), 1995), but that the central debates emphatically begin with the recognition that science *is* 'inside' history and is socially constructed (see Hammersley 1995). The dominant discourse of science does not question its historical and social character; rather the issues are to do with the implications of this widely accepted fact.

It is not possible to review in detail the development of debates in the 'post-empiricist philosophy of science', nor is it our main aim here, but it is relevant to the context of the argument to draw attention to the 'naturalized' philosophy of science represented by epistemological realists such as Boyd and Laudan (Papineau 1996). Papineau refers to the 'explosion of exciting work in the sociology of science':

This kind of sociology has been widely regarded as undermining any epistemological analysis of science, on the grounds that epistemology deals in *a priori* standards of rationality, while sociological studies seem to show that scientific theory choices aren't governed in this way at all, but rather by scientific power struggles and opportunistic manoeuvres. This rejection of epistemology presupposes, however, that epistemology traffics solely in *a priori* principles of theory evaluation. By contrast, if epistemology of science is conducted in the naturalistic mode, then the conflict disappears. Naturalized philosophers of science have no axe to grind for *a prior* principles over social processes. They can happily accept that social processes often determine theory choices. The only normative question they will want to ask is whether those processes are an effective means to scientific aims. Nor is this a question they can answer for themselves. For it is an empirical question, not an *a priori* one, and the philosophers will therefore need the help of sociologists and historians of science in order to answer it. (Papineau 1996, p. 16)

The currently 'dominant' discourse of science not only bears no relationship to the postmodernist straw man, but the naturalization of epistemology by philosophers of science such as Popper, Hanson, Hesse, Harre and others precedes the 'postmodernist revolution' by several decades. Contrary to Usher and Edwards' view that 'Relativism is feared precisely because in claiming that there is no uniquely privileged position from which to know but a number of different positions each with their own standards, the very possibility of an authorising centre is apparently destroyed' (1994, p. 37), relativism is not feared at all, but simply dismissed because its claims have no serious status (Fay 1996; Harre & Krausz 1996).

In addition to Papineau's comments about the convergence between philosophy and sociology of science, we can note also the increasingly powerful syntheses being produced by critical realist philosophers and social theorists such as Roy Bhaskar (1979) and Margaret Archer (1990, 1995). We would add the observation that the 'internalist' versus 'externalist' split in accounts of science can, from this point of view, be seen as fundamentally misconceived, in the sense that 'externalists' have tended to treat internalist reconstructions of the logic of science as equivalent to ethnographic descriptions of the social practice of science. We suggest that it might be more productive to see internalist models as explications of the 'rules' of science rather than descriptions of its social practice. In this way, we would no more expect practice to immediately exhibit a well-informed 'rule' than we would expect speech to transparently reveal language.

The significant point, here, is that no amount of 'thick' description can in itself supersede, negate or disallow theoretical excavations of the rules of practice understood as their generative principles and condition of existence. The strong sociological version of the critique of formalist versions of internalism was certainly correct in criticizing positivism on the grounds that its requirement of a theory-neutral pure observation language mirroring sense-data (as in Russell or the early Wittgenstein) was simply not possible and, furthermore, as Popper argued (and Durkheim before him), nothing like science anyway. But it is wrong to assume from the inevitable indeterminacies of science as a social practice that no formal epistemological account of science is possible. Although it is true that all social practices have an endemic degree of indeterminacy and, in this respect, science is like any other social practice, it does not follow that all social practices, including science, are therefore symmetrical and that there are no formal demarcation criteria between kinds of practices and discourses. Such a conclusion would follow only if a particular absolutist condition (disallowing indeterminacy in principle) is insisted upon in the definition of what is to count as science and reason more generally. It is precisely this condition that some postmodernists impose and is represented in Usher and Edwards' account. If science, or rationality more generally, cannot be absolute, then, according to this view, it cannot be at all. However, as James Bohman says, 'Even if interpretation is unavoidably indeterminate, it follows only that there is no unique best interpretation, not that there is no way to distinguish better from worse interpretations' (1991, p. 10). It is just such an 'all or nothing' argument that post-empiricist epistemology and philosophy of science has abandoned and, furthermore, did so from within its own tradition and within its mainstream critical discourse.

The sceptical and relativist conclusions of postmodernism regarding the possibilities of knowledge (or feminist moves to present this knowledge as in some *intrinsic* sense 'androcentric', or by multiculturalists as 'ethnocentric') follow only from the attribution of *absolutist* criteria to science and reason. The sociologizing of knowledge relations in a form that reduces them to no more than standpoints articulated within power relations holds only for as long as the 'all or nothing' principle holds. Post-empiricism, on the other hand, supersedes this opposition by demonstrating that there is no in-principle conflict between epistemology and sociology – that epistemology, to the degree that it must present an historically viable account of science, must be sociological; but sociology, to the extent that it must provide a viable account of science within history, must accommodate a naturalized epistemology that provides not 'the unique best interpretation', but addresses how we come to distinguish and institutionalize what Luntley (1995) calls the 'simple truth', which involves the recognition that some explanations are indubitably better than, or at least formally different from, others. As Gellner, Harre, Popper, Kuhn and others, in their various ways have recognized, the epistemological problem is an historical problem (classically, that of Weber). Although it is true that we do not know or agree about exactly how it is that some explanations are better than others or how we know this, the one thing we know beyond serious doubt is that all explanations are not equal. Whereas those fields centrally concerned with the problems of knowledge (epistemology, the philosophies of science and knowledge) have long recognized the need for sociology, it is a peculiar fact that key areas within sociology and the sociology of education in particular have systematically refused the converse – to acknowledge that a sociology of knowledge which cannot accommodate post-empiricist epistemology is, as Gellner (1992a) insisted, little more than intellectual affectation.

It is ironic that the postmodernists and those now sheltering under their wings are the only ones left with any interest in positivism. Their account holds only for as long as positivism stands. In this sense, positivism is their secret 'Other' – the orthodoxy that is the condition for their heterodoxy. It is, then, not surprising that they do so much to sustain it in their various accounts of the 'dominant discourse'. What is surprising and sociologically significant is that there should be an intellectual field doing this when nowhere else is positivism of anything other than passing historical interest. This is more serious than it sounds. As Bohman has observed, 'post-empiricism has removed the social sciences from their contentious and peripheral status and placed them directly in the centre of some new epistemological debates' (1991, p. 3). At the very moment that post-empiricist epistemology draws sociology into the centre, the position-taking logic of the field of sociology of education propels it, yet again, towards an intellectually and politically bankrupt 'sociology of knowledge' covertly grounded in assumptions and overtly in practices that can only maintain it at the periphery of serious debate.

What Kind of Thing: Voice Discourse as Pedagogic Device

In this section, we will characterize voice discourse in terms of what it does *positively* in terms of its basic discursive procedures. We will attempt to demonstrate how the intellectual moves within the argument of voice discourse operate as discursive positioning devices revalorizing the social relations between groups. The reduction of knowledge to the single plane of experience through the rejection of 'depth analysis' and its epistemology (that allows for and requires a separate and autonomous non-mundane language of theory) produces differences of identity alone, but differences that are, in essence, all the same. The postmodern proclamation that there is only 'surface' echoes the earlier phenomenological claim that science is simply another species of commonsense; an everyday accomplishment of members of the science community or form of life.

The pedagogic device (Bernstein 1990) of voice discourse promotes a methodology in which the explication of a method's social location precludes the need to examine the content of its data as grounds for valid explanation. Who says it, is what counts, not what is said. This approach favours an ethnography that claims to reveal the cultural specificity of the category – the 'voice' of membership. What is held to be the facts, is only so and can only be so, from a particular perspective. The world thus viewed is a patchwork of incommensurable and exclusive voices or standpoints. Through the process of sub-division, increasingly more particularized identity categories come into being, each claiming the unique specificity of its distinctive experience and the knowledge authorized by it.

The consequence of the abolition of the knowledge boundary that follows from the epistemological theses of postmodernism is the increasing specialization of social categories (see Chapter 2, this volume). Maton describes this process of proliferation in terms of the way such 'knower' discourses,

> base their legitimation upon the privileged insight of a knower, and work at maintaining strong boundaries around their definition of this knower – they celebrate difference where 'truth' is defined by the 'knower' or 'voice' . . . as each voice is brought into the academic choir, the category of the privileged knower becomes smaller, each strongly bounded from one another, for each voice proclaims its own privileged and specialized knowledge. The knower group will thus fragment, each fragment with its own representative . . . The result, in terms of the privileged knower, is an accretion of adjectives, the hyphenation which knower modes often proclaim as a sign of progress. . . . Thus, with the emergence of each new category of knower, the categories of knowers become smaller, leading to proliferation and fragmentation within the pedagogic discourse. (2000, pp. 92, 93; see also this volume, Chapter 2)

As Maton argues, this move promotes a fundamental change in the 'legitimation code', from *what is known* (and how) to *who knows it.*

The device that welds knowledge to standpoint, voice and experience, produces a result that is inherently unstable, because the anchor for the voice is an interior authenticity that can never be demonstrated, only claimed (Fuss 1990, 1995; Siegel 1997; Taylor 1992). Since all such claims are power claims, the authenticity of the voice is constantly prone to a purifying challenge, 'If you do not believe it you are not one of us' (Hammersley & Gomm 1997, para. 3.3) that gears down to ever more rarefied specializations or iterations of the voice category; an unstoppable spiral that Bernstein (1997, p. 176) has referred to as the 'shrinking of the moral imagination.[10]

As Bernstein puts it, 'The voice of a social category (academic discourse, gender subject, occupational subject) is constructed by the degree of specialization of the discursive rules regulating and legitimizing the form of communication' (1990, p. 23). If categories of either agents or discourse are specialized, then each category necessarily has its own specific identity and its own specific boundaries. The speciality of each category is created, maintained and reproduced only if the relations between the categories of which a given category is a member are preserved. What is to be preserved? The *insulation* between the categories. It is the strength of the insulation that creates a space in which a category can become specific. If a category wishes to increase its specificity, it has to appropriate the means to produce the necessary insulation that is the prior condition to its appropriating specificity (ibid.).

Collection codes employ an organization of knowledge to specialize categories of person, integrated codes employ an organization of persons to specialize categories of knowledge (Bernstein 1977, pp. 106–11). The instability of the social categories associated with voice discourse reflects the fact that there is no stable and agreed-upon way of constructing such categories. By their nature, they are always open to contestation and further fragmentation. In principle, there is no terminal point where 'identities' can finally come to rest. It is for this reason that this position can reappear so frequently across time and space within the intellectual field – the same move can be repeated endlessly under the disguise of 'difference'.

In Bernstein's terms, the organization of knowledge is, most significantly, a device for the regulation of consciousness.

> The pedagogic device is thus a symbolic ruler of consciousness in its selective creation, positioning and oppositioning of pedagogic subjects. It is the condition for the production, reproduction, and transformation of culture. The question is: whose ruler, what consciousness? (1990, p. 189)

The relativistic challenge to epistemologically grounded strong classifications of knowledge removes the means whereby social categories and their relations can be strongly theorized and effectively researched in a form that is other than arbitrary and can be challenged by anyone choosing to assert an alternative perspective or standpoint.

Languages of Theory and Experience

Horizontal knowledge structures (Bernstein 1999) of the voice sociology kind lack the procedures (theoretical language or syntax) for generating non-arbitrary knowledge claims (see also Muller & Taylor 1995). They all speak of the same thing: experience. They are all equally perspectively privileged. Whether we look at the literature of standpoint epistemology (Hartsock 1990; Harding 1991), new literacy studies (Street 1984), or ethno and constructivist pedagogies (Olssen 1997), among many others, what binds them together across their multiple differences is the belief that discourses, knowledge, all symbolic forms, because they participate in a world where all humans ought to be equal, are all fundamentally the same, on the same epistemological footing, of the same type and structure. Experiences are differentiated only in terms of their authenticity as expressions of their own subjecthood. In a world of difference, as Gayatri Spivak says, 'the place where indeed all human beings are similar is seen to be lodged in their being different' (1990, p. 228).

This arguments holds that in a constructed world, where constructors are all equal because all are equally human, constructions must be fundamentally of a kind. Demonstrating the equal validity, or fundamental worthiness, of lay, local and non-official forms of discourse is a major scholarly aim for many relativists on the grounds that because all people are equal, so is their knowledge. It is also a strategy of struggle that many local communities, taking their cue from the professional educators, have adopted as their own (Singh 1998).

Crucially, such a theory of structural equality of discourse forms denies the discontinuity of epistemological break, of a distinction between metaphor and concept, of the necessity for a retreat from practical utility in order to address the unthought and to effect a conceptual advance (Bernstein 1996, chapter 4). It promotes one kind of superficial difference at the expense of another that is fundamental. The difference it promotes is that of (tacitly constructed) membership as the means of defining experience and knowledge. As we pointed out, this position is inherently unstable because categories and associated authenticity claims are always open to challenge, expressed in the process of fragmentation that accompanies the iteration of identities and division of categories. Post-structuralism, as an emerging orthodoxy in the humanities, reflects this instability but redresses the problem by re-presenting it as a virtue in the celebration of 'difference'. Each new 'voice' is celebrated as another emancipation. What this celebration of difference disguises, and this is the basic source of the instability, is the actual theoretical dualism that these approaches deny. The position is thus grounded in a contradiction that denies the condition of its own existence.

All accounts have, first, to theoretically construct the world they go on to describe in various ways and, in principle, be able to demonstrate non-tautologically (Bernstein 1996, chapters 6 and 9) that the world is in fact as such. What voice discourses suppress is the manner in which they covertly exempt themselves from the condition they prescribe and hold to be true for everyone else. This exemption is always a form of the basic contradiction of relativism. The truth that all truths are relative must exempt itself in order to be true; there is one truth that is not relative: the truth that all truth is relative. But then, of course, it is not true that all truth is relative. Positions that deny that anything can be 'in fact' the case (because what is the case is only ever so from a particular perspective) implicitly suppress the claim that it is in fact the case that the world is *thus* and, furthermore, can be shown to be so. In fact, we know full well that it is not! The exemption that these discourses covertly claim is precisely the principle that they overtly deny – that there are, in fact, ways of warranting truth claims that are not merely reducible to perspectives, standpoints and forms of life (Hammersley & Gomm 1997). The condition, for instance, for establishing that knowledge may be, in some sense, degree or form, gendered is that there are some procedures and criteria that, in themselves, are not. It is not just that the world is not as the relativists claim, their world is an impossible one.

In these terms, what we call discourses of voice are those lacking a strong *internal* language of description. Their internal language does produce a world of objects and relationships, but its process of production lacks a stable, explicit and rigorous methodology of production (as is the case for what Bernstein terms 'hierarchical knowledge structures' exemplified by physics [1999]). For instance, feminism has the theoretical problem of defining the categories 'male' and 'female' independently of their various presumed realizations. Hence, although it is common to come across terms such as 'male epistemology' or even 'male conferencing', it is much rarer to encounter an instance of 'male' being defined independently in such a way that it can then become a methodological issue as to whether any particular case is *in fact* a realization of 'maleness' rather than some other thing (Pollert 1996).

It is important to stress that these discourses do not lack an internal language of description; their problem is that it exists only in a weak form, as 'orientations, condensed intimations, metaphors which point to relevancies' (Bernstein 1996, p. 137). Bernstein's use of literary terms, here, is completely appropriate. These weak languages of description can only produce accounts in which positions and relations are re-presented as characters and the drama of their relationships. Where experience replaces theory as the author of knowledge, the privileging of the mundane does not abolish theory; it systematically denies and obscures its own theoretical genesis.

Conclusion

We argued in the first section of this chapter that the force of 'voice discourse' depends upon the manner in which it positions itself in opposition to the allegedly mainstream, dominant or hegemonic discourse. There are three basic points.

First, as we have argued, voice discourse operates primarily as a debunking strategy. It attempts to displace a set of 'dominant' knowledge claims by revealing those claims to be epistemologically spurious: the disguised interests and standpoint of the dominant group. It does this by representing that dominant discourse as positivistic and absolutist. By constructing the dominant discourse in this fashion, it has no problems in pressing its claims because, certainly, any position that did assert epistemological privilege by these means would fail. The problem is, no one does. It is on the basis of this manoeuvre that voice discourse goes on to establish its positive (inclusive) attributes in terms of the representation of those voices previously silenced or marginalized by the hegemony of the dominant discourse.

Secondly, the dominant position in science begins with and has long acknowledged precisely those things which postmodernists and others claim as their distinctive, original insights: that science, and reason more generally, is socially constructed, 'inside' history and inevitably enmeshed with the complex of interests present within the context of production. But the sceptical, reductionist and relativist conclusions drawn by postmodernists and others from these facts simply are not warranted, or are only warranted in terms of the positivistic model that they insist upon representing as 'science'. The central programme within post-empiricist philosophy of science has successfully defended epistemology against the kind of rela-tivizing reductionism supported by postmodernists. Within the 'natural-ized' philosophy of science, epistemology and the sociology of knowledge are complementary, not antagonistic. The dominant discourse of science sustains *fallibilism* but avoids scepticism – indeed, claims to certainty and absolutism in knowledge (typically resented by postmodernists and certain feminists as definitive of foundationalism or androcentrism) are generally treated as the symptoms of ideology and disallow claims to scientificity or reasonable justification.

Thirdly, given that the present position in science is well known, well established and has been in place for so long, we suggest that the voice dis-course position, in its various forms over the past two decades and more, has been sustained by a form of knowledge that is symptomatic of a strongly insulated field position supporting a particular position-taking strategy.

Although these approaches make much of their self-acclaimed reflexivity, in fact it is just this quality that they lack (we are speaking here about the accounts not their agents). It is interesting to note how the use of ethno-graphy is associated with a preoccupation with biography, the writers write themselves into their world, they stabilize their 'voice' at the expense of revealing its conditions of production. They suppress the procedures by which they specialize their own voice and, hence, by which they produce their own descriptions of the world. This displaced 'reflexivity', re-presented as a claim to authenticity, cannot reveal the principles whereby these authors produce the world within which they locate themselves (i.e. the internal language of description that constructs the world to be theorized) but, rather, re-presents it as the first person of the narrative of description.

Although voices are claimed to be mundane (authored and authorized by the authenticity of the mundane [speech/experience]), they are, and can only ever be, esoteric because it is only within the esoteric (writing/theory) that the texts of voice can be produced. What voice discourse sup-presses is its own esoteric origins as 'a recontextualizing principle which selectively appropriates, relocates, refocuses, and relates other discourses to constitute its own order and orderings' (Bernstein, 1990) – the principle that first constructs the world it then goes on to describe. The 'voice' of voice discourse erases the text that writes the world of which it speaks.

Endnotes

[1] This tenet of the 'new sociology' was soon challenged. As Young writes, 'The "new sociology of education," as a set of ideas . . . was short-lived, partly on account

of its own theoretical limitations' (1998, p. 39), and 'The idea that knowledge is socially stratified in society and in schools . . . is powerful – unless it is seen as a total description of the origins and structure of the curriculum, when it becomes naive and misleading' (ibid., p. 5).

² This process roughly follows the social trajectory of educational expansion and the entry of 'non-standard' students into sites where they previously had only a limited representation (Hickox & Moore 1994, 1995).

³ See Popper (1994, chapter 2), and discussions in Fay (1996) and Bohman (1991).

⁴ Space does not allow us to substantiate this claim but a relevant comparison is between this type of contemporary postmodernist account of science and the phenomenologically inspired *New Directions in Sociological Theory* by Filmer et al. (1972, chapter 1).

⁵ Symptomatically, these approaches frequently draw upon literary forms such as narrative, biography and confession.

⁶ See Bernstein (1996, chapter 4) and Moore (2004).

⁷ It would have to be established empirically in any particular case that the inclusiveness or exclusiveness of a particular knowledge community had either positive or negative epistemic effects. Although the social composition of a knowledge community might influence the kinds of things about which it develops knowledge, it would make no sense to say that it influences how true or well-warranted is the knowledge it produced.

⁸ It is relevant to call attention here to the fact that *failure* of the scientific worldview to assume a hegemonic position within modern society is the more remarkable. Contrary to the expectations of many nineteenth century thinkers, it is the persistence (and, in recent times, intensification) of religious, mystical and other kinds of 'irrational' belief that has been the most striking feature of the twentieth century (regarding the debates around secularization, nationalism and 'the end of ideology'). In the particular case of English culture, the dominance of the humanities and, in particular, the enduring influence of an anti-scientific romanticism within the national culture and its education system, has been a longstanding cause of concern among those who argue that Britain's industrial decline is a consequence of a failure to modernize around a science-based culture and economy (Beck 1998; Hickox 1995; Mathieson & Bernbaum 1988).

⁹ For the influence of the nineteenth century Ahtur/Geisteswissenschaftn distinction on the debate about the relationship between the natural and social science, see Boham (1991). It is essentially this distinction that informs the discussion in Filmer et al. (1972).

¹⁰ This phenomenon is already part of popular culture, and commented on in ironic terms: 'I'd heard this described as the narcissism of Minor Difference at a seminar on fashion retailing', says the cynical anti-hero of David Huggins' *The Big Kiss* (1996).

Chapter 4

Promoting Official Pedagogic Identities: The Sacred and the Profane

John Beck
Cambridge University

Introduction

We have to recognize that the university is a ruined institution.

(Readings 1996, p. 169)

Knowledge as we know it in the academy is coming to an end . . . (and this represents) a crisis arguably more serious than those of finance, organization and structure.

(Griffin 1997, p. 3)

Basil Bernstein's most trenchant judgement on these developments was contained in a paper significantly subtitled 'The divorce of knowledge from the knower':

> Of fundamental significance, there is a new concept of knowledge and of its relation to those who create and use it. . . . Knowledge, after nearly a thousand years, is divorced from inwardness and literally dehumanized . . . what is at stake is the very concept of education itself. (2000, p. 86)

Bernstein's voice was, then, one of many claiming that in the last two decades of the twentieth century academe experienced a series of seismic shocks. The tone of these pronouncements quite as much as their content is highly revealing: not cool, detached appraisal; rather, apocalyptic warnings that something of great intrinsic value was threatened with extinction – a language of crisis, dehumanization and loss. Nevertheless, the content of these pronouncements *is* also significant. All these writers concur that the changes they describe have to do not only with the dominance of marketization and managerialization within education but more fundamentally – and as a *consequence* of intensified marketization and managerialization – with *knowledge* and a changed relation to knowledge on the part of knowledge creators and users. As always, Bernstein's analysis of these developments was highly distinctive and it enabled him to illuminate significances and implications sometimes overlooked by others. In this chapter, I shall try to highlight what was most original in Bernstein's account, and I shall, as he did, trace the story beyond the confines of the university to include, in particular, schooling and teacher training in England and Wales. The primary focus of the discussion will be on the structuring of *identities* and more particularly, on Bernstein's analysis of recent attempts 'at the State level' to 'project official pedagogic identities' of a distinctively new kind (Bernstein & Solomon 1999, p. 271).

Sources of Inwardness and Assaults upon Inwardness: The Sacred and the Profane in the Formation of Educational Identities

The evident alarm and dismay of the writers I have quoted suggests that they are reacting to something 'deep' – something experienced internally as an assault upon the self. As Bernstein saw it, a new and 'truly secular' conception of knowledge was displacing the humane relation to knowledge nurtured within western universities since Mediaeval times, creating a situation in which 'knowledge, after nearly a thousand years is divorced from inwardness', and 'separated from commitments, from personal dedication, from the deep structure of the self' (Bernstein 2000, p. 86).

Bernstein's way of understanding inwardness and the deep structures of the self was avowedly sociological – and drew its inspiration chiefly from Durkheim. Identity had to do primarily with ways in which order (and sometimes disorder) internal to the individual was related to and resulted from external orderings – both discursive orderings and the socially structured relationships in which they were embedded. (In his later work, he tended more often to talk about the structuring of identities in terms of the modalities of 'symbolic control', perhaps having become chary of the vocabulary of 'order' which had, in the past, led to his work being located at the 'wrong' [Conservative] pole of 'the two sociologies' dichotomy [Dawe 1970].)

Bernstein's discussion of inwardness and assaults upon it was also shaped profoundly by his use of the Durkheimian concepts of the sacred and the profane. In most of his writings, he offered a 'structural' account of the sacred in relation to identity, seeing the internalized sacred as an effect of exceptionally strong classification.[1] Indeed, in a paper published in 1990, Bernstein discusses the relationship between classification and identity in terms that are not merely structural but almost structuralist:

> [T]he form taken by educational practices – that is, their degree of specificity, the extent to which practices are specialized to categories – depends entirely upon the relation between these categories . . . If categories of either agents or discourse are specialized, then each category necessarily has its own specific identity and its own specific boundaries. The specialty of each category is created, maintained and reproduced only if the relations between the categories of which a given category is a member are preserved. What is to be preserved? The *insulation between the categories*. It is the insulation between the categories which creates a space in which a category can become specific. (1990, p. 23)

It is, then, the structuring of the relations between categories rather than any properties intrinsic to categories (based for example on divisions within knowledge which may be held to be logical in character), which defined the strongly bounded discursive entities to which sacredness could become attached. Similarly, for Bernstein, it was not historical scholarly doctrines such as the pursuit of knowledge for its own sake which were ultimately the source of identities which gave rise to a sense of purity and sacredness: this was insisted upon in his seminal early paper 'On the classification and framing of educational knowledge':

> A sense of the sacred, the 'otherness' of educational knowledge, I submit does not arise so much out of an ethic of knowledge for its own sake, but is more a function of socialization into subject loyalty: for it is the subject which becomes the linch-pin of identity. Any attempt to weaken or change classification strength (or even frame strength) may be felt as a threat to one's identity and may be experienced as a pollution endangering the sacred. (1971a, p. 56)

Essentially the same position is restated 25 years later, except that the language of collection and integrated knowledge codes has been replaced by the terminology of 'singulars' and 'regions':

> The sacred face (of singulars) sets them apart, legitimizes their otherness and creates dedicated identities with no reference other than their

calling . . . From this point of view singulars develop strong, autonomous self-sealing and narcissistic identities. (1996, p. 68)

Bernstein's conception of the sacred is, then, impeccably Durkheimian – at least in one respect: radical otherness and separateness were the hallmarks of Durkheim's definition of the sacred/profane polarity: 'a bipartite division . . . into two classes . . . which radically exclude each other' (Durkheim 1967, cited in Lukes 1975, p. 24). But from another aspect, Bernstein's appropriation of Durkheim's dyad was less 'pure' because Durkheim insisted that the sacred–profane separation divided 'the whole known universe . . . into two classes which embrace all that exists, but which radically exclude each other' (ibid., p. 25), whereas for Bernstein – at least in certain ways – the profane could *co-exist* with the sacred within the same individuals and the same modalities of identity. Those whose 'inner' identities were centred in dedication to the intrinsic value and purity of their scholarly pursuits were also always actors implicated (to different degrees) in the 'profane' world of what we would now call educational macro- and micro-politics. Bernstein employs an analogy of a coin with two faces: the inner 'sacred' face but also the 'outer' profane face turned towards 'external linkage and internal power struggles' in various organizational and political arenas (2000, p. 54). Although this creative appropriation of Durkheim's famous dichotomy may have been 'impure', it was, arguably a source of strength. In particular, by recognizing that a sacred dimension of identity could coexist with a profane aspect, Bernstein's analysis was able to acknowledge realistically that authentic inner dedication could coexist (and had coexisted) with a finely honed capacity to protect self interest where necessary – but that this did not ipso facto compromise the legitimacy of intellectuals of certain kinds seeing themselves as guardians of intrinsic educational values; rather the reverse. This, insofar as one can read the ambiguities correctly, seems roughly to have been the 'committed' position which Bernstein himself took, at least in his more polemical counterblasts, where, as we have seen, he did not flinch from announcing his own commitments and seeking to protect *his* sacred from 'pollution'. Such internal tensions in his work – between personal involvement and more distanced sociological analysis – are perhaps, in themselves, evidence of the potency of the social in the formation of human subjectivity. If so, then it may not be accidental either, that Bernstein used a set of *psychoanalytic* concepts to index the intra-psychic processes involved in such identity formation – introjection, projection, etc.)

From Nursery to Tertiary: The Rise of Market-Oriented Instrumentalism and the Promotion of New Pedagogic Identities

In the second part of this chapter, I shall examine some of the ideas which Bernstein began to develop in the late 1980s (see 1990, pp. 133–64) and continued to revise during the 1990s.[2] These are elaborated most completely in two chapters in Bernstein (2000), where the final part of the 1996 version of 'Pedagogizing knowledge' was extended to form a new chapter entitled 'Official knowledge and pedagogic identities'. Bernstein quite clearly regarded these papers, and especially the second, as work in progress – 'an embryonic outline, rather than a completed painting' (2000, p. 65). In the space available, it will not be possible to do justice to the scope and richness of his insights: as so often, he was engaged in formulating theories and models of general applicability, capable of analysing change in many different kinds of society and education systems. Here, the focus will be much narrower, referring mainly to his analysis of the inexorable progress of market-oriented instrumentalism in education and its consequences for educational identities. In outline, the core of his argument is succinctly summarized in the polemical section which concludes the essay on the Trivium and Quadrivium:

> Today, throughout Europe, led by the U.S.A. and the U.K., there is a new principle guiding the latest transition of capitalism. The principles of the market and its managers are more and more the managers of the policy and practices of education. Market relevance is becoming the key orientation for the selection of discourses, their relation to each other, their forms and their research. This movement has profound implications from the primary school to the university. (ibid., p. 86)

It was, then, the scope as well as the content of these changes that Bernstein saw as so dangerously threatening. A far-reaching revolution was in progress that threatened the structural conditions, which may be essential if commitments to the belief that knowledge, scholarship and free enquiry may have *intrinsic* value are to be sustained and passed on.

The basic structural condition in question was, in Bernstein's view, the maintenance of strong *insulation* between education and the 'profane' sphere of economic production. As early as the 1970s, he argued that in most Western societies, under both 'entrepreneurial capitalism' and 'twentieth century capitalism', there was normally *strong classification between education and production.* This was the key condition of the real (if always relative) autonomy of education which in turn was crucial to maintaining and legitimating the *indirect* rule of the dominant economic class, through the agency of a distinct cadre of specialists in *cultural* production and repro-duction (Bernstein 1977, pp. 174–200). The strong classification between the two spheres, Bernstein argued, also produced a sharp separation between the intrinsic/sacred and the extrinsic/profane aspects of educa-tion: 'this socially constituted division between the sacred and profane is integral to the form and process of cultural reproduction instituted in edu-cation'. Bernstein recognized, of course, that what *constituted* 'the sacred takes on different expression in different historical epochs', so that in terms of educational identities, it might at one time be embodied in the figure of the educated gentleman, and at a later point expressed in the idea of 'education for personal autonomy', etc. But as long as the classification between education and production remained strong, notions of intrinsic value to which 'sacredness' attached were always present – especially at the tertiary level (ibid., p. 190).[3]

In the last few decades of the twentieth century, the insulations between education and production began to weaken; indeed, increasingly they were stripped away by direct intervention. In part, Bernstein accounts for this, at least as far as tertiary education is concerned, in terms of 'singulars' being increasingly displaced by *'regions'* – a development which he seems to have regarded as a response to market conditions on the part of 'autonomous' higher educational institutions, rather than as being politically imposed. In a lecture delivered in 1988 he observed:

> [W]e are witnessing . . . a movement which started much earlier in the USA, towards the regionalization of knowledge: a good indicator of its technological orientation. We can see this . . . as a weakening of the strength of classification of discourses, and with this . . . a formation of less specialized professional identities whose practices are technological. (1990, p. 156)

Subsequently he speculated that 'it may be that regions will become the modal form (of discursive organization) from the late twentieth century onwards' with 'the classical university regions, medicine, engineering, architecture' being augmented by 'contemporary regions' as diverse as computer studies, business studies, cognitive science, film studies, and so on (ibid., p. 55). In emphasizing the association between this proliferation of regions and the increased dominance of technological and market imperatives, as well as the more direct connections (and sometimes controls) between the spheres of production and higher education, Bernstein is broadly in accord with commentators such as Gibbons et al. (1994) and Delanty (2001), who also stress the impact on traditional forms of knowledge organization within universities of developments such as 'the rise of the [corporate] knowledge user', or the fact that, increasingly, 'knowledge is being generated in its contexts of application' often *outside* universities, or that knowledge generation is more and more 'problem-specific', with commercial competition becoming 'the basis for the logic of discovery' (Delanty 2001, pp. 108–09).

Once more, one of the most penetrating aspects of Bernstein's exploration of these issues is his discussion of their implications for identity change. As we have seen, singulars, which were the modal form of discursive organization within universities throughout the nineteenth and much of the twentieth centuries, created through their strong insulations, identities which partook of the sacred and were experienced as worth pursing 'for their own sake'. Increasing regionalization of knowledge, especially in its recent strongly market-driven forms, Bernstein suggests, creates identities whose organizing principle is that they 'face outward towards fields of practice' with the result that 'their contents are likely to be dependent on the requirements of these fields' (2000, p. 55). As an earlier Bernstein might have put it, the extrinsic is raised above the intrinsic. Once again, there are significant parallels here with diagnoses offered by other writers. Delanty, for example, speaking of the 'modern university' and its Enlightenment heritage, characterizes its traditional model of knowledge as 'coherent, autonomous, transcendent, self-referential', conferring 'upon the university and its priestly caste of intellectuals the role of guardian of knowledge' (2001, p. 105) – and, as we have seen, he contrasts this with the effects of contemporary market-driven imperatives. Yet Bernstein offers us more, and he is more specific. In a telling formulation, he emphasizes that with growing regionalization, 'identities are what they are, and what they will become, as a consequence of the *projection* of that knowledge as a practice in some context: and the future of that context will regulate the identity'. He adds that 'the volatility of that context will control the regionalization of the knowledge and thus the projected identity' (ibid., p. 55).

In seeking to better understand the role of the *State* in the complex processes through which market principles have come to dominate education, especially in those societies whose economies are increasingly under the sway of neo-liberal principles, Bernstein began in the 1980s to develop a repertoire of new concepts. Some of these had much more general importance within his theory – notably the concepts of primary, secondary and recontextualizing contexts (briefly, the contexts of knowledge *production, re*production, and the *recontexualizing* processes that always accompanied the relocation of texts and practices from the primary to the secondary contexts) (1990, Appendix 1.6, pp. 59–61). And 'recontexualization', of course, became the linch-pin of the analysis of 'pedagogic discourse' developed in the key papers published from the 1990s onwards. For our purposes, however, the most important ideas to emerge at this time were those which sought to conceptualize more precisely the relationships between educational professionals and the agencies of the State. In another paper in the 1990 collection – a lecture originally delivered in Santiago as early as 1988 – Bernstein highlighted the phenomenon of increasing direct intervention by the State:

> [T]he crucial change is the State's increasing control over its own agencies of symbolic control, especially education, at all levels. . .. The change is a change in State ideology and regulation . . .

Significantly, he added:

> what is of interest is the State's indifference, even hostility, to its professional base. (1990, pp. 154–5)

Later papers, (notably 1996, chapter 3) offered a more elaborated analysis of the recontexualizing context, introducing the distinction between the Professional Recontexualizing Field (PRF) and the Official Recontextualizing Field (ORF), which enabled him to offer more nuanced analyses of 'the recontexualizing field and its dynamics' in relation to the State. This was explored with particular reference to Britain since the late 1970s (ibid., pp. 70–5). Essentially, and at risk of considerable simplification, these dynamics involved four things: the progressive exclusion or marginalization of independent educational professionals and the influence of the PRF; the intensification of direct regulation by State agencies of both the inputs and outputs of education at all levels below the tertiary sector; the introduction of financial and performance audits and a linked system of rewards and penalties for all education providers (from nursery schools to universities); and finally, new forms of institutional management with greatly enhanced powers over professional employees but themselves under great pressure to 'perform' within the newly created quasi-markets of the public sector. Bernstein's last paper to address these issues introduced a further key concept: *the Re-centred State*:

> [T]his refers to new forms of centralized regulation whereby the State de-centralizes and through (a) central setting of criteria and (b) the central assessment of the outputs of agencies, financially (and otherwise) rewards success and punishes failures: 'choice', selection, control and reproduction. (2000, p. 78)

These new concepts and the use Bernstein makes of them suggest that it is not unreasonable to see this work concerned with the role of the State in recent educational reform as broadly in line with mainstream 'policy scholarship' (Grace 1995). There will not, of course, be space here to discuss the *strengths and limitations* of Bernstein's various discussions of the State: his analyses are certainly incomplete; they could be criticized for a certain 'ad hoc' character; moreover, there is no general theory connecting his theorizations of class, pedagogic discourse, and the key concepts of power and control, to a comprehensive analysis of the State.

Instead of remaining at this general level of discussion, we shall in the remainder of this chapter, focus on just one instance of Bernstein's use of this new conceptual apparatus. Once again, what is most original and insightful is the way he goes beyond analysing organizational change to focus on the State's efforts to project pedagogic identities congruent with the new policy priorities. Broadly, the Recentred State is seen as employing its new repertoire of controls and incentives to project particular kinds of *prospective pedagogic identities*. Essentially, this involves '*selective* recontextualizing of features of the past to defend or raise economic performance' and Bernstein briefly speculates about the main elements of identity construction central to both the Thatcherite and Blairite political projects (2000, pp. 67–8). Of even greater interest, however, is the discussion of what he terms 'generic' pedagogic modes and their implications for identity. Generic modes, he suggests, had their origin in Further Education but have recently been extended much more widely, partly in response to the perceived need to functionalize education for a world in which futures are held to be increasingly unpredictable and where the capacity to react rapidly and appropriately to changing market demands is at a premium. Most importantly,

> Generic modes . . . are based on a new concept of 'work' and 'life' . . . which might be called 'short-termism'. This is where a skill, task, area

of work undergoes continuous development, disappearance or replacement . . . Under these circumstances it is considered that a vital new ability must be developed: 'trainability', the ability to profit from continuous pedagogic re-formations and so cope with the new requirements of 'work' and 'life'. These . . . it is hoped, will realize a flexible transferable potential rather than specific performances. Thus generic modes have their deep structure in the concept of 'trainability'. (2000, p. 59)

Although Bernstein never makes the point fully explicit, recent reforms of teacher training in Britain (especially initial training), seem in many ways to be a paradigm instance of generic modes. In the 1980s and 1990s, the introduction of competency-based training tightly linked to centrally specified performance criteria was accompanied by an increased emphasis on workplace-based learning and on 'mentoring' by practitioners. At the same time, the greatly enhanced powers of government agencies such as the Teacher Training Agency and Ofsted 'reduced the autonomy of the PRF and changed the positions of dominance within it' (2000, p. 58). And here it is crucial to recognize a further characteristic of generic modes: they insidiously suppress recognition of their own discursive base, that is, they suppress awareness of the fact that they are themselves tacitly rooted in theory, notwithstanding their claims to being based on practice and on experience in the 'real world'. In this sense, they involve misrecognition (2000, p. 53). As Jones and Moore (1995) so clearly demonstrated, the introduction of competency-based paradigms in teacher training in Britain not only involved the suppression of the discursive behaviourist base of this new generic mode, it also denied 'trainees' access to alternative discourses, especially education disciplines such as philosophy and sociology of education, which might have equipped students to become critically aware of the forces that were really structuring their professional re-formation. Significantly, this exclusion of certain discourses (and agents) within the PRF was achieved not by explicit censorship, but by filling the course time available with 'essential' (and audited) practice-related content.

In terms of *identity*, Bernstein points out that 'trainability' – the hidden central concept of generic modes – has a curious but highly significant characteristic: there is at its heart 'an emptiness which makes the concept self-referential . . .' (ibid., p. 59). Trainability as a desired disposition is *necessarily* empty because its whole point is the fostering of receptiveness to whatever set of objectives and contents comes along next (or is next imposed). The similarities with the identity-forming implications of regionalization discussed earlier should be clear. And in this regard, it is worth noting the remarkable resemblances between Bernstein's analysis of 'train-ability' and Bill Reading's critique of the corporate ideology of 'excellence' in contemporary American universities. Readings too diagnoses a revealing emptiness at the heart of slogans like 'the pursuit of excellence' which are so prominent in university mission statements and the like. 'Excellence', he contends, is a paradigm instance of 'dereferentialization' – that is, the use of terms having no intrinsic meaning but which can be mobilized to legitimize whatever priorities markets or managements require. He adds: 'the appeal to excellence marks the fact that there is no longer any idea of the University, or rather that the idea has lost all content' (Readings 1996, p. 39, quoted in Delanty 2001, p. 140). I have myself suggested that there is a similar dereferentialized hollowness in New Labour's deployment of terms like 'modernizing' – and even 'new' (Beck 1999, p. 229).

If this analysis is persuasive, and if generic modes of training prove successful in producing the disposition to welcome successive pedagogic reformation, then older bases of teacher identity which created deep, stable inner commitments – be they the subject identities associated with singulars or the 'therapeutic' identities associated with child-centred pro-gressivism – face not so much direct challenge as *evacuation*. Bernstein's underlying Durkheimianism leads him to argue that *something* must fill the socially empty space which successful inculcation of trainability would produce – in order that the actor can 'recognize him/herself and others'. He goes on to suggest that this focus of identity is likely to centre in 'the materialities of the market' and in commodified signifiers of success and worth (Bernstein 2000, p. 59). We may speculate that for certain teachers, this may go along with coming to see themselves as successful *managers* – of 'human resources' perhaps. But since management may itself be another intrinsically empty category having 'no superordinate goals or values of its own' (Newman & Clark 1994, p. 29), the salience of material signifiers of worth may, in such cases, become even more fundamental to identity construction. The upshot is likely to be that the profane 'outer' *becomes* the 'inner'.

Bernstein did highlight the paradox that the official discourse of the National Curriculum, especially in secondary schools, was a collection of 'singulars' and that this potentially offered an alternative basis for identity-formation. But his final verdict was nevertheless pessimistic:

The emphasis on the performance of students and the steps taken to increase and maintain performance for the survival of the institution, is likely to facilitate a state-promoted instrumentality. The intrinsic value of knowledge may well be eroded even though the collection code of the curriculum appears to support such a value. (2000, p. 61)

Endnotes

[1] The main exception is Bernstein's essay 'Thoughts on the Trivium and the Quadrivium' (2000) and the earlier paper from which it was derived 'Education, symbolic control and social practices' (1990, pp. 133–64). Here, he offered a much more *historicized* analysis which related both inwardness and sacredness to what he saw as the shaping influence of certain unique characteristics of *Christianity* on the form and content of the curriculum of the University of Paris in early Mediaeval times (as analysed by Durkheim 1977).

[2] There are two editions of Bernstein's *Pedagogy, Symbolic Control and Identity*: the original published by Taylor and Francis in 1996 and a revised edition by Rowman and Littlefield in 2000. Unless otherwise stated, all references in this paper are to the revised edition.

[3] It is important to recognize here that Bernstein was highly aware of the partially contradictory position of the agents of cultural reproduction and of their 'ambiguous consciousness' (1977, p. 199). They had the capacity to represent values which were in some ways independent of those of the dominant class yet they were also unavoidably implicated in reproducing and legitimizing the dominance *of* that class. Their celebration of the 'intrinsic' in this sense was compromised by the way in which this was often associated with their own class interests.

Chapter 5

Competency-Based Training, Powerful Knowledge and the Working Class

Leesa Wheelahan
Griffith University

Introduction

This chapter uses a modified Bernsteinian analysis to explore the way in which competency-based training (CBT) in vocational education and training (VET) in Australia excludes the working class and other disadvantaged social groups from access to powerful knowledge, because it denies students access to the structuring principles of disciplinary knowledge. First, I outline the distinction that Bernstein makes between sacred and profane or esoteric and mundane knowledge, and the role each plays in society. This includes discussion of Bernstein's analysis of the structures of esoteric and mundane knowledge as vertical and horizontal discourses, and the way in which each type of knowledge is acquired. This is the basis for Bernstein's social argument for democratic access to the disciplines. Bernstein's main focus was on the social relations of knowledge, and not the epistemic relations. However, access to disciplinary knowledge is important for epistemic reasons as well as social reasons, and the chapter draws on critical realism to establish this argument. Bernsteinian theory and critical realism constitute complementary approaches that together provide insights into the structures of knowledge, the content of knowledge and the relationship between knowers and knowledge, which includes exploration of the social conditions under which knowledge is produced, and the extent to which these processes are mediated by power. The second section explains the emergence of CBT in Australia, and situates these reforms to VET within broader processes of policy reform by Anglophone neo-liberal governments, which sought to structure VET as training for industry. Bernsteinian theory is used to analyse the way in which the language of progressivism was transformed through its incorporation into the 'new vocationalism', and resulted in the 'controlled vocationalism' of current

VET policy in England and in Australia, in ways that reinforce the power of employers (Bates et al. 1998; Jones & Moore 1995). The final section analyses VET policy and the structure of VET qualifications in Australia to demonstrate that, while these qualifications may provide access to procedural knowledge or to products of disciplinary knowledge, students do not gain access to the 'style of reasoning' within disciplinary structures of knowledge, which reduces the control students as workers have over knowledge in the workplace.

Esoteric and Mundane Knowledge

Moore and Muller (2002, p. 635) refer to Bernstein's approach as a 'form of sociological realism in the Durkheimian mode'. Bernstein's (2000, p. 29) theory of knowledge is indebted to Durkheim in arguing that all societies distinguish between sacred or esoteric knowledge on the one hand, and profane or mundane knowledge on the other. Esoteric knowledge is theoretical and conceptual knowledge, while mundane knowledge is 'knowledge of the other . . . knowledge of how it is (the knowledge of the possible)' (Bernstein 2000, p. 157). Durkheim and Bernstein imply that the distinction between esoteric and mundane knowledge is universal, while the content of each is culturally and historically specific.

Esoteric knowledge is sacred knowledge because, historically, religion was the paradigmatic form of theoretical and abstract knowledge, and mundane knowledge was profane knowledge because its concerns were the concerns of the profane, everyday world. Religions are in essence the collective representations of societies and reflect societies back to themselves. They express the general social relations of particular societies, and this is why religions differ between societies and epochs (Durkheim 1967, pp. 29–30). Religion was paradigmatic for theoretical, abstract knowledge, which was later expressed as specialized forms of knowledge most associated with academic disciplines, because of the way in which religion negotiated the boundaries between the material and immaterial worlds, but also because religion, philosophy and science share the same concerns: 'they are nature, man, society' (Durkheim 1967, p. 476).

The distinction between esoteric and mundane knowledge is the means through which society navigates between the concerns of everyday life (the mundane) and a 'transcendental' realm (Bernstein 2000, p. 29). Young (2003, pp. 102–03) explains that esoteric knowledge for Durkheim consists of 'collective representations' of a society that allow it 'to "make connections" between objects and events that are not obviously related' and 'to "project beyond the present" to a future or alternative world'. Collective repre-sentations are therefore the means societies use to transcend the limits of individual experience to see beyond appearances to the real nature of relations in the (natural and social) world. All societies need to connect the material and immaterial, the known and the unknown, the thinkable and the unthinkable, the here and the not here, the specific and the gen-eral, and the past, present and future. This capacity is a precondition for the existence of society.

Vertical and horizontal discourse

Bernstein elaborated Durkheim's distinction between esoteric and mun-dane knowledge through his exploration of the structures of knowledge in each case, and the social relations they are based on. He says that esoteric knowledge – or conceptual, abstract knowledge – is a form of vertical dis-course, whereas mundane or everyday knowledge is a form of horizontal discourse, with different social relations underpinning each.

Mundane knowledge is tied to specific contexts and events, so that the meaning of mundane knowledge is only understandable within that spe-cific context and the material base it rests upon (Bernstein 2000, p. 30). Because meaning is context specific, it is consumed by that context and cannot easily be applied elsewhere. This is why it is difficult for mundane knowledge to be a driver of change beyond the context in which it is enacted. The structure of mundane knowledge or horizontal discourse is segmented by the specific context in which it is realized (e.g. the workplace, home or local sporting club). This gives rise to segmental knowledges, which are not necessarily transferable to other contexts except where features of the context and social relations are similar. Bernstein (2000, p. 157) says that horizontal discourse is 'likely to be oral, local, context dependent and specific, tacit, multi-layered, and contradictory across but not within contexts'. The principle through which knowledge is selected and applied is relevant to the local context, and the local context is usually the site in which learning that knowledge (and how to apply it) takes place. This means that meanings, knowledge and competences acquired in one context (or segment) do not necessarily have meaning or relevance in another (Bernstein 2000, p. 159).

In contrast, Bernstein (2000, p. 30) argues that much esoteric knowl-edge is potentially powerful knowledge because it constitutes the site of the 'unthinkable' and the 'yet-to-be-thought'. Esoteric knowledge has the potential to challenge the social distribution of power, because of its (not always realized) capacity to transform knowledge and how that knowledge is used. Such knowledge is indirectly related to a material base, and this means that there is a potential for a gap to arise between that knowledge and its material base, which Bernstein (2000, p. 30) refers to as the 'potential discursive gap'. Bernstein (2000, p. 30) argues that this gap can 'become (not always) a site for alternative possibilities, for alternative realizations between the material and immaterial' and can 'change the relations between the material and immaterial'. This is the site of the 'unthinkable', the 'impossible' and the 'not-yet thought', and this is why esoteric knowledge has power and status, and why access to it is always regulated through a division of labour, and through distributive rules that provide access to some, but not others (Bernstein 2000, p. 31).

Esoteric or conceptual knowledge is structured as a vertical discourse because, unlike horizontal discourse, knowledge is not segmented by, and integrated through, the specific context in which it is realized. Rather, Bernstein (2000, p. 160) explains that vertical discourse consists of 'specialized symbolic structures of explicit knowledge' in which the integration of knowledge occurs through the integration of meanings and not through relevance to specific contexts. Bernstein says that, 'The procedures of Vertical discourse are then linked, not by contexts, horizontally, but the procedures are linked to other procedures hierarchically' (2000, p. 160). Vertical discourses take one of two main forms. The first form of vertical discourse 'takes the form of a coherent, explicit, and systematically principled structure, [and is] hierarchically organized, as in the sciences' (2000, p. 157).

Physics or other natural sciences are examples of vertical discourses with hierarchical knowledge structures. The other 'takes the form of specialized languages with specialized modes of interrogation and specialized criteria for the production and circulation of texts, as in the social sciences and humanities' (Bernstein 2000, p. 157). Unlike the acquisition of horizontal discourse (which is tied to specific contexts and largely only meaningful within that context), the process of acquiring vertical discourse is through induction into that strongly classified and insulated body of knowledge. The acquisition of vertical discourse requires the development of the capacity to integrate meanings so that these meanings 'are not consumed at the point of its contextual delivery' (Bernstein 2000, p. 160). Students need to acquire the capacity to integrate knowledge (and underpinning principles) through systems of meaning bounded by the discipline in ways that transcend the particular application of specific 'products' of disciplinary knowledge in specific contexts. Rather than learning the isolated and unconnected contents of disciplinary knowledge, students need to learn the systems of meaning.

A realist ontology

Bernstein's (2000, p. xx) analysis of the nature of esoteric and mundane knowledge, and the structure of the discourse that underpins each, demonstrates the reasons why access to abstract, disciplinary knowledge is important, and is the basis of his argument against the lack of democratic access to such knowledge. However, Bernstein was primarily concerned with the social relations of knowledge, and his argument does not, on its own, constitute an argument based on the epistemic relations of knowledge (Moore & Maton 2001). Beck and Young (2005, p. 185) explain that Bernstein was less concerned with the internal content of disciplinary structures of knowledge, and that he was agnostic about their epistemological standing. Moore (2004, p. 142) argues that Bernstein's insistence that theories generate languages of description about their objects of study 'in such a way that the theory is independently tested against reality and open to modification in light of that testing' means that Bernstein was insisting on 'an external ontological imperative'. I think Moore is right, but this is an area where Bernstein's argument was implicit and underdeveloped, because his focus was on the structures of knowledge, which he considered to be independent to questions concerning the content of knowledge.

Moore (2004, p. 148) explains that the sociology of education must be concerned about the production of knowledge, as well as its more traditional concerns about the way in which different fields of knowledge are classified within the curriculum. He compares and contrasts constructionist and realist approaches to the production of knowledge. Constructionism insists on the relativism of all knowledge; knowledge is defined through (and reduced to) the perspective of the knower, through denying the existence of an independent objective reality. Realist approaches concede that knowledge is a social product and that it is fallible as a consequence, but that an objective reality exists, and that the purpose of knowledge is to understand that objective reality, even if our knowledge is always impartial, socially mediated, and marked by the social conditions under which it was produced, which includes power and privilege (see also this volume, Chapter 1). My goal here is to argue for the latter, without engaging in debate with the former.[1]

Critical realists argue that we need to go beyond underlying appearances or events to understand the connections that produce the reality that we experience (Sayer 2000). This is because the world is complex and stratified. The outcomes we experience are always the product of co-determination of different causal mechanisms that interact in open systems (Bhaskar 1998). For example, Collier (1998, p. 263) explains that everything is governed by the law of physics; some, but not all things are governed by the laws of biology; and, more recently, some but not all things are governed by the law of capitalist economics. The causal mechanisms operating within these different strata (and others not identified here) interact to make factory production possible.

Critical realism is a relational philosophy because it examines the interplay between different objects and strata, arguing: that the world is characterized by emergence, that is situations in which the conjunction of two or more features or aspects gives rise to new phenomena, which have properties which are irreducible to those of their constituents, even though the latter are necessary for their existence. (Sayer 2000, p. 12). For example, even though societies comprise lots of individuals and could not exist without them, adding up all the individuals who live in a society does not express the totality of that society. Society is more than the sum of its parts, and the nature of society reacts back to affect the individuals and other factors (such as material and social resources) that make society possible. We have to go beyond our experiences and beyond the events that take place in the world to understand the nature of the generative mechanisms that cause these events and experiences. An example of a causal mechanism in the social world is social class, while gravity is an example in the natural world. However, even though critical realists argue that the natural and social worlds are characterized by stratification, co-determination and emergence, this does not mean that we can use the same methods to study each. This is because the objects we are studying do not have universal properties, and this means that it is not possible to use universal methods to explore those objects (Archer 1995).

Critical realists argue that knowledge arises from our practice in the world (Bhaskar 1998; Sayer 2000). As our practice leads to better knowledge of the world, changes ensue in the classification and structures of knowledge. Changes in the structure of the disciplines occur as a consequence of the interplay between social relations, our practice, and insights from already existing knowledge in other disciplines. This is because the academic disciplines are themselves complex realities.

They are partly constituted by arbitrary social relations because they are social products, but they are also partly constituted by the objects they seek to study, and this means that the division between the disciplines is not wholly arbitrary (Collier 1997, 1998). Some disciplines, such as physics or chemistry, provide insights into aspects of the world by identifying causal mechanisms in isolation of their operation in open systems. Other disciplines, like all the human sciences, focus on the emergent outcome of many causal mechanisms operating at different levels (Collier 1997, 1998).

Access to disciplinary knowledge is important for epistemic reasons because it provides students with access to the 'collective representations' about the causal mechanisms that the discipline studies, mechanisms that are not always accessible through direct experience (or problem-based learning). The disciplines provide students with access to the relational connections within a field of study and between fields, and students need access to the disciplinary 'style of reasoning' (Muller 2000, p. 88) to move beyond a focus on isolated examples of content. Specific content is the product of disciplinary knowledge; it is not knowledge about the generative mechanisms (and the relations between them) that the discipline studies. If the world is characterized by ontological depth, stratification, emergence and co-determination, then students need to understand these processes, and not have their understanding restricted to the level of events or experiences. These are the epistemic reasons why access to the disciplines is important. However, interdisciplinary research is necessary to understand concrete particulars (the things that exist or happen in the world), because concrete particulars are always a consequence of co-determination of many different mechanisms (as in the earlier example of factory production). Such interdisciplinary work takes place, however, through explicitly negotiating disciplinary boundaries rather than their negation.

Broad Context for the Introduction of CBT in VET in Australia

The introduction of CBT in Australia was as a consequence of similar neoliberal reforms as those in the United Kingdom (particularly England), which sought to recast education, and particularly VET, as an instrument of micro-economic reform. There are many parallels as well as differences between the two systems, as each nation sought to develop specific reforms in response to imperatives generated by the social, cultural, economic and technological changes associated with globalization (Priestley 2002).

Competency-based training was introduced in the 1980s and 1990s in Australia as part of broader industry restructuring to increase Australia's competitiveness in an increasingly globalized economy (Goozee 2001,

p. 62). It was introduced in VET in Australia by a Labour government, as part of broader reforms to all sectors of education through seeking to subordinate education to economic needs, and to align 'skill' development with the 'needs' of the economy. There was bipartisan support for the reconstruction of VET according to the principles of human capital theory. Labour and Conservative governments have, since that time, redefined VET as training for industry, according to industry-defined outcomes, as part of a broader reform process that sought the development of a competitive VET 'market' to make VET more 'responsive' to the needs of industry (Goozee 2001, p. 90).

Bates et al. (1998, p. 113), in discussing the introduction of the new vocationalism in England, explain that 'whereas the old vocationalism was about preparing trainees for specific jobs, the new vocationalism aimed at preparation for work in general'. I have applied their analysis to Australia, because the resonances are so strong. They explain that, despite the historical antipathy between vocationalism and progressivism, the 'new vocationalism' of the 1980s was infused with the language of progressivism.

The language of progressivism was strongly associated with the introduction of CBT in Australia. Indeed, the Australian Council of Trade Unions was among the most enthusiastic supporters of the introduction of CBT, and helped to develop and implement the new VET system and new VET qualifications through their participation in corporatist mechanisms established by the then Labour Government (Goozee 2001). The introduction of CBT would, it was argued, increase participation in education and training, provide unparalleled access to education and training for people from disadvantaged backgrounds, recognize and certify the skills of existing workers, create access to on-the-job and off-the-job training for workers, help to overcome occupational segregation based on gender divisions or outdated craft divisions, increase private and public investment in training, and improve the quality and flexibility of the training system (Goozee 2001, pp. 63–4).

Vocationalism drew from progressivism a rejection of 'the centrality of disciplinary knowledge and school subjects in definitions of the curriculum' (Bates et al. 1998, p. 111). This is because progressivism (in the tradition of Rousseau, Blake and the Romantic movement; Bates et al. 1998, p. 110) was concerned primarily with the development of the intrinsic capacities of the child/student. Consequently the task of the teacher was not to instil disciplinary knowledge, but to 'expose students to situations in which they could construct their knowledge of the world' (Bates et al. 1998, p. 111). Bloomer (1998, p. 168) explains that the reworked progressivism drew the language of 'consumer rights, freedom and individuality' from the liberal market ideologies that were driving the new vocationalism, because these were seen as 'inherently and morally good'. In Australia as in England, the 'new vocationalism' of the 1970s and early 1980s was transformed into 'controlled vocationalism' that granted increased control to the state and to employers in specifying the outcomes of VET (Bates et al. 1998, p. 114). An important difference between Australia and England is that the Learning and Skills Sector in England offers a range of general, second-chance and higher education programmes as well as VET qualifications, which are based on National Vocational Qualifications. However, under the new UK funding arrangements, these possibilities for non-competence-based programmes are fast disappearing as in the case of the workers educational associations. There are fewer options in Australia. In VET in Australia, publicly funded provision leading to qualifications must be based on training packages, which are the equivalent of National Vocational Qualifications. Some further education programmes still exist, but they are marginal and their future is threatened unless they can demonstrate a labour market outcome. In most cases, the only way that VET providers can escape these restrictions and offer a qualification normally accredited in another sector is through full-fee, and not publicly funded, programmes (Wheelahan & Moodie 2005).

Jones and Moore (1995, p. 81) explain that educational policy must be located within the political context in which it arises, and this helps us to understand the way in which the progressivism of the new vocationalism was transformed into controlled vocationalism. They explain that the

> political and policy context act selectively upon the realization of the various possibilities suggested by different approaches to competence . . .; Whether it is the controlling or emancipatory possibilities that come to be realized will be settled not by theoretical or definitional debates but within real world, institutional contexts. (Jones & Moore 1995, pp. 81–2)

The real world, institutional policy context acts by selectively borrowing from other discourses and constructs 'an approach appropriate to the particular objectives of the agency assembling it' (Jones & Moore 1995, p. 83).

In drawing from Bernstein, Jones and Moore explain that the broader policy context constitutes the regulative discourse through providing the principle of recontextualization that is used to construct the explicit, instructional discourse. The policy discourse of competence borrowed from theories 'originally developed within disciplines in the academic sphere [which] are taken out of that context and reassembled, in an appropriate form, within the institutional space of the agency concerned' (Jones & Moore 1995, p. 83). They explain that educational policy development is characterized by two processes: the first is the process of recontextualization, in which ideas and concepts are selectively appropriated into an instructional discourse, but the realization of the instructional discourse is always embedded in the regulative discourse, and the parameters of regulative discourse are shaped by the particular model of social order (in this case, neo-liberalism) pursued by government policy. The principle of recontextualization points backwards, to the different origins of the instructional discourse. It tells us where the discourse has come from. This was the way in which progressivism was reworked and transformed through the new vocationalism. The second process to which Jones and Moore (1995, pp. 83–4) refer is the process of incorporation, which refers to the way 'in which the discourse incorporates those aspects of social life that are the primary concern of the agency'. This tells us the direction in which the discourse is travelling, or where it is going. The introduction of CBT in England (and in Australia) 'incorporates "the world of work" according to its own particular principles and rules' (Jones & Moore 1995, p. 84).

The world of work imagined in policy (at least in Anglophone, liberal market economies) is the 'natural' free market populated by entrepreneurial, flexible workers who take responsibility for their firm's outcomes, but without the hierarchical (and expensive) management structures characteristic of Fordism (Bates et al. 1998, p. 116). Bates et al. (1998, p. 117) explain that 'All these arguments hinge upon the notion of improving an organization's competitive edge and imply a unitary model of employer–employee relations'. The outcomes of work are not problematized and policy takes for granted that the purpose of education is to 'revolve around the cultivation of appropriate skills and attitudes for employment' (Bates et al. 1998, p. 115). The outcomes of education (particularly VET in England and in Australia) were similarly redefined as unproblematic 'descriptions' of the skills needed by employers.

This process is being driven further in Australia, and all VET qualifications will be revised so that they incorporate the newly endorsed 'employability skills'. These skills must be 'front and centre' of VET qualifications as they are redeveloped (Department of Education Science and Training [DEST] 2005, p. 160). These employability skills will replace the existing broader 'key competencies' because the latter 'were too generic in their approach and no longer reflected the needs of contemporary workplaces'

(Cleary et al. 2006, p. 10). The new employability skills are even more tightly tied to work than were the previous key competencies, and are defined as follows (see DEST 2005, pp. 181–4):

- communication that contributes to productive and harmonious relations between employees and customers
- teamwork that contributes to productive working relationships and outcomes.
- problem solving that contributes to productive outcomes
- initiative and enterprise that contributes to innovative outcomes
- planning and organizing that contribute to long- and short-term strategic planning.
- self-management that contributes to employee satisfaction and growth
- learning that contributes to ongoing improvement and expansion in employee and company operations and outcomes
- technology that contributes to effective execution of tasks

Williams (2005, p. 45) explains that the discourse around employability skills is a normalizing exercise, in which the desired attributes of 'learner-workers' are defined according to the dominant values, beliefs and expectations of the dominant culture.

The definition of employability skills here shows that this is indeed the case, if we define dominant culture as the near-hegemonic dominance of employer interests in government policy and in the VET system.

VET Qualifications in Australia

As the previous section explains, the only qualifications that are accredited in the VET sector are training packages, which are the equivalent of the English National Vocational Qualifications, or programmes that consist of industry-specified units of competency if an argument can be made that there is no suitable training package. VET qualifications prepare students for occupations across all industries at different skill levels, and are not limited to the traditional trades.

The introduction of training packages caused fierce debate within Australia, so much so that Schofield and McDonald (2004) called for a 'new settlement' to underpin training packages in their report on the high level review of training packages in 2004. Training packages have been criticized for many reasons, but particularly by teachers because of concerns that they downplay the importance of underpinning knowledge (Smith & Keating 2003, p. 169). This section provides a theoretical explanation for teachers' concerns.

Training packages are developed for broad industry areas (such as community services), and each training package comprises a number of qualifications at different levels. Qualifications are made up of industry-specified units of competency that are specified in the training package, and many units of competency are shared between qualifications. Each unit of competency consists of a number of elements of competency, employability skills, performance criteria, a range statement that describes the probable contexts in which the competency will be deployed, and evidence guides to guide assessment. *The Training Package Development Handbook* (DEST 2005, p. 105) defines competency as follows: 'Competency comprises the specification of knowledge and skill and the application of that knowledge and skill to the standard of performance required in the workplace'.

Units of competency must be related to realistic workplace practices. The Handbook specifies the way in which knowledge should be handled in units of competency. The Handbook (DEST 2005, pp. 109–10) stipulates that: 'In recognition of the importance of knowledge in skills application and skills transfer, units of competency must detail the underpinning knowledge required for competent performance'. The application of knowledge is often the key to the transfer of competency to new situations. Underpinning knowledge will often need to be assessed in order to ensure that the person understands the 'why' as well as the 'how'. Clear articulation of the required underpinning knowledge will support training and assessment of the unit of competency.

However, while knowledge must be expressed, units of competency, their elements or performance criteria should not be entirely knowledge based unless a clear and assessable workplace outcome is described. Knowledge in units of competency:

- should be in context
- should only be included if it refers to knowledge actually applied at work

Later on, The Handbook says that, 'Competent performance must result in a realistic expression of knowledge through problem solving, prediction of outcomes, cause and effect, or similar dynamic process specific to the unit' (DEST 2005, p. 134).

This is a very fragmented, atomistic and instrumental view of knowledge. It is premised on positivist views of knowledge, in which knowledge is reducible to statements about correlation and prediction. Knowledge is not and cannot be always about prediction of outcomes, unless we are limiting our statements to observation of cause and effect in closed systems (Bhaskar 1998), and this certainly does not describe the world of work or any aspect of the social world. Knowledge is about understanding. Moreover, the Handbook posits an atomistic view of knowledge, which carves up the knowledge needed in a particular area, and then renders it all equal. For example, the unit of competency 'Advocate for clients', which is part of the Community Services Training Package (Community Services and Health Industry Skills Council 2005, p. 81), has three elements of competency:

1. assist clients to identify their rights and represent their own needs
2. advocate on behalf of clients on request
3. advocate for clients

There are nine performance criteria (although one of these has three components).

The 'essential knowledge' included in the evidence guide requires students to demonstrate knowledge of the following:

- organizations and services relevant to the nature of client service
- referral options and resources available to community
- organizational policies and procedures
- relevant legal and other rights/limitations
- social justice principles
- differences between negotiation, advocacy, mediation and conciliation (Community Services and Health Industry Skills Council 2005, p. 83)

Social justice principles and the difference between negotiation, advocacy, mediation and conciliation are not differentiated from the other components of necessary knowledge (or from each other even though social justice is at a different level of theorization than the applied concepts of negotiation, advocacy, mediation and conciliation), yet some of these elements are clearly procedural and of less importance than the underpinning broad sociological knowledge that is needed to successfully understand the context in which advocacy takes place. Not all knowledge is of equal importance or of the same type.

Moreover, this approach assumes conceptual knowledge can be unproblematically defined. Social justice principles are called for in the above example, yet the concept of social justice is related to the nature of the human actor. What kind of human actor is assumed? The designation of 'clients' suggests that a consumer relation is posited. This demonstrates the folly in assuming that it is possible and desirable to identify specific knowledge associated with work that is separated from the system of concepts that give it meaning, and then unproblematically teach and assess it. The capacity to use particular knowledge at work is an emergent capacity that emerges from broader knowledge, skills and attributes. In this case, some understanding about different ways in which philosophy or sociology define agents and their relationship to society seems to be essential knowledge that community workers use to 'know with' and interpret particular situations. Prior to the introduction of the training package, the students enrolled in a community development programme in which I used to teach, undertook subjects such as human rights and advocacy, sociology and politics, and students were required to explore the contests over different understandings of agency and the implications these had for practice.

In other words, the programme in which I used to teach stood at the interface between disciplinary knowledge and the field of practice (Bernstein 2000, p. 52), and while the field of practice provided the rationale for the selection and translation of knowledge in the curriculum, it was still based on explicit engagement with disciplinary knowledge.

Bernstein's insights allow us to see that CBT fundamentally transforms the nature of knowledge by delocating it from the vertical discourse in which it is classified and relocating it closer (if not completely) towards horizontal discourse.[2] This changes the nature of knowledge, and the processes through which it is acquired. Rather than integration of meanings we have integration within a context. Consequently, students are provided with access to specific content, and not the systems of meaning in disciplinary knowledge. However, the content of a discipline is the product of the discipline (and each discipline has lots of 'products'); it is not the generative principles used within the discipline to create new knowledge, and nor does a focus on content provide the criteria needed to select the knowledge needed in new contexts. Content is disaggregated so that it consists of isolated 'bits' of knowledge.

A focus on specific content for a specific context means that the meaning of that content is exhausted by the context. Unless students have access to the generative principles of disciplinary knowledge, they are not able to transcend the particular context. Students need to know how these complex bodies of knowledge fit together if they are to decide what knowledge is relevant for a particular purpose, and if they are to have the capacity to transcend the present to imagine the future.

Knowledge is not under their control. This simultaneously denies them epistemic access to the structures of knowledge relevant in their field and social access to the 'unthinkable'.

Critical realism extends these Bernsteinian insights, because a focus on the specific content of disciplines denies students access to the 'collective representations' that provide access into the stratified and emergent nature of the real. This 'absence' arises from the broader ontology and epistemology of CBT, which is a form of empirical realism (based on atomism in ontology and epistemology). By focusing on the knowledge and skills that people need to 'do' their job, and by insisting that assessment be directly aligned with these outcomes, CBT collapses the domain of the real (of generative mechanisms) and the domain of the actual (where events take place) into the domain of the empirical (that which is observable). It does so because CBT assumes that outcomes can be achieved by directly teaching to the outcomes, and in doing so ignores the complexity that is needed to create capacity, and this goes beyond the level of experience in the contextual and situated.

Teaching and learning must engage the real and the actual, and not just the empirical, because this is the only way to generate a varying and contextually sensitive performance in a variety of contexts. In contrast, CBT breaks skills down into discrete components, which can be packaged as competencies, then added up, moved about and reconfigured to make different qualifications, through common core competencies (and now employability skills). That is, the total equals the sum of the parts. This is the method that aggregates, and is less concerned with understanding the relationship between elements, and how these elements are transformed in the context of such a relationship.

The argument here says nothing about the way in which students should be taught the disciplines. Obviously teaching physics or mathematics to electricians should be different to teaching students undertaking degrees in these disciplines. This applies to all the regions of knowledge (which is where Bernstein locates the professions) that stand at the interface of a field of practice, on the one hand, and disciplinary knowledge, on the other, because the recontextualizing principle used to select knowledge from the field in which it was produced and relocated in curriculum is the demands of practice (Bernstein 2000, p. 54). However, just like those students studying elite professions in elite universities, students in VET should have access to the disciplinary boundaries and the capacity to nego-tiate these boundaries in their practice. CBT renders these boundaries invisible.

Conclusion

The social composition of the VET and higher education sectors is different in Australia. Students from low socio-economic backgrounds are under-represented in higher education, while the VET sector is more representative of the broader community (Wheelahan & Moodie 2005). The implications from the above analysis are that CBT in VET reinforces class divisions through differentially distributing access to 'unthinkable' knowledge, because it does not allow students access to a 'style of reason-ing' represented in disciplinary knowledge (Muller 2000), and conse-quently focuses on specific content rather than the generative principles that underpin disciplinary knowledge. Bernstein's analysis of the structures of knowledge and the way in which access to it is differentially distributed provides insights into the social reasons why access to disciplinary knowl-edge is important, while critical realism provides insights into the epistemic reasons. A social justice strategy in Australia must not be premised solely on increasing access to higher education for working-class students, although this is important. It must also be premised on overturning CBT as the man-dated model of curriculum for all VET qualifications, and emphasizing once again the importance of disciplinary knowledge as a component of VET qualifications. Electricians need to think like mathematicians, and community development workers like sociologists. We need to value the depth and complexity of knowledge needed for vocational practice the same as we do for professional practice.

Endnotes

[1] See chapter 6 of Moore (2004) for a critique of relativist theories of knowledge.

[2] Bernstein (2000, p. 113) distinguishes between the production of knowledge and the reproduction of knowledge. He says that all knowledge is delocated from the site in which it was produced (e.g. in research in physics departments) and relocated into pedagogic discourse (e.g. as part of the physics curriculum in school), because the whole field of knowledge production cannot be reproduced in entirety in the curriculum. This means that a process of selection and recontex-tualization must take place. However, while the field of physics production is

not the same as the field of physics reproduction in the curriculum, they are related by the way in which knowledge is classified within the discipline. My point here is different, because CBT severs the relationship between the field of knowledge production and its associated field of knowledge reproduction in curriculum.

Chapter 6

Knowledge and Truth in Sociology of Education

Michael Young
University of London and University of Bath

Johan Muller
University of Cape Town

Introduction

In his book *Truth and Truthfulness* (2002), Bernard Williams identifies the 'commitment to truthfulness' as a central tendency in current social thought that can be traced back to the Enlightenment and now stretches from philosophy and the humanities to 'historical understanding, the social sciences and even to the interpretations of discoveries and research in the natural sciences' (2002, p. 1). He describes this tendency as 'an eagerness to see through appearances to the real structures and motives that lie behind them' (p. 1). However he sees this 'commitment to truthfulness' as increasingly paralleled by a no less pervasive 'scepticism about truth itself', 'whether there is such a thing [as truth] . . . whether it can be more than relative or subjective or something of that kind' (p. 1). His argument is that the latter inexorably corrodes the former.

The two tendencies, towards truthfulness and against the idea of truth, are not for Williams, as for many, just a contradiction or tension that as sociologists or philosophers we have to live with. Rather he sees an acceptance of the notion of truth as the condition for a serious commitment to truthfulness. This chapter takes Williams's claim as a starting point for re-examining what kind of activities the sociology of knowledge (in educational studies, and more generally) is engaged in, bearing in mind that in most forms it has been an almost paradigmatic case of endorsing a scepticism about the truth (see this volume, Chapters 1 and 3).

Williams compares the sociology of knowledge to muckraking journalism with which it has some similarities. Both seek truthfulness, but more often are little more than forms of debunking. Muckraking journalism and some strands of the sociology of knowledge have little doubt about what truth is or where it lies – it lies in identifying the corruption of the powerful. This is the basis for the kind of moral self-righteousness and absolute certainty that we find in campaigning journalists such as John Pilger. Some sociologists of education have tried to resolve the tension between truth and truthfulness in similar ways, often by assuming that their identification with the powerless or with a particular disadvantaged group brings them automatically closer to the truth. Such positions are often referred to as 'standpoint' theories even if the grounds for claiming that a standpoint can be the basis for a theory are far from clear.[1] Though superficially attractive, such solutions, Williams argues, serve only to deflect us from facing the really difficult questions about knowledge and truth that we cannot avoid if sociology is to offer more than – as some postmodernists claim – a series of stories (Mendick 2006).

Williams also points out that the end of the 'science wars' and the 'culture wars' and the gradual collapse of any credibility that postmodernism had as a social theory (Benson & Stangroom 2006) has not led to a new commitment to exploring the inescapable links between truth and truthfulness. More commonly he suggests, the outcome has been 'an inert cynicism . . . [which] runs the risk of sliding . . . through professionalization, to a finally disenchanted careerism' (Williams 2002, p. 3).

In this chapter we focus largely on the sociology of knowledge as it has developed within educational studies. This is partly because this is the context within which we have worked. However, locating the question of knowledge in educational debates raises more fundamental questions for social theory that are not always recognized. As Durkheim and Vygotsky (and more recently Basil Bernstein) recognized, just as every theory of education implies a theory of society, educational theories always imply a theory of knowledge (Young 2006).

As sociologists of education, we are, as Floud and Halsey (1958) pointed out long ago, creatures of the rise of mass education and the range of attempts to resolve its particular contradictions. As an aspect of modernization, mass education faced and still faces what might be described as the fundamental pedagogic issue – overcoming the discontinuity (sometimes expressed as a conflict) between the formal, codified, theoretical and, at least potentially, universalizing knowledge of the curriculum that students seek to acquire and teachers to transmit, and the informal, local, experiential and everyday knowledge that pupils (or students) bring to school.

When most of the small proportion of each cohort who attended school shared the underlying cultural assumptions of those designing and delivering the formal curriculum, this discontinuity was barely acknowledged.

Nor was it seen as a problem, at least by policy makers, in the earlier stages of industrialization when schools prepared the majority for unskilled work, and knowledge acquisition was seen as only important for a minority. However, the clash between the democratizing, universalizing goals of mass education and the selection, failure and early leaving that was the reality of schooling for the majority in most countries was never going to remain unnoticed for long. Mass schooling was not achieving the social justice and equality goals set for it by the emerging democratic movements, nor fulfilling adequately the growing demand from a globalizing labour market for higher levels of knowledge and skills.

This was the context in the 1960s when the sociology of education was 'reestablished' in the United Kingdom, as a subdiscipline of sociology, and not, as it had tended to be, an aspect of social mobility and stratification studies.[2] At that time, the central problematic of the sociology of education became, and it has largely remained, the discontinuity between the culture of the school and its curriculum and the cultures of those coming to school. It was partly as a critique of existing approaches to access and equality, and partly to focus on the deeper cultural and political issues that underpinned the persistence of educational inequalities, that Bourdieu and Bernstein developed their early work on cultural capital, language codes and educability (Bernstein 1971b; Bourdieu & Passeron 1977). One outcome of their ideas was that a focus on the sociology of the curriculum became a key element in what became known as the 'new sociology of education' (Young 1971).

Despite starting with the theoretical goal of re-orienting the sociology of education towards the question of knowledge, the sociology of the curriculum in the 1970s took on many of the characteristics that Williams identified with muckraking journalism rather than with social science. It knew the truth – the link between power and knowledge – and set out to show how this truth manifested itself in the school curriculum.[3]

It is not our intention to dismiss the new sociology of education's 'commitment to truthfulness' or its attempt to 'go deeper' and explore the links between curriculum organization and the wider distribution of power.[4] Reminding educationalists that the curriculum, and indeed knowledge itself, is not some external given but a product of historical human activities – part of our own history – was an important task at the time and remains so. However, it would be foolish to deny that many of those working in the sociology of the curriculum at the time identified, albeit not always explicitly, with the prevailing scepticism about truth and knowledge itself (Jenks 1977). This led many to question the idea that a curriculum committed to the idea of truth could 'truthfully' be the aim of the sociology of educational knowledge. As a consequence, the 'new' sociology of education that began, in Williams's terms, with a radical commitment to truthfulness, undermined its own project by its rejection of any idea of truth itself. The aim of this chapter is to reflect on and explore the issues that Williams raises in the particular case of the sociology of education.

We started by showing, via Bernard Williams, that if a commitment to truth is paired with a scepticism about truth, the latter inevitably corrodes the former. We end by arguing that sociology of education must re-align itself with realism, either of a naturalistic kind (after Durkheim 1983 and Moore 2004) that relies on the natural sciences for its model of objectivity or a formalist kind (after Cassirer and, although less clearly, after Bernstein). Nor need there be that kind of choice. The primary choice, we will argue, is between objectivity and anti-objectivity. There was a time when the idea of objectivity in the social sciences seemed to be aligned with oppression, and the route to an acceptable objectivity politically blocked. The time is ripe, we argue, to consolidate and develop the considerable advances made by current developments in the sociology of education that demonstrate the case for its potential objectivity (Nash 2005).

Social Constructivism in the Sociology of Education: What Went Wrong?

Our answer to the question 'what went wrong?' begins by accepting the premise that the 'new sociology of education' and its social constructivist assumptions were an important, albeit a seriously flawed, attempt to establish a sociological basis to debates about the curriculum. It undoubtedly represented an advance on the uncritical acceptance in England of the idea of liberal education (Hirst & Peters 1970) and on the technicist tradition of curriculum theorizing prevalent in the United States at the time (Apple 1975). It created considerable interest within educational studies as well as much opposition; however, it did not provide a reliable basis for an alternative curriculum. Nor did it provide an adequate theory of how, in practice, the curriculum was changing. Why was this so?

First it is important to recognize the extent to which the sociological approach to knowledge and the curriculum which emerged in the 1970s, and the social constructivist ideas which underpinned it, were neither new nor isolated developments. This was true in two senses. First, despite its claims to novelty at the time, the apparently radical idea that all knowledge is in some sense a product of human activities and that this leads at least implicitly and sometimes explicitly to scepticism about the possibility of objective knowledge, was not itself new. It can be traced back to the sophists and sceptics in Ancient Greece and found a new lease of life in Vico's challenge to the emergent hegemony of natural science in the early eighteenth century (Berlin 2000), and it survives to this day among those, like Richard Rorty, whom Bernard Williams (2002) refers to as the 'truth deniers'. It is also true that very similar sets of ideas could be found at the time in every discipline within the social sciences and the humanities. In other words we are dealing as much with the context of the time as with the content of this supposedly 'new' sociology of education.

If there was anything new about the 'new sociology of education', it was the educational contexts in which the idea of 'social constructivism' was applied, and the particular conclusions that were drawn from the assumption that the educational realities of curriculum and pedagogy were socially constructed and could be changed by teachers – almost at will (Gorbutt 1972). The 'decisionism' that this displayed is typical of all cognate constructivisms.

For social constructivists, how we think about the world, our experience, and any notion of 'how the world is', are not differentiated. It follows that the idea that reality itself is socially constructed had two closely related implications as it was interpreted in the sociology of education. First, it provided the basis for challenging any form of givenness or fixity, whether political, social, institutional or cultural. It was assumed that challenging givenness was as applicable to science or knowledge in general as to the social rules, conventions and institutions that had traditionally been studied by sociologists.[5] Secondly, it was able to treat all forms of givenness as arbitrary and, given different social arrangements, potentially changeable. It followed that insofar as a form of givenness persisted it was assumed to express the interests (political, cultural or economic) of some groups *vis-à-vis* others. The intellectual battle was between those, the social constructivists, who saw their task as exposing the apparent givenness of reality for 'what it really was' – a mask to obscure the deeper reality of arbitrariness and interests – and those who opposed them by defending as given what was 'in reality' arbitrary. The distinction between 'constructivists' and 'realists' is inevitably an over-simplification.[6] The primary difference between them was that the constructivists claimed that the only reality was that there was no reality beyond our perceptions. With hindsight, what is puzzling is the combination of indeterminism – everything is arbitrary – and determinism – everything can be changed – that this led to.

Within the 'broad church' of social constructivism in educational studies, a range of different perspectives were drawn on that had little in common and sometimes directly contradicted each other. At different times, different theorists and traditions were recruited. Within the sociology of education, at least from the early 1970s, the dominant perspectives from which the idea of social constructivism was drawn were the social phenomenology and ethnomethodology of Schutz, Merleau Ponty and Garfinkel, the symbolic interactionism of Mead and Blumer, the eclectic social constructivism of Berger and Luckman, the cultural anthropology of Horton (and later Geertz), the neo-Weberian sociology of Bourdieu and, albeit slightly uneasily, the critical Marxism of the Frankfurt School. For Bourdieu, for example, the unmasking of arbitrariness was sociology's core problematic. What these writers had in common, or were interpreted as having in common, was a form of sociological reductionism. As everything was social, sociological analysis could be applied to and account for anything and everything – even though sociologists often disagreed about what the social was. In the 1980s these theoretical traditions were extended to include (and, for many, were replaced by) discourse and literary theories. The literary theories drew on writers such as Derrida, Foucault and Lyotard who treated the social as just another text, a discourse or, in the case of Lyotard, a language game. The reductionist logic, however, was the same.

Education was in a sense, a special – or even, one might say, an ideal – case for social constructivist ideas. This partly reflected the relative theoretical weakness of educational studies and hence its openness to (or inability to resist) any new theory that came along. However, the sociology of the curriculum and the idea that educational realities were socially constructed had a quite specific appeal in the often authoritarian, bureaucratic and always hierarchical world of schooling. It easily led to challenges to existing forms of school knowledge, subjects and disciplines and their familiar expression in syllabuses (Keddie 1971; Whitty & Young 1976). More fundamentally, social constructivism challenged and exposed what it saw as the arbitrariness of the most basic categories of formal education such as intelligence, ability and attainment (Keddie 1971, 1973) and even of the institution of school itself. If social constructivism could show that all such categories, rules and institutions were arbitrary, this also made them potentially open to change, even if social constructivism could not say how or to what. The links between social constructivist ideas and the political Left, or at least parts of it, were hardly surprising, although more often than not expedient.

Why did these ideas gain such a stranglehold in educational studies, and why later were they so easily criticized and rejected? Did this pattern of initial support but later rejection indicate some flaw in the basic idea of reality being 'socially constructed' or did the idea contain, as Marx said of Hegel, a 'rational kernel' that somehow got lost? Why were these ideas particularly seductive – and with hindsight we can see particularly disastrous – for educational studies and the sociology of the curriculum in particular?

Two different kinds of response to such questions can be given. One is an external or contextual argument. It is familiar, relatively uncontroversial and can be dealt with briefly. It is relevant only to the extent to which it reminds us of the non-unique aspect of particular intellectual fields and that the sociology of education is no exception. Two kinds of external or contextual factors are worth mentioning that shaped ideas in the sociology of education – one social and one cultural. The first was the massive expansion and democratization of higher education, the parallel expansion and diversification of the social sciences and humanities, and the assumption, at least in educational studies, that these new types of knowledge could be used to transform what was widely recognized as an inefficient and unequal education system. These developments, magnified since the 1980s by globalization and the emphasis on markets in every sphere of life, created a quite new context for intellectual work in education that had considerable affinity with the new, relativist and supposedly more democratic ideas about knowledge. This new context for educational studies brought in new and sometimes already radicalized students and new lecturers and provided fertile ground for a range of cultural changes which all played a role in shaping the sociology of education. These included a much wider critical and, for a time, highly politicized academic climate, an affinity with populist ideas, a sometimes uncritical respect for the cultures of subordinate and minority groups and those from non-western societies, and a parallel scepticism about the academy and all forms of authority including science and other forms of specialist knowledge. All these developments drew on, and were implicitly or explicitly supportive of, social constructivist ideas (Benson & Stangroom 2006).

It is the internal issues – developments within the intellectual field of educational studies – that we want to concentrate on in this chapter. From early in the 1970s, social constructivist ideas were challenged, usually by philosophers (Pring 1972) but sometimes by other sociologists (Demaine 1981; Gould 1977). However, it was relatively easy for the 'new sociologists' to dismiss these critics by labelling them as reactionary, reformist or 'social democratic' (Young & Whitty 1977).[7]

In developing a less superficial response to its critics, social constructivism in educational studies only had two ways to go, at least within the terms it set itself as a radical theory. One direction was towards a politics that linked constructivist ideas to the privileging of subordinate (as opposed to ruling class or official) knowledge. Subordinacy could refer to the working class and be linked to Marxism, it could refer to women and be linked to feminism or it could refer to non-white groups and what later became known as post-colonial or subaltern studies. In a response that was quite specific to the sociology of education, identification with subordinacy was linked to a celebration of the culture of those who rejected and failed at school. Their language and their resistance to formal learning were seen as at least potentially supportive of a new 'revolutionary' consciousness (Willis 1977).[8] The other direction for social constructivism was towards postmodern versions of a Nietzschean nihilism and the denial of any possibility of progress, truth or knowledge. Not only were such interpretations of Nietzsche somewhat dubious, as Williams (2002, chapter 1) shows but they also offered little that was substantive to educational studies beyond a continuing, if largely empty, role for theory (or 'theorizing', as it became known).[9]

To summarize our argument so far: social constructivism provided teachers and students of education with a superficially attractive but ultimately contradictory set of intellectual tools. On the one hand it offered the possibility of intellectual emancipation and freedom through education – we, as teachers, students or workers have the epistemological right to develop theories and to criticize and challenge scientists, philosophers and other so-called experts and specialists. Furthermore, in some unspecified way, this so-called freedom was seen as contributing to changing the world. This emancipation from all authoritative forms of knowledge was linked by many to the possibility of achieving a more equal or just world, which for some (but not all) meant socialism. On the other hand by undermining any claims to objective knowledge or truth about anything, social constructivism, at least in some of the ways it was (and could legitimately) be interpreted, denies the possibility of any better understanding, let alone of any better world. For obvious reasons, however, this denial tended to be ignored by educational researchers, at least most of the time.

The double bind that combined emancipation and its impossibility was particularly problematic in education. If not only the selection of knowledge in the curriculum, but even the rankings, reporting and everyday judgements made by teachers about pupils were treated as arbitrary, continuing to be a teacher (let alone an educational researcher), became deeply problematic, except in 'bad faith'. Furthermore such ideas have left their mark in today's fashionable language of facilitation, group work and 'teaching as a conversation'. All these pedagogic strategies can be seen as strands of an attempt to suppress hierarchy, or at least render it invisible (Muller 2007).This new 'language of practice' or activity in educational studies, increasingly linked to the 'promise' of e-learning, mobile phones and the Internet, is now with us and has close affinities with the language of the market. It is of course supported by many who know nothing of the original sociological critiques of pedagogic authority.

Why did such ideas persist and why are they resurrected again and again as if they were new? It is not because they are true, unless a fundamental contradictoriness and the consequent impossibility of knowledge can be the truth. Nor, as in the case of new ideas in physics and chemistry, can it be that the idea of reality being socially constructed is so powerful that it has been used to change the world in ways that no one can deny. At best social constructivism reminds us that, however apparently given and fixed certain ideas or institutions appear to be, they are always the product of actual human activities in history. They do not have their origins solely in the material world external to us, nor can we find their origins, as Descartes thought, in our heads. At worst, social constructivism has provided an intellectual legitimacy for criticizing and challenging any institution, any hierarchy, any form of authority and any knowledge as arbitrary. The superficial political correctness, and at times the idiocy, that this position leads to has been a heavy price to pay for the small 'moment' of emancipation that is expressed in the truth that reality is socially constructed. One response to this observation, widely if not always explicitly admitted, has been to reject the enterprise of the sociology of education and more particularly sociology as it is applied to the curriculum. This was the response of the political Right who labelled it as left-wing ideology (Gould 1977). A more pragmatic and technocratic version of this position has since been adopted by most teacher training programmes and an increasing number of higher degrees in educational studies in the United Kingdom today. Programmes of initial teacher education or professional development that include the systematic study of the sociology of education are increasingly rare. This rejection of the sociology of knowledge was also, with rather more justification, the position taken by the group of natural scientists who waged the science wars (Sokal 1998) and who had, by the 1990s, become massively impatient with the patent circularity of constructivism.[10] It is not unlikely that the latter provided the intellectual justification for the policy consequences of the former.

A more constructive alternative, in our view, is to begin by remembering something that was too easily forgotten in the heady days of the 1970s and often still is. That is that sociology itself, like all social life, institutions, knowledge and even science, has a history. It follows that we need not only to see society and education historically, but to recall the history of sociology and the sociology of education and to recognize that debates within one generation of sociologists always need to be extended to be debates with earlier generations.

The social constructivists were wrong, we have argued. However, as we shall see, like the pragmatists such as James and Dewey at the beginning of the last century and with whom they had much in common, they were not wholly wrong. They were right to emphasize the socio-historical character of knowledge (and therefore the curriculum) as against the prevalent view of its given-ness. Their flaws, we can see in retrospect, were (i) in not spelling out the limits of the theory and (ii) in failing to give substance to their opening claim. The theory remained, therefore, largely rhetorical. Let us take one example. It is one thing to claim that such an apparently unquestionable idea like that of a liberal education is a social construct, and therefore no more than an exercise of domination. It is quite another to document liberal education as a historically changing phenomenon – very different for Eliot, Leavis and C. P. Snow from what it had been for Arnold and Newman.

Social constructivism was fundamentally wrong in the conclusions that it drew about knowledge and the curriculum. The social character of knowledge is not a reason for doubting its truth and objectivity, or for seeing curricula as no more than politics by other means. Its social character is (even more truthfully) the only reason that knowledge can claim to truth (and objectivity) (Collins 2000) and therefore the only reason for preferring some curriculum principles to others. To begin to see where this idea leads, we will turn to Durkheim's argument in his far too little known lectures published as *Pragmatism and Sociology* (Durkheim 1983).

The remarkable thing about Durkheim's lectures is that, in the pragmatism of James (and to a lesser extent, Dewey), Durkheim confronted almost identical problems to those introduced by the sociology of education in the 1970s. He knew that pragmatism was an advance on the rationalism and empiricism of the time, just as social constructivism was an advance on the view of the curriculum and knowledge that treated it as an a-social given. At the same time he also saw that pragmatism's form of 'humanizing' or socializing knowledge and truth, if left unqualified, led to far worse problems than those it claimed to overcome. The following section draws heavily on Durkheim (1983) to suggest a basis for how we might develop an alternative to social constructivism for the sociology of education.

From Social Constructivism to Social Realism:
Some Lessons from Durkheim

There are significant but not complete parallels between our engagement with the social constructivist ideas that became part of the sociology of education in the 1970s and Durkheim's engagement with the pragmatist ideas that were sweeping French intellectual life 60 years earlier. However, our interest in finding an alternative to social constructivism is somewhat different from Durkheim's concerns about pragmatism. As many writers have commented (Lukes 1975), Durkheim was writing at a time of great social upheaval in France that had been triggered in large part by militant opposition to the powers of the Catholic Church. He saw pragmatism, with its antagonism to any notion of objective rationality and its linking of truth to its consequences, as adding to the disorder and providing no basis for the consensus that for him underpinned any just social order. His primary concern therefore was to develop an objective basis for the moral values that could constitute a new consensus.

Ideas of truth and knowledge were important for Durkheim not primarily for themselves but on account of their moral role. He saw them as binding people together as members of society. Without denying the moral role of knowledge and truth, our concern is rather different – it is with the intellectual basis of the curriculum and the nature of knowledge, and the way the former was undermined and the latter avoided by the relativist implications of social constructivism.

Both pragmatist and social constructivist approaches to knowledge arose as responses to the weaknesses of existing epistemologies – rationalist and empiricist. Both rationalist and empiricist epistemologies led to static and dualist assumptions about knowledge and its relationship to the world. In trying both to overcome this dualism and to 'humanize' knowledge by locating it 'in the world', Durkheim argued that pragmatism (and by implication, social constructivism) treats concepts and the world of experience as part of one seamless reality. In other words pragmatists assume that knowledge is undifferentiated from human experience. In contrast, for Durkheim, the humanness of knowledge can only be located in society and in the necessity of concepts being both 'of the world' (a world that includes society and the material world) and differentiated from our experience of it. The social was 'objective' for Durkheim at least in part because it excluded the subjectivities of the ego and the, for him, 'profane' world of individual action and experience.

Durkheim agrees with the pragmatists in not treating knowledge or truth as in some way independent of human society and history. However, this does not mean, as James assumed, that truth is subjective – or no different from people's feelings and sensitivities. Truth and knowledge have a givenness but it is a givenness that is historical and social. We create knowledge, Durkheim argues, just as we create institutions: in relation to our history and on the basis of what former generations have discovered or created.

Perhaps surprisingly for someone so concerned with consensus, it is Durkheim, rather than the pragmatists with their obsession with problem solving, who, by recognizing the tension between knowledge as a social given and this givenness being historically formed, provides the basis for a social theory of innovation. The body of work in the sociology of science inaugurated by Robert Merton (1973) makes this plain. Furthermore, it was in the differentiation between the 'sacred' as an internally consistent world of concepts and the 'profane' as a vague and contradictory continuum of procedures and practices, that Durkheim found the social basis of science and the origins of speculative thought (Muller 2000).

Another parallel between pragmatism and social constructivism is exemplified in Durkheim's argument about how pragmatism resorts to an instrumental theory of truth, what he referred to as 'logical utilitarianism'. Knowledge was true for the pragmatists if it satisfied a need. Similarly, social constructivism, although not explicitly concerned with satisfying needs, emphasizes the situated-ness of all knowledge, and therefore locates it in practice (hence we have the origins of what became known as 'the practice turn' in social theory). Furthermore social constructivism has also associated itself with the importance of knowledge 'being socially relevant' – a utilitarianism thinly veiled beneath a moral correctness. As Durkheim pointed out, satisfying a need could never account for the essential impersonality of truth that is not related to any specific individual, standpoint, interest or need.

A related problem with pragmatism, for Durkheim, was that if the truth can only be verified by its consequences – that is, *a posteriori* – it always depends on what may (or may not) happen. As he points out, something cannot logically be judged true on the basis of what may happen; that is like relying on hope or 'wishful thinking', a tendency that has bedevilled much Marxist writing. To claim that because something works, it is true, is to confuse (or blur) two distinct categories – truth and utility. If something is true because it works, this either relies on an implicitly subjective and *a priori* criterion of 'what works' or it points to the need for a complex consideration of what working means and for whom, and on its own tells us little. Durkheim argued that truth must be *a priori* – not *a priori* in the Kantian sense, which makes it rigid and abstracted from human life, but *a priori* in the social sense – it is prior and it relies on what society has demonstrated to be true. Likewise for social constructivists, as for standpoint theorists, knowledge and truth are located in who the knowers are and in their interests (cf. this volume, Chapters 2 and 3). Just as with pragmatism we are left with consequences, so with social constructivism we are left only with interests. In each case, both truth and knowledge disappear.

Durkheim's strongest objection to pragmatism was that it neglected what he saw as the unique character of truth – its external, constraining, obligatory and, for him, moral force. When applied to social contructivism, Durkheim's insight emphasizes the limits that the social (for him, society) imposes on our ability to socially construct reality. It is those limits – the boundaries as Bernstein would put it – that free us to search for the truth. To paraphrase Durkheim, we feel the pressure of the truth on us – we cannot deny it even if we do not like it. Satisfying a need or relating to an interest are ultimately subjective criteria and can never be adequate as criteria of truth. Sometimes the truth does exactly the opposite to satisfying a need and does not seem to be in one's interest; however, that does not stop it from being true.

To summarize this section, we have argued that in his critique of pragmatism Durkheim offers us at least the beginning of an alternative to social constructivism that retains the idea that knowledge has a social basis but does not reduce the idea of 'the social' to interest groups, activities or relations of power. At the same time, in his sacred/profane distinction, which underpins the separation of objective concepts from practical subjective reality, and in his recognition of the continuity in modern societies of both mythological and scientific truths, his theory recognizes the crucial importance of the social differentiation of knowledge.

Finally, there remains the issue that we touched on earlier. For Durkheim, the social is the moral: it is about values. Insofar as knowledge (and the curriculum) are social, they too for Durkheim are primarily moral issues. This makes it difficult to use his framework to explore questions of knowledge content and structure that are avoided by the reductionist implications of social constructivism. Is Durkheim right in equating the social with the moral, even when it comes to the question of knowledge? Or can we envisage a non-moral concept of the social? We think the answer to the latter question must be yes; furthermore, a cognitive as well as a moral concept of the social is essential if we are to develop an alternative to social constructivist sociologies of knowledge (Chapter 1, this volume; Schmaus 1994).

Durkheim seems to focus more on the shared values on which the objectivity of knowledge depends rather than the nature of the knowledge itself. A clue to this feature of Durkheim's work may be found in his indebtedness to the Kantian tradition of *apriori-ism*. In his short book with his nephew

Marcel Mauss (Durkheim & Mauss 1967), Durkheim makes clear that it is not knowledge in the sense of what we know about the world that he is concerned with but the foundations of that knowledge – how it is possible. In other words he is interested in the social basis of notions such as logic and cause without which knowledge would not be possible. For Durkheim the objectivity of morality and logic have the same basis: society.

Paul Fauconnet, in his introduction to Durkheim's *Education and Sociology* (1956), offers an interpretation of Durkheim's sociology of education which gives more attention to his intellectual (or cognitive) concerns. In commenting on Durkheim's rejection of pragmatism's utilitarian concept of education, he writes that the transmission [of knowledge] through the teacher to the pupil, the assimilation by the child of a subject seemed to him [Durkheim] to *be the condition of real intellectual formation* . . . [our emphasis]. One does not recreate science through one's own personal experience, because [science] is social not individual; one learns it (Durkheim 1956, p. 48).

So much for ideas like 'pupil as scientist' (or theorist) popularized by constructivists (Driver 1982). Fauconnet continues: Forms (of the mind) cannot be transmitted empty. Durkheim, like Comte, thinks that it is necessary to learn about things, to acquire knowledge. (Durkheim 1956, p. 48). For us, therefore, despite Durkheim's stress on the moral basis of society, issues of the structure and content of knowledge must lie at the heart of the sociology of the curriculum. Although Fauconnet notes that Durkheim prepared lectures on specialist pedagogies in mathematics, physics, geography and history, no texts survive.

Durkheim leaves us, therefore, with only some very general propositions about the social basis of the foundations of knowledge and its differentiation. However, it is precisely the issue of differentiation, so crucial to a sociology of the curriculum, that the English sociologist Basil Bernstein addressed in his early papers on classification and framing, and in a paper published towards the end of his life in which he introduces the distinction between hierarchical and horizontal knowledge structures. It is therefore to Bernstein's ideas that we turn in the following section.

Bernstein's Typology of Hierarchical and Horizontal Knowledges

This section begins with a brief description of Bernstein's ideas on the differentiation of knowledge. He intervened decisively in the discussion about the form of symbolic systems (or knowledge) and set out to delineate the 'internal principles of their construction and their social base' (Bernstein 2000, p. 155). As is by now well known, he distinguishes between two forms of discourse, horizontal and vertical, and within vertical discourse, between two kinds of knowledge structure: hierarchical and horizontal.

For Bernstein, knowledge structures differ in two ways. The first way is in terms of what may be called verticality. Verticality has to do with how theory develops. In hierarchical knowledge structures, it develops through the integration of propositions, towards ever more general sets of propositions. It is this trajectory of development that lends hierarchical knowledge structures their unitary triangular shape. In contrast, horizontal knowledge structures are not unitary but plural; they consist of a series of parallel and incommensurable languages (or sets of concepts). Verticality in horizontal knowledge structures occurs not through integration but through the introduction of a new language (or set of concepts) which constructs a 'fresh perspective, a new set of questions, a new set of connections, and an apparently new problematic, and most importantly a new set of speakers' (Bernstein 2000, p. 162). Because these 'languages' are incommensurable, they defy incorporation into a more general theory.[11] The level of integration, and the possibility for knowledge progress in the sense of greater generality and hence wider explanatory reach, is thus strictly limited in horizontal knowledge structures.

Before we proceed to discuss grammaticality, the second form of knowledge variation, it is worth making a few observations on verticality. The first is that it artfully incorporates and recapitulates the fierce dispute in the philosophy and sociology of science between the logical positivists and the non-realists. Bernstein is implicitly asserting that the logical positivists (or realists) were right, but only in respect of hierarchical knowledge structures, and that the non-realists (Kuhn and those who followed him) were likewise right, but only in respect of horizontal knowledge structures. In other words, encoded into Bernstein's principle of verticality are the terms of the debate in the philosophy of science.

Secondly, we note that horizontal knowledge structures span a surprisingly broad range; they include not only sociology and the humanities but logic and mathematics. The anomaly is that in the latter exemplars of horizontal knowledge structures, we have a form of verticality that is almost equivalent to that obtained in hierarchical knowledge structures. The germane question then becomes, not so much what hinders progression in all horizontal knowledge structures, but rather what internal characteristics distinguish those horizontal knowledge structures that proliferate languages (such as the social sciences) from those like mathematics where language proliferation is constrained. It was in search of a sociological answer to this question and to provide an alternative to Bourdieu's sociological reductionism (Bernstein 1996), that Bernstein began by setting out his distinction between hierarchical and horizontal knowledge structures.

We turn now to the second form of knowledge variation: grammaticality. We have suggested that verticality has to do with how a theory develops internally (what Bernstein later referred to as its 'internal language of description'). In contrast, grammaticality has to do with how a theory deals with the world, or how theoretical statements deal with their empirical predicates (what he later referred to as its 'external language of description', Bernstein, 2000).The stronger the grammaticality of a language, the more stably it is able to generate empirical correlates, and the more unambiguous, because it is more restricted, the field of referents is. The weaker the grammaticality, the weaker is the capacity of a theory to stably identify empirical correlates, and the more ambiguous, because it is much broader, the field of referents becomes. Thus knowledge structures with weak grammars are deprived of a principal means of generating progress (or new knowledge), namely empirical disconfirmation. As Bernstein puts it, 'Weak powers of empirical descriptions remove a crucial resource for either development or rejection of a particular language and so contribute to its stability as a frozen form' (2000, pp. 167–8). To summarize, whereas grammaticality determines the capacity of a theory to progress through worldly corroboration, verticality determines the capacity of a theory to progress integratively, through explanatory sophistication. Together, we may say that these two criteria determine the capacity a particular knowledge structure has to progress.

However, for all its rigour and suggestiveness, this analysis merely starts the ball rolling, so to speak. What it provides is a survey of the range of variation, but even the charitable must admit that the poles remain clearer than the intermediate zones of the range. This is partly because the precise nature of, and relation between, verticality and grammaticality is unclear. A plausible surmise could be the following. On the one hand, verticality is a categorical principle; it consigns knowledge structures to either a theory-integrating or a theory-proliferating category. On the other hand, grammaticality is an ordinal principle, constructing a continuum of grammaticality within each category, or perhaps across the entire spectrum. Although at one point Bernstein depicts grammaticality as a feature only of horizontal knowledge structures (2000, p. 168), at another point he refers to physics, his paradigm of verticality, as having a 'strong grammar' (2000, p. 163). What this means is that Bernstein at times uses the 'grammar' metaphor to refer to the internal language, though mostly it refers to the external language.

However, even if we grant the surmise, anomalies persist, none more so than in the case of mathematics. In Bernstein's account, mathematics is a horizontal knowledge structure with a strong grammar. However, the principal criterion of strong grammaticality – how the theory deals with the world – doesn't quite fit. As Bernstein (2000, p. 163) concedes, mathematics does not progress by empirical corroboration, like physics does. It is a deductive system, and its grammar appears to be a purely internal one. This depicts mathematics as a knowledge structure with a strong internal but weak external language of description – the latter categorizing it as similar in type to the social sciences. However, the history of mathematics suggests this picture is far from adequate. As Penrose argues in *The Road to Reality* (Penrose 2006), time and time again, mathematical concepts at extraordinary levels of abstraction (one of his examples is the patterning of prime numbers) and with no apparent relationship to the material world turn out to be integral to our understanding of both the structure of the universe and the structure of matter. Such examples are not evidence of a 'weak external language of description' but perhaps of the need for a more developed sense of what grammaticality involves. Perhaps, as O'Halloran (2007) suggests, mathematics is the language the empirical sciences must use to generate verticality in their internal languages. If that is so, then its lack of an external language ceases to be strange.

The difference between sociology and mathematics is strikingly brought out by Moore and Maton's (2001) example of the epistemic continuity displayed in the story of the proof of Fermat's last theorem:

> What is so striking about this story is its sheer scale in historical time and in geographical and cultural space. It tells a story of a mathematician in late-twentieth century England effectively communicating with a French judge at the court of Louis XIV, and through him with Babylonians from three millennia ago. It represents an epistemic community with an extended existence in time and space, a community where the past is present, one in which, when living members die, will be in turn the living concern of future members. (Moore & Maton 2001, p. 172)

Things could not look more different in sociology.[12] However, mathematics also shares this temporal feature with literature. Markus (2003) has remarked that the 'tradition' in the Arts is 'ever expanding' and 'of great depth in time' (p. 15), a feature he contrasts to science which has a 'short-term' tradition, because it is ever 'evolving' (p. 15). Which knowledge form is nearer to which? Maths and science in one sense; and maths, literature and perhaps sociology in another? The fact is, which forms comprise the middle of the knowledge range is not clear at all. Is geography closer to physics than to biology, for example, and how would we know? Would we count their respective numbers of languages? It is certainly the case that empirical study would help to shed light on the theory, but it is also likely that the theory stands in need of some elaboration.

Towards a Logic of the Social and Human Sciences

As we saw in the previous section, Bernstein develops a language of description for dealing with variations in knowledge structure that provides us with tools for discussing variation that are so far unmatched in sociology, with the possible exception of Collins (2000). Bernstein's main intent was to develop a way of discussing how different symbolic ensembles become socially distributed. In so doing, he had also to confront the age-old question as to how knowledge progresses. The conciseness of the concepts of verticality and grammaticality has taken us a considerable way towards those goals. And yet the long shadow of physicalist idealism falls over this attempt as it does over practically all other attempts in the history of philosophy and social thought. When the chips are down, Bernstein's model for knowledge progression is ineluctably that of physics, or more precisely, as Cassirer expresses it, that of the mathematical sciences of nature. Here the recurrent problem for sociology rears its head again: is there only one ideal form of objectivity, namely that of physics? Or is there another?

Bernstein certainly strives to distinguish the form of progression in hierarchical knowledge structures from that in horizontal knowledge structures. But the difficulty is apparent in the name he gives to the latter. These progress, says Bernstein, by developing parallel theoretical languages, that is, horizontally. It is not hard to see that, while this might account for how knowledge elaborates, it cannot account for how it grows. The pathos of this description is sharpened when we consider it in the light of Bernstein's own strenuous attempts to develop a more vertical and robust language of description for sociology. Yet according to his own account of how sociological knowledge develops, his attempt can at best contribute another parallel language. It is not expressly said in these terms, but it is hard to avoid the conclusion that, unless and until sociology can stiffen its vertical spine and develop more powerful worldly corroborations – that is, become more like physics – sociological knowledge will not progress.

We return inevitably to the dilemma that we raised earlier. We argued that Bernstein characterizes hierarchical knowledge growth in a way that parallels the accounts of the logical positivists, and horizontal knowledge growth after the accounts of Kuhn and the constructivists. This effectively rules out the possibility of growth or progress in the social sciences. We are thus left with a position that is uncomfortably close to the relativism of pragmatism and constructivism, a position that Bernstein in his larger intents certainly did not align himself with. As we saw at the beginning of this chapter, for Bernard Williams the two views – a commitment to verticality or truthfulness on the one hand and scepticism about its realization on the other – do not coexist happily. The latter must inexorably corrode the former.

The Sociology of Knowledge in Educational Studies: A Way Forward

Arising from the tension between being truthful and the idea of truth that was identified by the philosopher Bernard Williams, this chapter has taken three steps in the journey to find an adequate basis for the sociology of knowledge in educational studies (and more generally). First we set out to document the weaknesses of the social constructivist position as it emerged in the 1970s, and which, with few changes, is still with us today and largely, but not entirely, unchallenged (Weiss et al. 2006; Young 2006). To do this we drew on the remarkable parallels between Durkheim's diagnosis of the weaknesses of pragmatism and the problems that the 1970s social constructivism gave rise to. Our second step was to extend the discussion to Durkheim and establish his two fundamental insights for the sociology of knowledge. The first was that the sociality of knowledge does not undermine its objectivity and the possibility of truth, but is the condition for it. The second is the key role that he gives to differentiation (for him between the sacred and the profane) as the origins of speculative thought and the growth of knowledge. Despite these insights, Durkheim was more concerned with the conditions for the possibility of knowledge – the Kantian question expressed in sociological terms – than the development of knowledge itself. Furthermore, just as Kant's model of truth was Euclid's geometry, so for Durkheim it was the natural sciences. This limits the extent to which Durkheim's sociology of knowledge can, on its own, provide an adequate alternative to pragmatism and social constructivism.

Our third step was to turn to the work of the leading contemporary Durkheimian, Basil Bernstein, and his highly original analysis of knowledge structures and their variation. Bernstein takes Durkheim's insights further than anyone else. However he is, like Durkheim, trapped in the assumption that physics represents the model for all knowledge growth. Ironically this leads to his inability to provide the grounds for the progress that his own theory makes.

To return to Williams one last time, in his most artful way, Williams suggests that a commitment to truthfulness shorn from a commitment to truth ends up in a bogus valorization of sincerity, that principle most prized by the image industry. To imagine that sincerity, a commitment to knowing our inner selves, is sustainable without a commensurate commitment to knowing our external world, natural or social, is possibly the central illusion of our age. As Harry Frankfurt puts it in his unexpected and heartening bestseller, *On Bullshit*,

> The contemporary proliferation of bullshit also has deeper sources, in various forms of scepticism which deny that we can have any reliable access to objective reality . . . [which leads to the] pursuit of an alternative ideal of sincerity . . . Our natures are, indeed, elusively insubstantial – notoriously less stable than the natures of other things. And insofar as this is the case, sincerity itself is bullshit. (2005, pp. 64–7)

It is the world beyond bullshit that is the one worth exploring. Further, it is (or should be) the world that education is about. The nature of that world and the conditions under which it shapes the curriculum defines the project of the sociology of educational knowledge.

Endnotes

1 See Nozaki (2006) and Chapters 2 and 3 of this volume for useful discussions of the problems that 'standpoint' theories give rise to.
2 It was of course over half a century since Durkheim made the theoretical case for the sociological study of education (Durkheim 1956). In the United Kingdom, Karl Mannheim had been appointed as the first Professor of Sociology of Education in 1946. However, he died within a year and, despite the efforts of those like Jean Floud and A. H. Halsey in the 1950s, it was not until the late 1960s that sociology of education in the United Kingdom became a distinct field of research and teaching within educational studies.

[3] Perhaps the most sophisticated and influential example of this genre is the work of Michael Apple (1975).

[4] One of the authors of this chapter was personally involved in these developments (Whitty & Young 1976, 1977).

[5] An example of the time is the Reader edited by Beck et al. (1977) in which there were chapter headings such as 'education, rationality, ability and childhood as social constructs'. We are not denying such categories are, and can be usefully seen as, social constructs, but that social constructivism set no limits on what could and could not be constructed in a particular context or over time. As Hacking (1999) noted, the idea of anything being a social construct is always true at a trivial level; the conceptual issue is in what circumstances is this of more than trivial significance.

[6] The terms 'radical' and 'moderate' social constructivism are frequently found in the literature. However, from the point of view of our argument, this differentiation misses the point that for even moderate forms of social constructivism, the limits on what can be 'constructed' are always only implicit.

[7] Philosophers were easily seen as merely defending their professional interests; an example of what later became generalized as standpoint theorizing! The idea of 'non reformist reforms' was popular among left educationalists at the time, but never given much substance.

[8] The idea of 'resistance' took on a life of its own far removed from Willis's original study and became elevated to the status of a 'theory' (Giroux 1983).

[9] Whereas in North America this 'theorizing' took the overtly political form of the 'critical pedagogy' associated with writers such as Peter McLaren and Henry Giroux, in England a less clearly defined body of 'educational theory' emerged that was exemplified by such work as Usher & Edwards (1994).

[10] For a more measured commentary on these issues, see Haack (1998).

[11] This is not to say such incorporation has not been attempted in a horizontal knowledge structure. From Max Weber and Talcott Parsons onwards, sociological theory is strewn with largely unsuccessful attempts to integrate diverse sets of concepts into a single whole.

[12] Or could they? Is not an epistemic community within sociology in which 'the past is in the present' assumed when we, in the first decade of the twenty-first century, engage with Durkheim's concept of anomie or Weber's concept of bureaucracy?

Chapter 7

Knowledge Structures and the Canon: A Preference for Judgements

Rob Moore
Cambridge University

Introduction

This chapter addresses from the perspective of *aesthetic* concerns a set of issues more usually approached in terms of epistemology. Essentially, the concern is with the production of *judgements* – the evaluation of the relative merits of art objects and the discrimination of some as being 'better' than others. It must be stressed that this is an exercise in *sociology*, not in aesthetics or criticism. No claims are made about any particular art object relative to any other. To say it is sociological is to indicate that the focus is upon the *sociality* of the production of aesthetic judgements, that this production is something that people *do* within a special type of socio-historical context (a field or arena) that can be described in terms of its structural features, its generative principles (its 'powers') and understood at the level of the individual in terms of the mediation of *habitus*. This type of context is conventionally termed a 'canon' and its distinctive feature is that it is extensive in space and time. Such a thing is not simply an accumulation of items (artworks) but a dynamic arena of the formulation of endlessly contested and disputed judgements. Artworks, schools, movements and so on, are nodes within an extended matrix that is energized through time and space by a distinctive form of human sociality and provide the reference points and material for that activity. Specifically, this chapter will address the 'sociality of judgement' through a sociological defence of the concept of the *canon*.

In terms of Bernstein's ideas, the concern is with how the concepts of 'horizontal' and 'vertical' discourse, and 'horizontal' and 'hierarchical' knowledge structures (1999) might be applied to the ream of artistic judgement. Bernstein's exemplar of a hierarchical knowledge structure was physics, but within the arts the features that physics represents for Bernstein are not clear cut (see Chapter 6, this volume). At the extreme, an argument often presented within and without academia is that artistic judgement is ultimately a matter of personal taste; that is, of the 'horizontal'. This position denies the possibility of *judgements* in the aesthetic realm having in some sense an 'objectivity' independent of personal preference. To a major extent, the root problem has been an assumption that to argue for judgements apart from preferences is to commit to some form of 'essentialism'; that is, that art works of superior worth are so by virtue of some feature intrinsic to them as things-in-themselves, as art objects. My argument is that judgements are the product of *procedures* of a particular collective kind. This is a form of what Brian Fay (1996) terms 'procedural objectivity' (see also Moore 2009) which enables social realism to be an alternative to essentialism that preserves the possibility of judgements in the aesthetic by defining the material form of the *sociality* of artistic production and criticism.

The Canon Under Fire

For some time, the idea of a canon has been challenged from a number of quarters. The essence of this 'critical' challenge is that the basic principle of a canon – that it enshrines those things (art objects, ideas, etc.) that are of autonomous, superior worth – is fundamentally false. Canons are seen as arbitrary constructions reflecting no more than the tastes and fashions of dominant social groups or, at worse, as ideological forces that legitimate and reproduce the position and power of dominant groups. Critical approaches tend to assume two forms: reductionism and relationalism.

Reductionism has its origins in Marxist ideology analysis and standpoint theory. It operates by identifying the social base of a work of art or movement, the standpoint that it reflects and the interest it serves. In the traditional Marxist form artistic movements might be classified as 'bourgeois art'; more recently feminist examples of standpoint theory might describe the 'male literary canon'.

Relationalism is best represented in the work of Pierre Bourdieu (e.g. 1993). In this case, items are distributed in a 'field' (e.g. the cultural field) and are related to each other in terms of their synchronistic positioning and are structured between high and low (that which is deemed to have distinction and confers 'cultural capital' and that which is vulgar). Aesthetic value is generated through the relationships *between* positions rather than through the art object in itself. To attribute intrinsic aesthetic value to an art object is 'essentialism' that involves 'misrecognition' and entails 'symbolic violence'. Values are ultimately arbitrary in that they reflect no more than the social distribution of taste and the structure of the field represents no more than the system of power relations and economic interests of society.

Although relationalism is conceptually more sophisticated than reductionism, they ultimately say the same things: criteria of judgement within cultural and intellectual fields are arbitrary and have no *intrinsic* values that can be considered independently of external social relations, interests and power. Once the social base has been revealed and the interest it serves and the standpoint it reflects exposed, there is no more to say – nothing in terms of truth or beauty in their own right.

In recent years these debates have been fiercely expressed in the culture and science 'wars' (Brown 2001; Graff 1992). Richard Hoggart has asked:

> Why are the arguments so angry? Why are so many people so violently disinclined to admit any differences in the value of different works of art; or between human choices as to activities? This is the most revealing of our multiple cultural hang-ups. It involves many people – the conclusion is inescapable – almost entirely rejecting 'great' works of art in any form (people who dismiss George Eliot as 'merely a reflection of nineteenth century bourgeois values' and clearly have not read her work). Such people as these are well-versed in one or the other art, but unwilling any longer to make value-judgements between them. By extension, they are uneasy about talk of art's possible relation to 'meaning'. They avoid any vertical judgements, in favour of the endlessly horizontal. By the Nineties a senior official with Radio 3 [the BBC's classical music station] could announce: 'There is no art; only culture'. A spiritual mate adds: 'Each man is his own culture.' (1995, pp. 57–8)

Basically, the problem is that of *relativism* – cognitive, moral and aesthetic. The argument in this chapter is that relativism is the consequence of a mistaken preoccupation with *absolutes* in relation to values and with a failure to properly understand the *sociality* of knowledge.

The Mind Inside Itself – The Endlessly Horizontal

Because the field of debate is so broad, the focus here will be on one particular recent text in order to provide a central reference point. The emeritus professor of English Literature at Oxford University, John Carey, published a book provocatively entitled: *What Good Are the Arts?* (2005). This book has been extensively reviewed and caused considerable controversy. Carey explicitly endorses the view cited above that 'Each man is his own culture'. His central argument is, 'Anything can be a work of art. What makes it a work of art is that someone thinks of it as a work of art' (2005, p. 29). In more substance, there is a distinction between those who,

> . . . assume the existence of a separate category of things called works of art . . . which are intrinsically more valuable than things which are not works of art, and which accordingly deserve universal respect and admiration. These assumptions, we can now see, belong to the late eighteenth century, and are no longer valid. The question 'Is this a work of art? – asked in anger or indignation or mere puzzlement – can now receive only the answer 'Yes, if you think it is; no, if not.' If this seems to plunge us into the abyss of relativism, then I can only say that the abyss of relativism is where we have always been in reality – if it is an abyss. (2005, p. 30)

Carey's position is allied with postmodern relativism. For Carey and others, relativism simply is *not* a problem. However, Carey does have a problem because his book contains two arguments, the second of which is a defence of literature on the grounds that it is 'superior to the other arts, and can do things they cannot do' (2005, p. 173). Carey is not unaware that this argument seems at odds with the relativism that precedes it, but he does not in any satisfactory manner resolve this tension. The reason is not simply because Carey presents two contradictory arguments, but because he draws upon or implies two quite different theories of knowledge in doing so. In the first instance there is the subjectivist relativism he explicitly espouses, but in his second argument there are the elements of a radically different approach. In Bernsteinian terms, Carey 1 argues in 'horizontal' mode (*who* knows), whereas Carey 2 argues in 'vertical' mode (what is *known*). The first task, though, is to demonstrate the wider implications of Carey's position for the issues being addressed.

The argument will begin by drawing attention to how Carey believes the arts *would have to be* if they were indeed to be special: 'a separate category of things called works of art . . . which are intrinsically more valuable than things which are not works of art'. He grounds this, as he sees it, elitist and mistaken approach to the arts, in the ideas of Kant:

> It is easy to identify the dictates of Kant and his followers in the notions about art that are still in circulation today. That art is somehow sacred,

that it is 'deeper' or 'higher' than science and reveals 'truths' beyond science's scope, that it refines our sensibilities and makes us better people, that it is produced by geniuses who must not be expected to obey the same moral codes as the rest of us, that it should not arouse sexual desire, or it will become pornography, which is bad – these and other superstitions belong to the Kantian inheritance. So does belief in the special nature of artworks. For Kantians, the question 'What is a work of art?' makes sense and is answerable. Works of art belong to a separate category of things, recognized and attested by certain highly gifted individuals who view them in a state of pure contemplation, and their status as works of art is absolute, universal and eternal. (2005, p. 14)

Compare Carey's statement with this example of a postmodernist account of science:

The ascendancy of scientific method as the means of establishing knowledge has resulted in a consistent failure to examine science as a social practice and as a historical and cultural product. Science has instead been seen as transcendental and decontextualized. Knowledge, as well as the knowing subject, therefore, becomes context free. Rationality is cast as universal and transcendental, operating across all historical and social contexts and practices but independent of all of them. The result is an individualistic epistemology where the solitary individual confronts an independent reality of objects. (Usher & Edwards 1994, p. 36)

Carey himself does not set out to present a critique of science. Indeed, at a number of points his argument is precisely that aesthetics cannot do what science does (and in this respect Carey does not appear to be an out-and-out *cognitive* relativist). The point is that in both cases these writers present the same basic logic of argument for rejecting truth claims in the areas of aesthetics and science. To put it succinctly, essentialism is to aesthetics what foundationalism is to epistemology. In both cases it is argued that truth claims or value judgements can only be such if they are 'universal and transcendental, operating across all historical and social contexts and practices but independent of all of them', and are 'absolute, universal and eternal'. Similarly, there is the (basically Cartesian) model of the 'privileged knower' as 'certain highly gifted individuals who view them [artworks] in a state of pure contemplation' where 'the solitary individual confronts an independent reality of objects'. In both cases these writers present *absolutist* or *infallibilist* definitions of truth whether aesthetic or epistemological and atomistic, contemplative models of the self. They both provide strong demolitions of absolutist claims. The problem is they *then* conclude that because truth claims cannot be absolute – 'universal and transcendental, operating across all historical and social contexts and practices but independent of all of them' – then we cannot have valid truth claims *at all*. In this crucial respect, both sets of writers are wrong. The fact that we cannot produce truths that are absolutely infallible in the areas of epistemology, aesthetics or morals does not mean we cannot intelligibly produce relatively objective or at least non-arbitrarily justifiable *judgements* that some things or practices are better than others.

The all-or-nothing fallacy

It is important to note that Carey advances his position on the basis of a particular set of alternatives:

> The champion of high art would have to mean not just that his experience were more valuable *to him*, for that would not prove the superiority of high art, only his preference for it. He would have to mean that the experiences he derived from high art were in some absolute and intrinsic sense more valuable than anything the other person could get from low art. (2005, p. 25)

We are allowed here only the choice between a *preference* or an *absolute*. This is a form of what Alexander called the 'epistemological dilemma' – that is, the only choices apparently available to us are those of relativism or absolutism (1995). For Carey, if we cannot provide absolute ('divinely decreed') support for our judgements then we cannot have any judgements at all, but merely preferences and tastes. Niiniluoto makes an observation similar to Alexander when describing 'dogmatic scepticism':

> This mode of thinking could be called the *All-or-Nothing-Fallacy*. Its different forms propose a strong or absolute standard for some category . . . and interpret the failure or impossibility of satisfying this standard as a proof that the category is empty and should be rejected. (2002, p. 81)

This is precisely Carey's approach. Carey's thinking is an example of a wider mode of thought that has been identified and critiqued by a number of commentators (Moore 2004).

Preferences and judgements

In a key statement, Carey displays not only the manner in which his approach parallels a number of other kinds of relativism in the social sciences and cultural studies, but also indicates the kernel of the problem at the centre of such perspectives – essentially, a confusion over the difference between a preference and an informed and weighed judgement. Carey declares himself as follows:

> I have suggested that those who proclaim the superiority of high art are saying, in effect, to those who get their pleasure from low art, 'What I feel is more valuable than what you feel.' We can see now that such a claim is nonsense psychologically, because other people's feeling cannot be accessed. But even if they could, would it be meaningful to assert that your experiences were more valuable than someone else's? The champion of high art would have to mean not just that his experience were more valuable *to him*, for that would not prove the superiority of high art, only his preference for it. He would have to mean that the experiences he derived from high art were in some absolute and intrinsic sense more valuable than anything the other person could get from low art. How could such a claim make sense? What could 'valuable' mean in such a claim? It could have meaning only in a world of divinely decreed absolutes – a world in which God decides which kinds of feelings are valuable and which are not – and this, as I have said, is not the world in which I am conducting my argument. (2005, p. 25)

There are four symptomatic points to take from this that apply equally across the range of relativisms (cf. Chapters 2, 3 and 8, this volume):

- The first is its *subjectivism*: claims are specialized to the experience or *feelings* of the knowing subject or to categories of people sharing a particular inter-subjective framework reflecting their position in society and constitutive of some core identity and identification.
- The second is that, as a consequence, knowledge relations are rewritten as *relations between social groups* – groups of 'knowers' or, indeed 'feelers'.
- The third is that statements of judgement are no more than statements of group *tastes or preferences* (Carey devotes three pages (117–20) to Bourdieu's classic study, *Distinction* – albeit with some reservations).
- The fourth is that the only alternative to taste is divinely decreed *absolutes*.

In these respects, Carey's position in aesthetics reproduces the basic propositions that underpin postmodern scepticism, feminist standpoint theory and a wide range of other forms of contemporary relativist perspectivism. Knowledge is no more than what different knowers *know*. This results in a kind of social embarrassment in which it is taken that to judge some things, values or practices to be better than others is to imply that some *people* are better than others. Because we cannot detach judgements about knowledge from judgements about knowers we cannot judge the one without judging the other (or 'Other' in the post-structuralist, semiotic version). This at least partly answers Hoggart's question as to why the arguments are so angry: people are taking them *personally*. What is to one an aesthetic judgement is to another a cultural snub.

Carey's view is that we are limited only to preferences or absolutes in the area of aesthetic judgement and because we cannot have absolutes we are left with nothing but preferences – assertions of *taste* alone. However, it is a commonsense observation that there is no major problem in distinguishing between the exercising of a preference and the production of a judgement. The claim by any individual that they *prefer* to read P. D. James' murder mysteries but *judge* the novels of Henry James to be of superior literary significance is perfectly intelligible as would be the statement that, 'I *prefer* to listen to Chuck Berry, but *judge* Beethoven to be musically superior'. Preferences and judgements are different things that operate in different ways. In the main, preferences are acquired in an ad-hoc and contingent kind of way whereas judgements are actively produced according to publicly shared rules of various kinds. For any particular individual, it is simply a matter of life-history whether they prefer beer to wine and, if beer, traditional English ales to Continental lagers. The world of preferences is the world of relativism, of taste, because in many areas of life there is no good *reason* why anyone should do any one thing rather than any other. But, as Carey makes very clear in his second argument in defence of literature, it is not the same in the world of *judgements*.

Carey acknowledges that his attempt to demonstrate the 'superiority' of Literature as a form of art sits strangely with his argument that art is simply what anyone wants it to be. He presents his intention in this way:

In the rest of this book I intend to make out the case for valuing literature, taking examples for the most part, but not exclusively, from English literature – a branch of knowledge which, in recent years, has been progressively devalued in schools and universities, and regarded as rather shamefully parochial and old-world compared to, say, media studies or

cultural history. In opposition to this, I shall also try to show why literature is superior to the other arts, and can do things they cannot do.
Just in case anyone should seize on these aims as inconsistent with the
relativist cast of the first part of my book, let me emphasize that all
the judgements made in this part, including the judgement of what
'literature' is, are inevitably subjective. (2005, p. 173)

The crucial point at the end of this is the reference to the 'inevitably subjective' nature of Carey's judgements. He immediately goes on to say that
his definition of literature is: 'writing that I want to remember – not for its
content alone, as one might want to remember a computer manual, but
for itself: those particular words in that particular manner' (ibid). At this
early stage of the argument, it could be retorted that somewhere there
could be someone for whom the computer manual does in fact produce
'artlike' experiences, and, hence, for *them* it is an artwork – they prefer
reading computer manuals to reading Keats' odes and, indeed, experience
equally valued experiences as do poetically inclined ode readers when
reading Keats (though, according to Carey, we could never actually know
this). Though it would be consistent with his first argument, this is not the
path that Carey follows in his second. Instead, he hopes that his argument
will '*persuade* some or all of my readers' (2005, p. 174, my emphasis). The
point is that Carey's readers should not be persuaded simply by reading a
list of Carey's *preferences* because, as he notes, the simple fact that *someone*
prefers one thing to another is in itself neither here nor there. A statement
of preference is a statement *about* the person preferring (i.e. 'I am the *kind
of person* who likes this'), *not* about the thing preferred (i.e. 'Given that
this is an instance of *a thing of this kind*, it is better than that other instance
of its kind, but not as good as this one of its kind'; in the way that hunters
in a hunter-gather society might say, 'This is a particular spear and, given
how we understand spears to be the kind of thing they are, we judge that
it is a better spear than this one, but not as good as that one). Carey's
preferences in life might be relevant to the circle of people who buy
him birthday presents but not to the majority of his readers who do not
actually know him – our interest is in his *judgements*. The 'subjectivity' in
producing his argument in support of literature is not, simply, 'I just
happen to *prefer* it', but, 'I judge it to support my *argument*'. If Carey's
wish is to 'persuade' his readers, then he does so by producing reasoned
judgements, not merely by telling us about his preferences (i.e. telling us
things about him, Carey, as opposed to providing us with *good reasons* why
we might come to share his judgements concerning what it is that he is

judging). And this is precisely Carey's own argument for the superiority of literature.

The Mind Outside Itself – The Possibility of Verticality

A central dimension of Carey's argument throughout the book is that we cannot compare artworks because we cannot compare the *experiences* that people have of them because we cannot access the minds of others. Carey suggests, first, that to compare artworks is invidious because it is to compare people and, secondly, that it is impossible anyway because the minds of others are closed to us. The latter is a peculiar argument from a teacher, critic and public intellectual. At least a certain aspect of Carey's consciousness is available to us – that which is intentionally expressed in his book in order to engage our consciousness. We must assume that Professor Carey, as a teacher in Oxford University, made aspects of his consciousness available in an intelligible and comprehensible way to his students. Perhaps we are seeing again a problem of dogmatic scepticism – of course we cannot access Carey's consciousness *absolutely or exhaustively*; not even he, he admits, can do that. But we don't have to. We only have to access each other's consciousness *well enough*, from the most intimate to the most fleeting encounter, to maintain normal human social interaction. A problem with Carey's extreme subjectivism is its neglect of the structured character of *inter-*subjectivity and its variety and the forms it might adopt.

Carey quotes the metaphysical poet John Donne and goes on to say:

> To take a proper, diagnostic look at your own mind, Donne reasons, you would need to *get outside your own mind – and that cannot be done*. The instrument you must use to probe your mind is already bent, for it is your mind. (2005, p. 182, my emphasis)

This is the very heart of the problem. Emile Durkheim took the opposite view to that of Donne and Carey. He said when defining a 'thing':

> A thing is any object of knowledge which is not naturally controlled by the intellect, which cannot be adequately grasped by a simple process of mental activity. It can only be understood by the mind on condition that the *mind goes outside itself* by means of observation and experiments, which move progressively from the more external and immediately

accessible characteristics to the less visible and more deep-lying. (1956, pp. 58–9, my emphasis)

At one point, Carey quotes Durkheim approvingly:

Philosophers have often speculated that, beyond the bounds of human understanding, there is a kind of universal and impersonal understanding in which individual minds seek to participate by mystical means; well, this kind of understanding exists, and it exists not in any transcendental world but in this world itself. (Durkheim, cited in Carey 2005, p. 252)

Carey appears unaware, when invoking Durkheim, that the, 'kind of universal and impersonal understanding in which individual minds seek to participate by mystical means', that Durkheim wishes to relocate in, 'this world itself', is precisely the Kantian, 'mysterious realm of truth, which he [Kant] called the "supersensible substrate of nature", where all such absolutes and universals resided' (Carey 2005, p. 9). Carey's reductive subjectivist relativism could not be further removed from Durkheim's emergent historical materialism and the manner in which he translates Kant's 'mysterious realm of truth' into, 'this world itself'. Durkheim did this by arguing for the *sociality* of knowledge and for the *social* origins of Kant's transcendental categories (Moore 2004). It is in this manner that for Durkheim the mind can go 'outside itself' and it is in Carey's *second* argument, 'in defence of literature', that we can develop a sense of how this is so.

In support of literature

How, then, does Carey advance the cause of literature and what are the broader implications of his second argument? The essence of his case is that,

. . . literature gives you ideas to think with. It stocks your mind. It does not indoctrinate, because diversity, counter-argument, reappraisal and qualification are its essence. But it supplies the materials for thought. Also, because it is the only art capable of criticism, it encourages questioning and self-questioning. Its function as a mind-developing agency gives it especial relevance in our present culture. (2005, pp. 208–9)

The language employed here is quite different from that of Carey's first argument. In the extract preceding the above, he refers to literature as, 'a branch of knowledge' and in the above this is explicated in terms of, 'ideas to think with', 'counter-argument, reappraisal and qualification', 'materials for thought', 'criticism . . . questioning and self-questioning', 'a mind-developing agency'. Furthermore:

> Literature is not just the only art that can *criticize itself*, it is the only art, I would argue, that can criticize anything, because it is the only art capable of *reasoning*. Of course, paintings can convey implicit criticism – Hogarth's *The Gate of Calais*, say, or Ford Madox Brown's *Work*. But they cannot make out a *coherent critical case*. They are locked in inarticulacy. Operas and films can criticize, but only because they steal words from literature, which allows them to *enter the rational world*. When literature criticizes other arts its target is often their *irrationality*. (2005, p. 177, my emphases)

This passage contains the key terms: literature can criticize *itself* (it is reflexive), it is capable of *reasoning*, it can make out a *coherent critical case*, it is part of the *rational world* and can target the partial *irrationality* of other arts.

Once again, Carey's argument comes up against the problem of his prior assumption that truth claims can only ever be absolute and he assumes that this is the case in the natural sciences and that it is in this respect that they differ radically from the humanities and social sciences:

> [O]nce belief in a God is removed, moral questions, like aesthetic questions, become endlessly disputable. Indeed, moral questions could be defined as questions to which no answers are available. Consequently, agreement about them is not to be expected. In this they differ from scientific or mathematical questions. Disagreement is, in other words, a necessary condition for the existence of ethics as an area of discourse. (2005, p. 172)

But moral and aesthetic questions do *not* differ from scientific and mathematical questions in this way (though they do differ in other ways) – they also are 'endlessly disputable'. It is the possibility of *falsification* and paradigm change that drives knowledge in these areas. Carey appears to be wedded to a strangely anachronistic, positivistic model of the natural sciences. He might well be correct in claiming that, 'moral questions could be defined as questions to which no answers are available' (though this could scarcely constitute an adequate *definition*), but, given the absolutist way in which he defines an 'answer', this is not the same as saying that these are questions about which no justified *judgements* can be made.

Carey is much closer to what is really significant in these areas when he says, 'it is not being right or wrong that makes a scientist. It is respect for proof and freedom from prejudice (2005, p. 184). What he says, here, about the scientist is as true for the critic. Certainly, what counts as 'proof' will differ for the critic (and also for the mathematician). But this does not provide the scientist with *infallible* truths that are absolute and certain and the critic must provide textual evidence to support his or her argument (as Carey, of course, does throughout his book and we take for granted that he does so in an honest and truthful and *rigorous* scholarly way rather than just inventing writers and quotations as it suits him). Although the mathematician, the scientist and the critic will employ different models of 'proof', they do not employ different models in the *respecting* of proof and each must be equally free from prejudice (as far as that is ever humanly possible).

In college bars throughout the world there will be groups of mathematicians, scientists and critics sitting around tables arguing about problems in their respective fields. In key respects, they will be doing things differently, but in the most fundamental respect they will all be doing the *same* thing – producing, not necessarily agreements, but informed, rigorous judgements grounded in 'respect for proof'. Crucially, 'respect for truth' is not simply a slogan. It is an internalized value, acquired through a methodology of 'education' (the systematic formation of a *habitus*), embedded within and manifested through shared, collective procedures, principles and criteria. And in doing this they are doing something qualitatively different from the first thing they all did when entering the bar; namely, ordering their drinks – the exercise simply of their personal preferences. In the course of their discussions over their drinks, certain of these individuals might judge that they should 'change their minds' on particular issues, but they could not in the same way be *reasoned* into changing their preferences about what to drink. Preferences are simply personal, but judgements are intrinsically *collective* in character and presuppose collectivities of certain kinds.

In support of knowledge

Carey's second argument can now be the starting point for the exploration of an alternative theory of knowledge that draws upon a different understanding of the *sociality* of knowledge than that which sustains the variety of relativisms of which Carey's first argument is an instance. The key question is: how does the mind, 'go outside itself'?

Consider Carey comparing aesthetics with ethical theory:

> In aesthetics, likewise, there are no absolutes, we have to choose. Even in choosing to have no interest in the arts at all is a choice. But though preferences between arts, and decisions about what a work of art is, are personal choices, that does not mean they are unimportant. On the contrary, like ethical choices, they shape our lives. Nor does it mean that they are unalterable. Just as we can be argued out of or into moral convictions (as, for example, in cases of religious conversion), so our aesthetic preferences may change. This may be sudden and dramatic . . . Or it may be the result of *gradual discovery and persuasion – a process we generally call education.* (2005, p. 172, my emphases)

We see here once again the fatal muddle concerning preferences and judgements and the way in which this is associated with the preoccupation with absolutes. We have, on the one hand, 'preferences that are personal choices', but on the other it is acknowledged that we 'can be argued out of or into moral convictions', but there is no rigorous conceptual distinction between these two things in Carey's book. The reason being, that in the absence of absolutes in the areas of ethics and aesthetics, then, for Carey, there *is* no difference.

What is important for Carey is that in both ethics and the aesthetic, 'we have to choose'. He is correct, but changing preferences is not the same thing as being, 'argued out of or into' something. To change a preference is simply to decide to *opt* for one thing rather than another. Someone might decide that they are bored with Indian food and will start eating Chinese instead, but they need to tell their friends no more than, 'I just happen to feel like doing it'. If, by contrast, someone declares that they have been *persuaded* into changing their *judgement* about the relative literary merits of P. D. James and Henry James and have come to accept that P. D. is the better writer they would be required to provide *reasons* – that is, to do all those things that Carey believes make literature 'superior' and which he himself, of course, as a critic, does in his book. Furthermore, there would be nothing in principle unintelligible in this person also declaring that in the course of being persuaded in this judgement, they have also found that they now *prefer* to read Henry rather than P. D. and *opt* to do so. Preferences and judgements and opting and choosing are different things gone about in different ways.

Carey's first argument collapses *judgements* into *preferences* and *choosing* into *opting*. His second argument does the opposite – judgements regulate and have priority over preferences and we are *persuaded* rather than merely *opt*. There could well be an argument to the effect that, in the liberal humanist tradition, the purpose of education is to articulate preferences with judgements (and this could be implicit in what Carey says above), but this is a big question for another time.

To proceed, then, in the very different direction indicated by Carey's second argument and his recognition of a process of, 'gradual discovery and persuasion – a process we generally call education'. Implicit in this can only be an acknowledgement of the fact that in certain areas our preferences can be refined by judgements (and in others operate independently) and that this process ('education') occurs when we interpellate our personal preferences into public arenas of collective judgement (though this does not necessarily imply that in all cases we have to – we may choose to be left to our own devices as to our choices of football team, footwear, sexual orientation or alcoholic beverages). We *interpellate* our preferences and opinions in order to actively engage with explanations and reasons in a field of, 'counter-argument, reappraisal and qualification'. Fields of judgement are not those of the purely personal subjectivity of preferences, of *opting*. They are fields of *inter-subjectivity* of a special kind. They are essentially *interlocutory* in character and their purpose is the formation of judgements according to publicly shared procedures and criteria.

Coalitions of the Mind

Unlike the exercise of preference, the formation of judgement is a particular kind of inter-subjectivity (of sociality) structured within specialized communities of interlocutory interpellation. Interlocutory in that they are grounded in *dialogue* and intepellationary in that these are dialogues concerning *reasons and explanations* – '*why?*' discourses: precisely those procedures that Carey identifies as constituting the 'superiority' of literature among the arts. The problem that this presents for relativist thinkers such as Carey (in aesthetics) and Usher and Edwards (in epistemology) has been well summarized by Randall Collins:

> That ideas are not rooted in individuals is hard to accept because it seems to offend against a key epistemological point . . . It is assumed that objective truth itself depends on the existence of a pure observer or

thinker, untrammelled by anything but insight into truth. The notion is that the social is necessarily a distortion, an alien intrusion in epistemology; if ideas are determined by social interaction, then they cannot be determined by truth. This objection comes so naturally that it is hard to think except within this dichotomy: either there is truth that is independent of society, or truth is social and not objectively true. There are two prejudices here. One is the assumption that constructing an idealized individual, outside of the social, provides a vantage point that social networks cannot provide just as well. On the contrary: there is even more difficulty in connecting such a disembodied individual to the world than there is in connecting a social group to the world, since a group is already to some degree extended in the world of time and space.

The second prejudice or tacit assumption is that the criterion of truth exists in free-floating reality, along with the free-floating thinker–observer. But the very concept of truth has developed within social networks, and has changed with the history of intellectual communities. (2000, pp. 7–8)

The 'prejudices' described by Collins are those exhibited by Carey and by Usher and Edwards and are symptomatic of relativism in general – they are the prejudices of 'dogmatic scepticism', of the 'all-or-nothing fallacy'. The core problem is the assumption that, 'if ideas are determined by social interaction, then they cannot be determined by truth'. The irony is that this proposition, assumed dogmatically by relativists, is precisely the foundationalism that underpins the positivism and essentialism that they are out to refute, but which they themselves presuppose in their sceptical conclusions. In the Durkheimian tradition, Collins' argument is that truth *is* social in that it is the product of a distinctive form of structured and enduring sociality: 'thinking consists in making "coalitions of the mind," internalized from social networks, motivated by the energies of social interactions' (Collins 2000, p. 7). These 'coalitions of the mind', as Collins' work demonstrates, as *canons* of various kinds, are extensive in time and space (Moore & Maton 2001): a group grounded in a tradition sharing certain standards and procedures, and so on and a corpus of canonical works. The philosophical canons of Europe, Islam, India and China, for instance, have endured, and interacted, over many centuries and intellectual networks today are global and transcultural. Collins opens his argument in a manner that indicates how things that for Carey and others like him are fatally problematical can be approached in a different way:

Intellectuals are people who produce decontextualized ideas. These ideas are meant to be true or significant apart from any locality, and apart from anyone concretely putting them into practice. A mathematical formula claims to be true in and of itself, whether or not it is useful, and apart from whoever believes. A work of literature, or of history, claims the same sort of status, insofar as it is conceived as art or scholarship: part of a realm that is higher, more valid, less constrained by particular circumstances of human actions than ordinary kinds of thoughts and things. Philosophy has the peculiarity of periodically shifting its own grounds, but always in the direction of claiming or at least seeking the standpoint of greatest generality and importance. This continues to be the case when the content of philosophy is to assert that everything is transient, historically situated, of local value only; for the relativist statement itself is asserted as if it were valid. This is an old conundrum of the skeptical tradition, discussed at great length in Hellenistic philosophy. Skeptics in attempting to avoid making assertions implicitly stand on a meta-distinction among levels of assertion of varying force. This illustrates the sociological point admirably, for only the intellectual community has the kind of detachment from ordinary concerns in which statements of this sort are meaningful. (Collins 2000, p. 19)

This statement contains much of the kind of thing that Carey dislikes: 'A work of literature, or of history, claims the same sort of status, insofar as it is conceived as art or scholarship: part of a realm that is higher, more valid, less constrained by particular circumstances of human actions than ordinary kinds of thoughts and things'. Collins also points to the unavoidably self-refuting logic of the relativist position. But what is significant, here, is his view that, 'Intellectuals are people who produce decontextualized ideas'. And what is important is that it is the *ideas*, not the *intellectuals* that are 'decontextualized'. The key relationship is that between 'particular circumstances' and the 'higher realm'. It is the idea of a 'higher realm' that Carey's first argument rejects (but which is smuggled back within the second argument). How does Collins underpin this 'higher realm' and how might the way in which he does so connect with Carey's second argument?

Collins notes that, '. . . if one refuses to admit anything beyond the local, one arrives at some version of scepticism or relativism; if one idealizes what happens in situations as the following of rules and uses these inferred rules as a tool for constructing the rest of the world, one arrives at a type of idealism' (pp. 20–1). Carey's world of preferences as the only alternative to absolutes is the kind of relativistic localism described and entails the *parochialism* of the horizontal that his second argument rejects and which, he argues, literature can take us beyond. Collins' purpose is to understand the sociality of knowledge in a way that is neither relativistic nor idealist.

> Let us begin at the site of all action: the local situation. All events take place in a here-and-now as concrete and particular. The perspective of micro-sociology, which analyzes the structures and dynamics of situations, is all too easily interpreted as a focus on the individual actor or agent. But a situation is just the interaction of conscious human bodies, for a few hours, minutes, or even micro-seconds; the actor is both less than the whole situation and larger, as a unit in time which stretches across situations. The detached agent who makes events happen is as artificial a construction as the non-social observer, who represents the idealized vantage point of classical epistemology. The self, the person, is more macro than the situation (strictly speaking, the person is meso); and it is analytically derivative because the self or agent is constructed by the dynamics of the situation. (Collins 2000, p. 20)

The fact that all human embeddedness, consciousness and action is, in the first instance, local does not mean that it is nothing *but* local: 'The local situation is the starting point of the analysis, not the ending point. The micro-situation is not the individual, but it penetrates the individual, and its consequences extend outward through social networks to as macro a scale as one might wish' (Collins ibid.). It is through 'extension' (as to some extent with Bernstein's 'verticality') that Collins moves from the particular, the local, to the 'higher' realm. However, he makes a crucial conceptual adjustment to the spatial metaphor:

> To deny that anything exists other than the local is true in one sense, misleading in another. It is true that nothing exists that is not thoroughly local; if it did not exist locally, where possibly could it be found? But no local situation stands alone; situations surround one another in time and space. The macro-level of society should be conceived not as a vertical layer above the micro, as if it where in a different place, but as the unfurling of the scroll of micro-situations. Micro-situations are embedded in macro-patterns, which are just the ways that situations are linked to one another; causality – agency, if you like – flows inward as well as outward. What happens here and now depends on what happened there and then. We can understand macro-patterns, without reifying them as if they were self-subsisting objects, by seeing the macro as the dynamics of networks,

the meshing chains of local encounters that I call *interaction ritual chains*. (Collins 2000, p. 21)

The sociality of judgement

Carey's second argument is not, actually, that far removed from that of Collins (in fact, for him to intelligibly *do* what he does in his book presupposes a Collins type condition). The crucial difference lies in Carey's preoccupation with personal *subjectivism* as opposed to Collin's sociological concern with the sociality of *inter*-subjectivism. This difference can be illustrated by contrasting Collins above with Carey below:

> Since every reader's record of reading is different, this means that every reader brings a new imagination to each book or poem. It also means that every reader makes new connections between texts, and puts together, in the course of time, *personal networks of association*. This is another way in which what we read seems to be *our creation*. It seems to *belong to us* because *we assemble our own literary canon*, held together by *our preferences*. The networks of association we build up will not depend on spotting allusions or echoes, though sometimes we may notice these, but on imaginative connections that may *exist only for us*. (2005, p. 242, my emphases)

As the added emphases illustrate, Carey's view is unremittingly egocentric. He is in a certain sense quite correct in what he says, but what he says is not *all* that can be said. Carey's description would apply *only* to a completely *non-communicative* reader who keeps his or her views entirely to themselves and assiduously avoids encountering or engaging with the views of others. The canon of 'personal preference' that exists 'only for us' applies only to that detached, asocial, contemplative self that Carey and the epistemological relativists reject. In principle there is no reason why any particular individual might not opt to adopt this position (it is not uncommon to encounter committed individual readers who resolutely proclaim that they do not want to 'study' literature because it would destroy the pleasure they derive from it). It can also be the case, however, that other readers enjoy *talking* to each other about what they have read (as the current enthusiasm for readers' groups demonstrates). There is a distinctive form of sociality in which individuals come together precisely in order to trade and exchange those, 'personal networks of association' – in just the way in which Carey in his book does with those who read his book. The fundamental point in this is that these, 'networks of association', are *inter-subjective* not solipsistically or paradigmatically sealed and incommensurable.

The imaginative nexus

There are two important points, here. The first is one that Carey himself makes and extensively illustrates in his book: writers operate *intertextually* within a tradition, a *canon*. They write against the background of what Harold Bloom (1996) calls the 'anxiety of influence' – they draw on a tradition, but, crucially, want to be judged to be *original*, as speaking in their own voice, and not merely repeating that which others have said before. This is the force that drives *all* modern fields of intellectual production: the quest for novelty and originality (it is, historically, their radically distinctive feature [Whitley 2000]). The second is that readers' preferences flow into each other. Carey's, 'personal networks of association' translate, communicatively, into Collins', 'coalitions of minds', into participation in enduring, *structured* forms of sociality: 'The focus is on *a particular kind of speech act*: the carrying out of a situation-transcending dialogue, linking past and future texts' (Collins 2000, p. 28, my emphasis).

The novelist Ian McEwan effectively conveys the sense of this 'situation-transcending dialogue' in the following:

> Those who love literature rather take for granted the idea of a literary tradition. In part, it is a temporal map, a means of negotiating the centuries and the connections between writers. It helps to know that Shakespeare preceded Keats who preceded Wilfred Owen because lines of influence might be traced. And, in part, a tradition implies a hierarchy, a canon; most conventionally it has Shakespeare dominant, like a lonely figurine on top of a wedding cake, and all the other writers arranged on descending tiers. In recent years, the canon has been attacked for being too male, too middle class, too Eurocentric; what remains untouched is the value of a canon itself: clearly, if it did not exist, it could not be challenged.
>
> But above all, a literary tradition implies an active historical sense of the past, living in and shaping the present. And reciprocally, a work of literature produced now infinitesimally shifts our understanding of what has gone before . . . Ideally, having read our contemporaries, we return to re-read the dead poets with fresh understanding. In a living artistic tradition, the dead never quite lie down. (2006, p. 4)

As this suggests, what Carey calls, 'the imaginative nexus' (2005, p. 243) is not simply an aspect of individual consciousness, but in the Durkheimian sense, of a *collective consciousness* extended in time and space and that embraces both reader and writer – 'the unfurling of the scroll of micro-situations'. According to Collins, although all intellectual exchanges are grounded in the local,

> Texts do not merely transcend the immediate particulars of the here-and-now and push toward abstraction and generality. To be oriented towards the writings of intellectuals is to be conscious of the community itself, stretching both backwards and forwards in time. Intellectual events in the present – lectures, debates, discussions – take place against an explicit backdrop of past texts, whether building upon them or critiquing them. Intellectuals are peculiarly conscious of their predecessors. And their own productions are directed toward unseen audiences. Even when they lecture to an immediate group, perhaps of personal students, disciples or colleagues, the message is implicitly part of an ongoing chain, which will be further repeated, discussed, or augmented in the future. (2000, p. 27)

Carey tells us that the 'essence' of literature is: 'diversity, counter-argument, reappraisal and qualification . . . questioning and self-questioning'. But these things entail *community*, they entail, as Collins says, '*a particular kind of speech act*' – the interpellation of, '*why?*' within a collective arena.

The problem in Carey's book is not where he ends up, but with where he begins. The problem being that he cannot actually get to the one via the other – he needs to observe the ancient advice to the traveller asking directions in a strange land: 'don't start from here'. Carey, in his first argument, wishes to avoid snubbing people by making cultural judgements and retreats into a critical diffidence that says, in matters of literature, your feelings are just as good as mine (an *emeritus* professor of English Literature at Oxford University). But it is not Carey's *feelings* that interest us, it is his *judgements*. However, in his second argument, Carey advances the view that, 'Like drugs, drink and antidepressants, literature is a mind-changer and an escape, but unlike them it *develops and enlarges the mind* as well as changing it.' (2005, p. 210, my emphasis). In order to sustain this view, he needs to start from somewhere else.

Carey says of literature: 'Once its words are lodged in your mind they are indistinguishable from the way you think' (2005, p. 245) – they contribute to the *habitus* that links the individual to society and the present to the living past. As Collins stresses, it is the *activity* that is important and, on that basis, the lesson of Carey's book, perhaps, is do as Carey *does*, not as he says.

Conclusion

It was stated in the Introduction that this essay is a work of sociology, not of criticism or aesthetic theory. It is *sociological* in that it takes as its focus what I have termed the 'sociality of judgement' – that is, a particular form of structured inter-subjectivity associated with a distinctive form of activity that occurs within a distinctive type of supra-individual social arena that is extended in time and space: a canon. Bernstein's theory of knowledge structures allows us to begin the modelling of the forms, principles and possibilities of such fields of symbolic production.

The canon *enables* a particular type of activity and its principles are *generative* – it is the arena of endless though not limitless dispute. Understood in this social realist way, it is possible to avoid the false extremes of absolutism and relativism by enabling a new focus on the *sociality* of judgement. Judgements are less than absolutes in that they acknowledge their fallibility. They are more than preferences in that they submit themselves to historically evolved rules of collective evaluation. It is the *knowledge* not the *knower* that counts (cf. Chapters 2 and 8, this volume). It would be wrong, however, to restrict this distinctive mode of sociality to the realms of academic scholarship, criticism and science where it assumes its most rigorous forms in what Bernstein calls hierarchical knowledge structures with stronger grammars. Its principles extend further into the public sphere and constitute the discursive rules of civil society in modern, secular, liberal democracy (Ahier et al. 2003).

More formally a canon is the type of *thing* that might be called a 'Durkheimian emergent social kind'. Durkheim describes such 'things' in the following way:

Collective representations are the product of an immense cooperation that extends not only in space but also through time; to make them, a multitude of different minds have associated, intermixed, and combined their ideas and feelings; long generations have accumulated their experience and knowledge. A very special intellectuality that is infinitely richer and more complex than that of the individual is distilled in them. (1995, p. 15)

It is this 'very special intellectuality' (an enduring structured form of sociality with generative powers, *habitus*) that has been the focus of this essay. The major work of thinkers such as Basil Bernstein and Randall Collins (among others) have opened up new avenues for the sociology of knowledge and the promise of breaking the deadlock that has vitiated theoretical advance in that area for so long.

Chapter 8

Canons and Progress in the Arts and Humanities: Knowers and Gazes

Karl Maton
University of Sydney

Introduction

In humanist study the age of innocence is lost. Over recent decades few academic debates have been as intense as the 'culture wars' over the rationale, role and form of the arts and humanities. These battles have reached far beyond the walls of the academy. Books such as *The Closing of the American Mind* (Bloom 1987), *Cultural Literacy* (Hirsch 1987), *The Western Canon* (Bloom 1996), *The Great Books* (Denby 1996) and *What Good are the Arts?* (Carey 2005) have become international best-sellers. Central to this controversy has been a 'canon brawl' (Morrissey 2005) not simply over what should be considered great cultural works but also over whether canons can and should exist at all (e.g. von Hallberg 1984b; Stone 1989). This has raised questions concerning the basis of aesthetic valuation of cultural works, the possibility of progress in the arts and humanities, the existence of artistic or humanist 'knowledge', and who can be said to 'know'. Such debates thereby raise questions of originality, innovation and progress, as well as of inclusion and access to knowledge.

These questions were raised from a different angle by Basil Bernstein's work on forms of discourse and knowledge structures (1999). One key feature distinguishing the 'hierarchical knowledge structures' of the natural sciences from the 'horizontal knowledge structures' of the arts, humanities and social sciences is how they develop. Hierarchical knowledge structures are explicit, coherent, systematically principled and hierarchical organizations of knowledge which develop through the *integration* and *subsumption* of knowledge. They exhibit a high capacity for 'verticality' (Muller 2007) or cumulative knowledge-building. In contrast, horizontal knowledge structures are a series of segmented, strongly bounded approaches that struggle to achieve verticality and develop by adding another segment or approach horizontally. A second key feature distinguishing knowledge structures is the strength of their 'grammar', or their capacity for generating unambiguous empirical referents. For Bernstein, the arts and humanities are characterized by a weaker grammar which removes a crucial resource for cumulative knowledge-building: the ability to compare competing explanations with consensually agreed upon evidence.

Bernstein's model offers a fresh perspective on questions raised in debates over the arts and humanities. However, the model also raises questions of its own. First, can horizontal knowledge structures progress and grow vertically or are they confined to only segmental development? Are the arts and humanities simply characterized by weakness (weaker verticality and weaker grammars) or does their strength lie elsewhere? Secondly, are all horizontal knowledge structures the same or are some more capable of knowledge-building than others, and how might their particular kind of progress shape this capacity for knowledge-building?

In this chapter I address these questions. Substantively, building on Chapter 7 of this volume, I argue that radical critiques of canons obscure the possibility of working critically *within* a canonic tradition, and that retaining the notion of a (rather than 'the') canon enables the *possibility* of building knowledge over time in more democratically accessible intellectual fields. Theoretically, I argue that, contrary to what a cursory reading of Bernstein's model might suggest, progress is possible in fields with horizontal knowledge structures but that to grasp the form this progress takes we need to develop his model. Specifically, we need to view intellectual fields differently by exploring not only their knowledge structures but also their *knower structures* and, crucially, how they define a legitimate 'gaze'. I begin by illustrating how radical critiques of canons and critical engagement within a canonical tradition represent horizontal knowledge structures with differing capacities for developing cumulative knowledge. Secondly, I argue that we cannot understand such fields by focusing on their knowledge structures alone, for their basis lies elsewhere: in the 'gaze' of a legitimate knower. I introduce the notion of knower structures with stronger and weaker *knower-grammars* as a means of analysing the different forms taken by this gaze. I then explore what light this perspective can shed on knowledge-building in the arts and humanities by exploring debates over canons and specifically different kinds of 'gaze' characterizing the history of cultural studies.

Critiques, Canons and Contexts

The 'culture wars' have often been portrayed as a struggle between two principal positions: conservative defences of an essentialist and singular canon and radical critiques of the possibility of such canons. These critiques often portray the traditional belief in Western cultural understanding, following Kant's *Critique of Judgement*, as maintaining that if someone judges something as, for example, beautiful 'he [sic] supposes in others the same satisfaction, he judges not merely for himself, but for everyone, and speaks of beauty as if it were a property of things' (1790/1951, pp. 46–7). This position views the canonical status of a cultural work as immutable, universal and transhistorical. A canonical work is thereby seen as freely-floating; it transcends all boundaries of time and space. Such a view 'insists on an orthodoxy that ought to be discernible at any time whatever, because of its essential perpetuity' (Kermode 1983, p. 21). Crucially, its value and meaning is intrinsic and essential. Such a view is said to be commonplace. Warburton, for example, claims it is tempting to view works of art 'as having intrinsic value, being valuable in themselves, independently of the experiences they give rise to' (2004, p. 47). Dworkin suggests many people succumb to this temptation: 'We say that we want to look at Rembrandt's self-portraits because it is wonderful, not that it is wonderful because we want to look at it' (1993, p. 72). According to critiques, this essentialist position portrays the reader or viewer as possessing a pure gaze and enjoying an unmediated, immediate relationship with the Beauty or aesthetic value of the cultural work.

Challenges to this view have been made across the arts and humanities by a variety of positions, including feminist, postcolonial, Marxist, Foucauldian, deconstructive, post-structuralist and postmodernist approaches. Despite their many differences, one argument common to these positions is that the essentialist vision of an objective basis for judgement is asocial and ahistorical and so fails to recognize that taste and knowledge vary over time and across cultures. Highlighting the variety of meanings of the same work generated by different readers or viewers, such critiques argue that there is no universal yardstick of 'Beauty' (or 'Truth' in epistemology or 'the Good' in ethics) but rather a series of different beauties or truths. Such critiques relate cultural values to their temporal and social contexts and shift emphasis from the intrinsic form of culture to its extrinsic function. In the face of such arguments one literary critic could lament *The Death of Literature* (Kernan 1990) and claim this leads instead to a fluid plurality of different literatures or definitions of art.

Particularly vocal in the culture wars have been standpoint critiques which go further to argue against not only specific canons but also the possibility of canons *per se* (see Chapters 2, 3 and 7, this volume). These emphasize the contingent, subjective and arbitrary nature of cultural valuations and view canonical status as reflecting the needs and interests of dominant social groups, so that

> A canon is commonly seen as what other people, once powerful, have made and what should now be opened up, demystified, or eliminated altogether. (von Hallberg 1984a, p. 1)

For example, feminist critiques portray 'Western culture' as

> a grand ancestral property that educated men had inherited from their intellectual forefathers, while their female relatives, like characters in a Jane Austen novel, were relegated to modest dower houses on the edge of the estate. (Gilbert 1985, p. 33)

When underpinned by standpoint theory, such critiques proclaim that not only the contents but also the basis of choice of a canon is, for example, Western, bourgeois or patriarchal.[1] Rather than being chosen for their cultural value as literary or artistic works, the canonical status of great works reflects their social value. Such standpoint critiques claim that 'the Master's tools will never dismantle the Master's house' (Lorde 1984, p. 112) and different knowers necessarily have different tools and cannot live together; each social group has its own basis of insight. Any specific canon is held to be one of many of equal cultural value but which enjoy different levels of social sponsorship.

This move towards relativism reaches its zenith in a highly individualistic form. Carey, for example, proclaims that the Kantian view is 'patently untrue' and instead the value of art 'is a statement of personal taste' (2005, p. 9). This decapitalizes the basis of knowledge claims: it argues not simply that Truth or Beauty have yet to be fully attained or realized but rather there is no *possibility* of Truth or Beauty. Where it goes further than standpoint critiques is to claim that one cannot say a cultural work is better or worse than any other except in terms of one's own *individual* personal preferences (Chapter 7, this volume). The legitimate meanings of cultural works are restricted to the individual's experiences which cannot be compared because we cannot access the minds of others. To differentially value art is to differentially value personal experiences. There is thus no basis for a *cultural* hierarchy of works or knowledge.

Contexts and knowledge structures

This choice between essentialism and relativism has often been portrayed as defining the terrain of the 'culture wars' (Graff 1992). One can redescribe these positions in terms of context-dependency: aesthetic judgements as wholly decontextualized or wholly context-bound. They are the polar extremes of *semantic gravity*, the degree to which meaning is related to its context (Maton 2008, 2009a). Here symbolic products are either freely floating or context-determined. Essentialism denies the existence of semantic gravity – the meaning of cultural works are entirely independent of contexts of production and reception, transcending time and space. Immutable, invariant and context-free, they are contemplated by a decontextualized knower with a pure aesthetic gaze. In contrast, relativist critiques portray semantic gravity as crushing. Each particular time, place, social group or individual represents a black hole – one cannot see in from outside, nor sweetness or light can escape. The valuation of cultural works is nothing but a reflection of their social contexts.

Despite being portrayed as oppositional, essentialism and relativism thereby share a denial of the *re*contextualization of knowledge and thus of the possibility of cumulative knowledge-building. Knowledge is either complete, for the value of a work is self-evident and resides within the work itself (essentialism), or exhausted by the social context it reflects (reductionism). One can, therefore, either add a new transhistorical work into the canon horizontally alongside existing works or one cannot have a canon for long. In Bernstein's terms, what they share is a portrayal of the arts and humanities as flat and segmented: extremely horizontal knowledge structures.

The canonic tradition

As Moore (Chapter 7, this volume) argues, the choice between essentialism and relativism obscures a third position, a different form of critique that holds open the possibility of knowledge-building: working critically *within* a canonic tradition. This capacity for verticality is illustrated by a depiction in 1756 of the poet Christopher Smart in the frontispiece of his periodical *The Universal Visitor, and Memorialist* (see Ross 2000, p. 34). The author is shown working at a desk, looking up at a mantle on which are positioned five busts surrounded by a large laurel wreath: Chaucer, Spenser, Shakespeare, Waller and Dryden. Each bust has a verse inscribed on its base, which are reprinted below the frontispiece :

TO CHAUCER! who the English Tounge design'd:
TO SPENCER! who improv'd and refin'd:
TO Muse-fir'd SHAKESPEAR! who increas'd its Praise:
Rich in bold Compunds, & strong-painted Phrase,
TO WALLER! Sweetner of its manly Sound:
TO DRYDEN! who is full Perfection found.

Behind the busts are bookshelves, including the works of a host of English authors and above which is a Latin inscription declaring this to be Apollo's Temple of the English. This image illustrates a number of the typical characteristics of a literary canon: a focus on authors; a story of writers building on the achievements of previous authors to enrich the language and understanding; the intertwining of a literature with a national culture; the dominating but inspiring shadow cast on the modern author by the past; and veneration of the sacred. Crucially, it represents a canonic *progression* ('improved and refined', 'increased', 'sweetener of') rather than the canonic succession suggested by essentialism. It thereby suggests cumulative knowledge-building, such that writers can argue 'that Dante understood more than Virgil, but Virgil was a great part of that which he understood' (Kermode 1983, p. 25) or, as T. S. Eliot proclaimed:

Someone said: 'The dead writers are remote from us because we *know* so much more than they did.' Precisely, and they are that which we know. (1980, p. 16)

Here semantic gravity is acknowledged – a cultural work is located in its ongoing social contexts – but not insurmountable. Cultural works are context-laden rather than context-determined; we may be remote from the context of production but not cut off from the product. It allows for the possibility of recontextualization and thereby of integration and subsumption of knowledge over time.

The two forms of critique briefly outlined here – reductionist relativism and working within a canonic tradition – offer different pictures of the capacity for knowledge-building in the arts and humanities. Yet both, Bernstein argues, represent horizontal knowledge structures; in literary criticism, for example, different approaches to literary analysis may build knowledge but each approach can remain strongly bounded from others and proclaim its own canonic tradition. This raises the question: wherein lies the difference between such fields? Put another way, how do these forms of critique differ in terms of their capacity for progress? I shall argue that to explore these issues we need to look at not only their knowledge structures but also their *knower structures*.

Knower Structures: A Second Dimension of Fields

In distinguishing different 'discourses' and 'knowledge structures', Bernstein focuses on one dimension of social fields: their discursive or ideational formation. This reflects a longstanding focus of the theory. For example, Bernstein's analysis of the sociology of education (1977, chapter 7) explores the ideological stances of intellectual approaches within the field. Similarly, fields of intellectual production are conceptualized in terms of their structurings of knowledge (1999). This focus on the knowledge formation of social fields is one of Bernstein's key contributions – his approach enables us to see knowledge as an object (Chapters 1 and 6, this volume). However, at the same time this focus makes it difficult to fully understand fields where knowledge is less explicit. For example, in Bernstein's analysis of educational knowledge codes (1977), the identities of actors are said either to reside in the possession of subject knowledge (collection code, where boundaries between academic subjects are stronger) or to be less certain and require constant negotiation (integrated code, where boundaries are weaker). Similarly, markers enabling actors to know they are operating within a hierarchical knowledge structure are explicit: 'the acquirer does not have the problem of knowing whether she/he is speaking physics or writing physics, only the problem of correct usage. The strong grammar visibly announces what it is' (Bernstein 1999, p. 164). However, in horizontal knowledge structures (especially with weaker grammars) where knowledge-based markers are less visible, the recognition and construction of legitimate texts is said to be more problematic. Wherever knowledge is explicit (collection codes, hierarchical knowledge structures), Bernstein's analysis is explicit: identity, insight and so on flow from this knowledge formation. Wherever knowledge is less explicit (integrated codes, horizontal knowledge structures), Bernstein's analysis becomes less explicit. For fields like the arts and humanities, the basis of insight, recontextualization and pedagogy is unclear. The question becomes: if they are not based on explicit structures of knowledge specialized to objects of study, then what are they based on?

Bernstein's model provides clues. He argues that for such fields:

> The social basis of the principle of this recontextualising indicates whose "social" is speaking. The social basis of the principle of the recontextualising constructs the perspective of the horizontal knowledge structure. Whose perspective is it? How is it generated and legitimated? (1999, p. 164).

As this suggests, the basis of these fields resides in something other than the formation of knowledge. However, to see what this might be requires a change of focus: one needs to see there are two analytically distinct structures that *together* shape educational and intellectual fields. In other words, fields comprise more than a formation of knowledge; they also comprise a formation of knowers. This represents a shift of perspective because the existing framework explores knowers only indirectly – using it one analyses the knowledge formation and then reads off implications for knowers as an epiphenomenon. Thus where knowledge is less explicit, the basis of the field becomes harder to see. I am arguing that for such fields this basis resides in a formation of knowers, and that this *knower structure* is not an epiphenomenon of the knowledge structure but rather has structuring significance of its own.

Fields as knowledge-knower structures

Building on Bernstein's approach, a series of papers in Legitimation Code Theory (LCT) has progressively conceptualized these two dimensions of social fields.[2] This approach suggests that for every knowledge structure there is also a knower structure; that is, fields are *knowledge-knower structures*. These structures are empirically inseparable as a social field of practice but analytically distinguishable. Where 'knowledge structures' conceptualizes the arrangement of knowledge within fields, 'knower structures' conceptualizes the arrangement of knowers. Crucially, the forms they take are not necessarily the same: each may be independently arranged hierarchically or horizontally.[3] For example, Maton (2007) illustrates how science can be characterized as possessing not only a hierarchical knowledge structure but also a *horizontal knower structure*: a series of strongly bounded knowers, each with specialized modes of being and acting, with non-comparable habituses or embodied dispositions based on different social trajectories and experiences. The social profile of scientists is often held to be irrelevant for scientific insight – anyone can ostensibly claim legitimate knowledge so long as they follow scientific procedures. So, in terms of their non-scientific dispositions, scientists can represent a segmented series of knowers strongly bounded in terms of their non-scientific gaze. This can be visually represented as follows, where each segment represents a different primary habitus (Kr1, Kr2, etc):

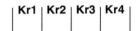

In contrast, the humanities can be characterized as possessing not only a horizontal knowledge structure but also a *hierarchical knower structure*: a systematically principled and hierarchical organization of knowers based on the construction of an ideal knower and which develops through the integration of new knowers at lower levels and across an expanding range of different dispositions. The position and trajectory of knowers within the field's hierarchies are arranged in relation to the ideal knower. This can be represented as a triangle of knowers:

(There may be more than one ideal knower and triangle of knowers). Here specific procedures for accessing a delimited object of study are less significant than possessing the legitimate dispositions.

Alongside hierarchical and horizontal knowledge structures one can thus speak of hierarchical and horizontal knower structures. These can vary independently, giving four modalities of fields as knowledge-knower structures. This describes the form taken by intellectual and education fields. The principles underlying these forms can be analysed in terms of *legitimation codes of specialization* (see Chapter 2, this volume), where each form is generated by a different code modality (Figure 8.1). The code is given by the epistemic relation to the knowledge structure (ER) and social relation to the knower structure (SR). Each may be more strongly or weakly classified and framed; or more briefly, each may be more or less emphasized (+/−) as the basis of claims to legitimate insight, identity and status. This gives four principal code modalities (ER+/−, SR+/−). Typically, a stronger relation ('+') indicates a hierarchical structure; for example,

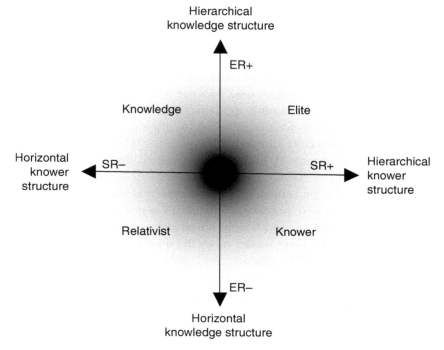

FIGURE 8.1 Knowledge-knower structures and legitimation codes

a stronger epistemic relation (ER+) is associated with a hierarchical knowledge structure. So, if the sciences exhibit a hierarchical knowledge structure and a horizontal knower structure, these are underpinned by emphasizing knowledge, skills and procedures and downplaying the dispositions of knowers – a *knowledge code* field (ER+, SR–). Conversely, if the humanities embody a horizontal knowledge structure and hierarchical knower structure, these are underpinned by placing less emphasis on procedures and more on aptitudes, attitudes and dispositions – a *knower code* field (ER–, SR+). In addition, one can describe an *elite code*, where both possessing specialist knowledge and being the right kind of knower are emphasized (both structures are hierarchical; ER+, SR+), and a *relativist code*, where neither is significant (both structures are horizontal; ER–, SR–).

This brief summary highlights that LCT brings together knowledge structures and knower structures. It should be emphasized that in intellectual and educational fields there are always knowledges and always knowers; they are *knowledge-knower* structures. For example, scientists do not merely follow procedures, they also develop a specialized gaze, 'a developed sense of the potential of a phenomenon arising out of practice' (Bernstein 1999, p. 165). Conversely, the arts and humanities are not knowledge-free; they have their own theories, methodologies and so on. The key distinction between these kinds of fields is in how knowledge and knowers are articulated. For knowledge-code fields the principal motivation is developing knowledge, and training specialized knowers is a means to this end. For knower-code fields the principal motivation is developing knowers, and creating specialist knowledge is the means. Thus, adding 'knower structures' to the framework builds on rather than displaces 'knowledge structures'.

The approach thereby enables fields to be seen along two dimensions, revealing issues that were previously obscured. For one thing, it shows that a field's hierarchy may not reside in its knowledge structure (Maton 2007). Put another way, Bernstein's model raises the question of what is 'vertical' in a horizontal knowledge structure. By conceptualizing fields as knowledge-knower structures one can see that *in vertical discourse there is always a hierarchy somewhere* – something is serving as the principle of production, recontextualization and evaluation. In distinguishing between fields the question becomes: where is the 'vertical' in different forms of vertical discourse? Or more accurately: what is hierarchical? where is the '+' in the legitimation code (ER+/−, SR+/−)? Is it in the knowledge structure (knowledge code), knower structure (knower code) or both (elite code)? (If neither, a relativist code, the field has no vertical discourse).

A second issue the approach reveals returns us to the issue of progress in the arts and humanities. These concepts suggest that the 'hierarchical' may reside in the knowledge structure for the sciences but in the knower structure for the arts and humanities. Bernstein states that hierarchical knowledge structures develop through the subsumption and integration of knowledge: 'verticality'. We can now add that fields with horizontal knowledge structures may develop through the subsumption and integration of habituses: 'sociality'. In other words, where one kind of field develops through knowledge-building, another kind develops through knower-building. Knower structures can thus be distinguished by the degree to which they integrate and subsume new knowers, their *sociality*, highlighting whether they develop through integration or accumulation of habituses.[4] So, while the knowledge structure of the humanities might exhibit lower levels of verticality, progress and growth of a different kind may be found in their knower structures.[5] This is not to argue that fields like the humanities must *necessarily* develop in this way or cannot build knowledge (different issues entirely) but rather to provide a way of seeing how actually existing progress may be occurring within such fields.

Gazes and knower-grammars

The issues brought into view by thinking in terms of knowledge-knower structures – that the primary basis and locus of growth of fields may reside in their knower structure – in turn raise two further questions. First, what is the basis of insight, recontextualization and evaluation in these fields? As mentioned earlier, for hierarchical knowledge structures this resides in their strong grammar; for example, truth claims can be judged against available evidence using shared criteria. In contrast, Bernstein argues:

> In the case of horizontal knowledge structures, especially those with weak grammars, 'truth' is a matter of acquired 'gaze'. (1999, p. 165)[6]

I defined knower structures as based on constructed knowers; each of these ideal knowers possesses a privileged 'gaze'. As Bernstein puts it, a '"gaze" has to be acquired, i.e. a particular mode of recognising and realising what counts as an "authentic" . . . reality' (1999, p. 165). For knower-code fields, this gaze embodies the principle underlying production, recontextualization and evaluation in the field – 'to know is to "gaze"' (ibid.). One can, I suggest, analyse this 'mode of recognizing and realizing' in terms of its strength of *knower-grammar* (Maton 2007, 2008). Analogous to Bernstein's 'grammar' of knowledge structures, knower-grammar refers to the degree to which this gaze is related to a specific base. We can redescribe Bernstein's concept as 'knowledge-grammar', the strengths of classification and framing of objects of study and their specialized procedures (or, using LCT, the epistemic relation). Knower-grammar refers to the strengths of classification and framing of privileged knowers and their dispositions (or social relation).

One can then conceptualize different kinds of gaze underlying fields in terms of their strengths of knower-grammar (or social relation). Here I shall identify born, social, cultivated and trained gazes (Figure 8.2). (I have used 'gaze', but one could also talk of 'ear' in music and 'taste', 'smell', 'touch' or 'feel' and 'voice' in various arts). The relatively strongest knower-grammar is illustrated by notions of 'natural talent' and 'genius'

FIGURE 8.2 Knower-grammars and gazes

(e.g. in debates over musical ability), or genetic inheritance and biological explanations of practice, where the privileged knower is held to possess a *born gaze*. Less fixed but still relatively strong is where ideal knowers possess a *social gaze* determined by their social category, such as standpoint theories based on social class or on race, gender and sexuality when constructed as social categories. Weaker is the *cultivated gaze*, where insight is held to arise from the socialized dispositions of the knower but these legitimate ways of thinking and being can be inculcated through education; for example, in literary or art criticism insight has often been held to result from prolonged immersion in great cultural works. Relatively weakest is the *trained gaze*, where legitimate insight is gained through prolonged training in specialized methods and procedures. For example, in the sciences the source of the privileged gaze is less the knower than the knowledge they possess, and in principal anyone can be trained into the legitimate gaze.[7]

This brings us to a second question: why might some kinds of fields have greater capacity for progress and growth than others? The different kinds of gaze outlined here trace a continuum from fixity of knower categories towards increasingly changeable features, and from knowers towards knowledge. They also trace a continuum of increasing openness to potential knowers. Strengths of knower-grammars help shape the conditions for entry, position and trajectory within a field's hierarchies. The stronger the knower-grammar, the more tightly restrictions are placed on membership of and ascension through a knower structure hierarchy. The born gaze is the most difficult to attain for those not already a member of the privileged knower group; the social gaze restricts potential knowers to social categories that may be difficult to join; the cultivated gaze holds out the possibility of attainment of legitimacy through prolonged immersion in a way of being, seeing or acting; and the trained gaze proclaims openness to anyone willing to be trained in specialized procedures. (They thus also trace a continuum of strengthening ER and weakening SR: a movement from knower-code to knowledge-code fields). The kind of gaze underlying the knower structure of fields may thus be crucial to the degree of extension of its epistemic community through time and space (Moore & Maton 2001): gaze may shape sociality and capacity for growth of the knower structure. Moreover, sociality may in turn affect verticality, the capacity for knowledge-building in a field; that is, knower structures may affect knowledge structures. It is to these issues that I now turn, using the concepts to explore the effects of different gazes on progress in the arts and humanities.

Gazes and Critiques

Earlier I outlined two forms of critique – reductionist critiques and working within a canonic tradition – that offer different pictures of the capacity for knowledge-building in the arts and humanities. These can be redescribed as representing different forms of legitimate 'gaze': a social gaze and a cultivated gaze, respectively (see Figure 8.3). To illustrate the effects these forms of gaze have for a field's capacity to embrace new knowers and build cumulative knowledge, and to build on Chapter 2 of this volume, I shall now focus on an example of each gaze from within the history of an intellectual field: British cultural studies.

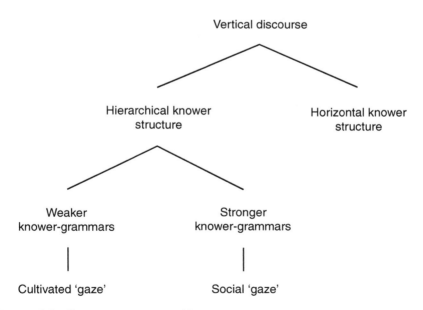

FIGURE 8.3 Knower structures and knower-grammars

The cultivated gaze

An example of a critique of a canon based on a cultivated gaze can be found in the early history of British cultural studies. Faced with the rise of new commercial forms of mass media, many educators argued in the early 1960s for teaching young people how to 'look critically and discriminate between what is good and bad in what they see' (Newsom Report 1963, p. 156). The founding figures of cultural studies – Richard Hoggart, Raymond Williams, E. P. Thompson and Stuart Hall – argued that such calls for discrimination were often accompanied by a devaluing of working-class interests and made cases for the cultural value of the 'popular arts' (Hall & Whannel 1964, pp. 23–37). They agreed with the need to cultivate critical discrimination and retained a conviction that much 'high' culture was of value, but highlighted that existing canons excluded the experiences of many people and the basis of choosing such canons could be extended to include new forms of culture. Through their work in adult education and the first New Left movement, they aimed to enable working-class learners to critically appreciate both new media and 'high' culture and so bring them into a cultural conversation from which they had been excluded. This was an 'attempt at a majority democratic education' (Williams 1989, p. 154) where the aim was to democratize access to a means of 'discrimination': a cultivated gaze.

At the same time, the founders of cultural studies argued that the means of ascending towards the critical literary gaze needed overhauling. New forms of media needed new forms of pedagogy and a new 'critical method for handling these problems of value and evaluation' (Hall & Whannel 1964, p. 15). In particular, they emphasized the need to build on the experiences of students; as Williams stated: 'I believe that communication cannot be effective if it is thought of as simply transmission. It depends, if it is to be real . . . on real community of experience' (in Hoggart & Williams 1960, p. 30).

Though early cultural studies began from and engaged with learners' experiences, it did not, however, end with those experiences. Williams (1968), for example, argued that 'the teacher who pretends he [sic] is not a teacher . . . is a pathetic and irrelevant figure' and Hoggart emphasized that it 'is a joint matter, but one in which the tutor has primary responsibility for keeping the lines braced' (1969, in 1982, p. 9). It thus aimed to integrate the interests and experiences of learners without slipping into 'that sloppy relativism which doesn't stretch *any* student because "they are all, in their own ways, doing wonderfully"' (Hoggart 1969, in 1982,

p. 12). They thereby aimed to provide an explicit and 'thoroughly-planned syllabus' to help 'fill out the sense of a coherent journey' towards the appreciation of cultural works in which neither

> the tutor nor the student should be in doubt about the overall aims of the course and its larger pattern of working over the session; nor about the place of each week in that pattern; nor about the shape of any one week in itself. (Hoggart 1982, p. 9)

This explicit path for ascending towards legitimate insight remained focused on achieving a literary gaze and was still to be attained through engaging with exemplars of aesthetic excellence, expanded to include new forms of culture. Hoggart, for example, proclaimed:

> [F]irst, without appreciating good literature no one will really understand the nature of society; second, literary critical analysis can be applied to certain social phenomena other than "academically respectable" literature (for example, the popular arts, mass communications) . . . the first is the more important and the second the less obvious. (1966, p. 277)

Progress and growth with a cultivated gaze

The kind of critique exemplified by early cultural studies is based on a hierarchical knower structure, one which works to integrate different habituses through cultivation into legitimate dispositions (see Figure 8.4). The tip of

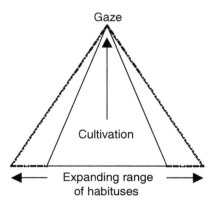

FIGURE 8.4   Progress and growth of knower structure under a cultivated gaze

the triangle is the ideal knower's gaze; the base represents the range of habituses integrated through education. Progress and growth of this knower structure can be understood along two dimensions: first, the horizontal expansion of the range of habituses embraced by the field; and secondly, the vertical ascension of knowers towards the gaze through the cultivation of their dispositions. The basis of progress thereby resides in the belief that a wide range of potential knowers can be inculcated into the legitimate gaze. This represents a knower-grammar (or social relation) that is relatively weaker than those of born or social gazes (though stronger than a trained gaze). Bernstein describes hierarchical *knowledge* structures as motivated towards integrating the greatest number of empirical phenomena into the smallest number of axioms; one can describe hierarchical *knower* structures as motivated towards integrating the greatest number of habituses into the smallest number of gazes.

It is notable that, as discussed earlier, the position illustrated by early cultural studies is often neglected by portrayals of the 'culture wars'. Radical critiques often present the essentialist understanding of canons as the historically dominant position. Yet this little reflects the common practice in the humanities of reinterpreting and critiquing an evolving canon rather than treating canonical works as universally transcendent. As an introduction to a collection debating the literary canon puts it:

> Indeed, traditions are made up of debates, diachronically (as past addresses present, and present the past), anachronically (as something ancient seems to matter for the present, and vice versa), and pluralistically (as an extraordinary range of voices make up a tradition, and the readings of that tradition). (Morrissey 2005, p. 1)

Though radical in many ways, early cultural studies was continuing a long tradition of such debates over authorities and models. The first writer known to have called such choices 'classics' is Aulus Gellius of the second century, who pronounced '*Classicus . . . scriptor, non proletarious*': the classic writer is distinguished from the rabble (Kermode 1983, p. 15). The genesis of canonization in English literary criticism dates back to at least the eighteenth century and to such texts as Samuel Johnson's *Lives of the English Poets*. In these debates writers engage with the opinions of contemporary and earlier writers on the value of particular texts (Beer 1989; Morrissey 2005). Such debates extend across time and space; they embrace other past and present thinkers and offer the possibility of cumulative knowledge-building.

A key to this potential sociality and knowledge-building resides in the cultivated gaze. This is based on the belief that knowers are not born but made through the re-formation of their habituses in prolonged exposure to great cultural works. Pedagogy thereby initiates learners into ways of knowing rather than explicit states of knowledge, instilling what Hughes called 'an invisible tribunal':

> Every writer carries in his or her mind an invisible tribunal of dead writers, whose appointment is an imaginative act and not merely a browbeaten response to some notion of authority. This tribunal sits in judgement on our own work. We intuit standards from it. . . . If the tribunal weren't there, every first draft would be a final manuscript. (1993, p. 111)

Cultivation also provides a shared library that enables allusions, references, intertextual play and the myriad effects of what Bloom (1973) called the 'anxiety of influence' – the desire to go beyond what has come before – to be assumed and left tacit. Sociality resides in the degree to which this invisible tribunal and library is shared, for possessing the gaze represents a gateway to the public sphere of such fields. This in turn affects their potential for knowledge-building, for the definition of 'art' or 'literature' is projected by the artistic or literary gaze onto a canon which provides the Archimedean point for debate. Thus, canons and cultivated gazes may represent for the arts and humanities the knower-based equivalents of the objects of study and specialized procedures of the sciences: they provide a focus and basis for intersubjective debate. Because the cultivated gaze is based on a canon, immersion in which helps develop what Williams called a 'community of experience', it both enables the possibility of debate over something (a canon) and a shared means of conducting that debate (the shared sensibilities of knowers).

The social gaze

A second form of critique begins from a similar position to early cultural studies. It rightly highlights that dominated social groups have historically been denied access to the means of creation and circulation of symbolic products and their experiences often excluded from the shared library. However, this form is based on a social gaze. Such a form came to dominate later cultural studies.

In the early 1970s, the highly influential Centre for Contemporary Cultural Studies (CCCS) engaged on a major project of trying to 'distil the field in terms of a basic set of core-texts' along with critical commentaries, with the goal of producing *A Reader in Cultural Studies* to 'prevent succeeding generations of students having to start again at first base' (Hall 1971, p. 5). This shared library aimed to provide a basis for cumulative knowledge-building and cultivating cultural studies knowers. However, this project was disrupted when the field moved to broaden its base further. Having attempted to include working-class learners among the range of knowers accessing a literary gaze, cultural studies increasingly focused on women. As Stuart Hall, Director of the CCCS during the 1970s, later recounted: 'we tried to buy it in, to import it, to attract good feminist scholars' (1992, p. 282). However, 'many of the women in cultural studies weren't terribly interested in this benign project' and, rather than 'good, transformed men', scholars such as Hall were portrayed as 'fully installed patriarchal power, which believed it had disavowed itself' (ibid.). The practices and beliefs of male practitioners were redefined by feminist critics as gendered and rooted in unequal relations of power. This became particularly salient when deciding the 'shared library':

> There are no leaders here, we used to say; we are all graduate students and members of staff together, learning how to practice cultural studies. You can decide whatever you want to decide, etc. And yet, when it came to the question of the reading list . . . Now that's where I really discovered about the gendered nature of power. (1992, pp. 282–3)

The influence of standpoint theory saw feminist critiques of the emerging canon of cultural studies proclaim that not only its contents but also its basis of choice was patriarchal, denying the legitimacy of the gaze and those who possessed it. The personal nature of struggles at this time echo in Hall's proclamation: 'Talking about giving up power is a radically different experience from being silenced' (1992, p. 283). The cultivated gaze was thus redefined as socially based: a male gaze. From this perspective, integrating women into the field was attempting to inculcate them into social ways of knowing other than their own – symbolic violence. One response was thus to call for 'a literature of our own' and 'a criticism of our own' or 'gynocriticism', a female framework for analysing literature written by women (Showalter 1977, 1989). This set in train a series of similar debates over the imperialist, Western, racialized and sexualized nature of knowledge in the field with new, previously excluded social groups often proclaiming their own gaze and derailing the project of building a fully shared library.

Progress and growth with social gazes

Critiques based on a social gaze correct the essentialist temptation to misrecognize a cultivated gaze and its canon as asocial and ahistorical. However, as early cultural studies illustrates, this can be achieved while maintaining belief in the value of canons and cultivated gazes. Contrary to many accounts of the 'culture wars', the move to a social gaze is not necessarily integral to critiquing canons. Reductionist critiques take the fact that cultivated gazes have been socially laden and historically associated with specific social groups to mean that it is socially determined and knowers can possess only a pre-existing social gaze. This move has consequences for intellectual and educational fields. Where cultivated gaze critiques aim to integrate previously excluded knowers by broadening the knower structure's base (Figure 8.4), those based on social gazes create their own, new triangle. The former aim to inculcate more potential knowers into an established conversation; the latter aim to carve out a new space for already legitimate knowers to find a voice and speak to each other. While the field remains based on a knower code, this move strengthens the social relation underpinning the code, affecting the nature of the field.

The social gaze restricts a field's capacity for sociality and knowledge-building along two dimensions. First, the range of potential knowers is diminished. If the knower structure begins as a single triangle (Figure 8.5, no. 1), rather than expanding this triangle a social gaze adds a second, separate triangle (no. 2). Where a cultivated gaze may be shared by

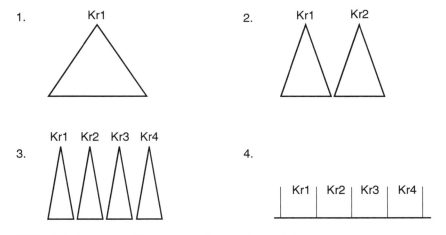

FIGURE 8.5 Progress of knower structure under social gazes

knowers originating from a range of different social backgrounds, a social gaze is shared by those who possess it already, unless they successfully change gender, social class, ethnicity and so on. With such a broad social category as 'women', this may at first appear to dramatically expand the field as a whole: a new space is carved out for a previously excluded social group. However, the new triangle can be maintained only so long as its social category remains unified, and the tendency is for it to be fragmented as more adjectives are added based on other social categories (see Chapters 2 and 3, this volume). With each successive adjective (e.g. white-female-heterosexual-Western-etc.) more separate knower structures emerge within the field, one for each new social gaze. This adds more triangles with successively smaller bases (no. 3). Though embracing more knowers, each new group has their own knower structure, fragmenting the field. The result is to move towards a horizontal knower structure (no. 4). If the field also has a horizontal knowledge structure, this diminishes the capacity of members to engage in fruitful debate and build knowledge over time. Different social groups have their own gazes and so their own objects, their own canons – each a literature or culture or art of their own. There is thus no Archimedean point, no shared object of study over which debate between segments can be engaged and no shared means of doing so.

A second dimension concerns the triangle's height: the distance between entry as a novice and achieving the ideal gaze may diminish. Pedagogy is less likely to focus on a prolonged apprenticeship for inculcating sensibilities and more on removing ideological obstacles (including prior cultivation) to enable the authentic social self to shine forth and so raise to consciousness one's social gaze. The gaze is still a gateway to a public sphere but now more restricted; one cannot enter or ascend the knower structure unless one is already an ideal knower. This also fragments the educational experience. For example, Richard Johnson (CCCS Director 1979–88) describes the early 1980s as witnessing 'the apparent splitting up of the field of cultural theory by the often separated and even antagonistic claims of different political movements', illustrated by a Masters degree course being 'organised around the political sequence of class, gender, and "race" rather than some more synthesizing account of tensions and best options in the field' (1997, p. 65). Instead of a coherent journey towards a cultivated gaze, students may experience segmented learning as they move between approaches; indeed, a common criticism of the Masters course was its lack of 'coherence' (Johnson 1997, p. 65).

The endpoint of this process is subjectivist relativism, the notion that there is nothing beyond the different subjective knowledges of a potentially infinite number of different knowers. The social category underpinning the gaze is thus broken down and replaced by individual gazes, as illustrated by such arguments as:

> The art-world has lost its credibility. The electorate has extended, has, indeed, become universal. My answer to the question 'What is a work of art?' is 'A work of art is anything that anyone has ever considered a work of art, though it may be a work of art only for that one person.' Further, the reasons for considering anything a work of art will be as various as the variety of human beings. (Carey 2005, p. 30)

From this perspective discrimination is only misrecognized social power. There is no hierarchy, no sequencing of achievements and nothing to be taught or learned. There is only the horizontal addition of new lists of personal preferences (Chapter 7, this volume). The 'invisible tribunal' results from individual biography: 'we assemble our own literary canon, held together by personal preferences' (2005, p. 242). Though critics such as Carey believe this is democratic as it overthrows the rule of 'the art-world', it does so by emptying 'art' of meaning. Moreover, there is no 'electorate' for there is no election. From this position, anything goes: 'If this seems to plunge us into the abyss of relativism, then I can only say that the abyss of relativism is where we have always been in reality – if it is an abyss' (2005, p. 30).

Returning to the question of finding the 'hierarchical' in vertical discourse, this is to move from a knower code towards a position without hierarchy (a relativist code or ER–, SR–) with a segment of knowledge for each segmented knower – both knowledge and knower structures become horizontal.

Conclusion

I began with questions raised by both the culture wars and Bernstein's model of knowledge structures: what is the basis of humanist knowledge, do the arts and humanities progress and, if so, how? Bernstein's model highlights the 'horizontal' form of development taken by the knowledge structure of such fields; they have weaker verticality and weaker grammars than hierarchical knowledge structures. This, however, leaves unanswered where their 'strength' may lie, how such fields might differ, and whether and how they might progress hierarchically. I argued that Bernstein's approach enables knowledge to be analysed but this focus means the basis of fields where knowledge is less explicit remains unclear. The question became: if the arts and humanities are not based on explicit structures of knowledge specialized to clearly defined objects of study, then what are they based on? To address this I introduced the notion of knower structures based on the gazes of ideal knowers, and suggested that where knowledge structures are characterized by verticality and knowledge-grammars (ER), knower structures are characterized by sociality and knower-grammars (SR). The forms taken by fields can then be analysed in terms of legitimation codes, which bring these grammars together (as ER+/−, SR+/−). Intellectual and educational fields were thereby described as knowledge-knower structures. Focusing on knower structures, a number of different gazes were defined in terms of the strengths of their knower-grammars.

These concepts were used to compare two states of a field both of which Bernstein's model would define as horizontal knowledge structures: cultural studies before and after the mid-1970s. The first was based on a cultivated gaze and characterized by a hierarchical knower structure; in the second the basis of insight, recontextualization and evaluation was redefined as a social gaze and the knower structure increasingly horizontalized. This strengthening of knower-grammar (and so SR) was shown to have implications for a field's ability to extend across time and space. The cultivated gaze affords greater opportunities for cumulative knowledge-building (greater verticality) because a greater number of habituses can be integrated and subsumed (greater sociality). This verticality is, however, of a particular form: it is limited to *within* the knower-defined field, to those deemed sufficiently cultivated to judge the aesthetic or literary merits of a work in relation to other cultural works. Nonetheless, defining the ideal knower's gaze as something that can be taught and learned enables this segment to be potentially more inclusive, allowing the possibility for (though not by itself guaranteeing) cumulative knowledge-building. In contrast, the social gaze restricts sociality and verticality because access into and ascension through the field's hierarchy of knowers is restricted to a particular social group. Moreover, this may begin a process of fragmenting the field into a series of separate knower structures, moving towards subjectivist relativism. The underlying rule of the cultivated gaze is 'habituses must be brought together', that of the social gaze is 'habituses must be kept apart'. More broadly, the trained gaze (of science, for example) reflects a hierarchy of knowledge; the cultivated gaze reflects a hierarchy of knowing; and the social gaze reflects a hierarchy of being (though positions proclaiming a social gaze typically deny hierarchies of being and so move towards horizontalism).

The capacity for a segment-limited form of verticality within fields like the arts and humanities thereby depends on their knower structures. In short, the knower structure of a field can affect its knowledge structure. This is also the key to understanding differences among fields with horizontal knowledge structures – they are not all the same nor are they confined to a strictly horizontal form of development. So, while Bernstein's framework allows us to see knowledge and provides most insight into fields such as the sciences, to fully understand intellectual and educational fields, and in particular the arts and humanities, we also need to see knowers. LCT embraces knowledge *and* knowers (Maton 2009c). Using LCT it becomes clear that fields with horizontal knowledge structures may progress 'vertically' through their knower structures (if operating a knower code); their 'strength' lies within these structures; their basis of insight, recontextualization and evaluation resides in a 'gaze'; and some fields are more capable of sociality and verticality than others, depending on the nature of this gaze.

Theorizing fields in this way also brings more firmly into view a position often obscured by accounts of the culture wars: critical engagement with a canonic tradition based on a cultivated gaze. Against essentialism, this position highlights the veracity of arguments that definitions of culture are related to actors located in socio-historical contexts rather than universal and transcendent. It also highlights, against relativism, that there can be intersubjective, rational bases for judgement that may be taught and learned. In a passage quoted earlier, Robert Hughes described invisible tribunals as imaginative acts rather than simply the result of browbeaten responses to social power. Such acts are not made outside society by decontextualized knowers but rather result from articulating the personal 'inner' with the social 'outer' via cultural authority, that is, from a cultivated gaze. The key to avoiding the Scylla and Charybdis of symbolic violence and relativism is thus to discover a gaze and a means of cultivating that gaze capable of embracing knowers from a multitude of social backgrounds. This is an urgent task facing the arts and humanities if we are to forge a culture peace, one characterized not by an unchanging, socially imposed canon, factional trench warfare or relativism, but by an enlarged cultural sphere in which everyone is able to join a living and visible tribunal. Reductionist critiques construct a false dichotomy of either pure gaze or social gaze. In denying the possibility of a democratic cultivated gaze, they give up hope too soon. That humanist culture has historically been associated with a limited social base does not negate hope of discovering such a gaze. In humanist study the age of innocence is lost, but not the age of hope and, to paraphrase Walter Benjamin (1919–22, p. 356), it is for the sake of those without hope that we are given hope.

Endnotes

[1] I am not suggesting all critiques make this argument – see further below on the different bases of critiques.

[2] See, for example, Chapter 2 of this volume, Maton (2007, 2008, 2009c) and Moore & Maton (2001). For examples of research using LCT, see Carvalho et al. (2009), Doherty (2008) and Lamont & Maton (2008).

[3] Horizontal knowledge structures are not necessarily based on knowers; mathematics is an obvious counter-example. One needs to explore the knower structure as well as the knowledge structure when describing fields.

[4] Moore (Chapter 7, this volume) uses 'sociality' to highlight that knowledge claims are practices people do within a special type of socio-historical context that can be described in terms of its structural features. Here I redefine 'sociality' as the degree to which this field integrates and subsumes habituses and conceptualize the structural features of this special type of context in terms of knower-grammars (see below).

[5] Lacking the dimension of 'knower structures', Bernstein's model can be criticized as overly focused on progress in the sciences and offering a deficit model of the humanities (see Chapter 6, this volume). The approach offered here overcomes such criticisms and does so through a cumulative and integrative development of the existing theory rather than horizontally accumulating another approach.

[6] 'Gaze' refers to the acquirer not to the discourse to be acquired, and to the outcome of the principles underlying fields not to the principles themselves (cf. Bernstein 1999, pp. 171–2). For example, I shall argue that the 'cultivated gaze' shapes and is shaped by canons, rather than is the gaze of the canon itself, and is the result of a knower code with a particular strength of knower-grammar. The necessity of these distinctions becomes clear when considering the move to a 'social gaze', which elides them both.

[7] All fields are knowledge-knower structures, so all include a gaze. Where the cultivated gaze makes possession of a specialized sensibility the basis of legitimacy, the trained gaze emphasizes possession of specialist knowledge as the criteria for membership of a field and the means of inculcation into its principles of organization (cf. Moore & Maton 2001). One emphasizes knowers over knowledge; the other emphasizes knowledge over knowers.

Acknowledgements

The editors wish to thank Alison Clark of Continuum – her arrival made the task of creating this book considerably easier, thanks to her enthusiasm and efficiency; and Nicole White, who studiously helped us with proofreading, bringing disparate styles into alignment, and numerous other tasks. Lastly, we thank Homerton College and the Faculty of Education in Cambridge University for supporting *Social Realism in Education: The First International Colloquium* in 2008.

The editors also wish to thank the publishers of journals for permission to draw on previously published material.

Chapter 1 was originally published as: Moore, R. and Young, M. F. D. (2001), 'Knowledge and the curriculum in the sociology of education: Towards a reconceptualisation'. *British Journal of Sociology of Education*, 22, (4), 445–61.

Chapter 2 is a revised version of: Maton, K. (2000), 'Languages of legitimation: The structuring significance for intellectual fields of strategic knowledge claims'. *British Journal of Sociology of Education*, 21, (2), 147–67.

Chapter 3 was originally published as: Moore, R. and Muller, J. (1999), 'The discourse of "voice" and the problem of knowledge and identity in the sociology of education'. *British Journal of Sociology of Education*, 20, (2),189–206.

Chapter 4 was originally published as: Beck, J. (2002), 'The sacred and profane in recent struggles to promote official pedagogic identities'. *British Journal of Sociology of Education*, 23, (4), 617–26.

Chapter 5 was originally published as: Wheelahan, L. (2007), 'How competency-based training locks the working class out of powerful knowledge: A modified Bernsteinian analysis'. *British Journal of Sociology of Education*, 28, (5), 637–51.

Chapter 6 is an abridged version of: Young, M. F. D. and Muller, J. (2007), 'Truth and truthfulness in the sociology of educational knowledge'. *Theory and Research in Education*, 5, (2), 173–201.

Chapter 7 is an abridged version of: Moore, R. (2007), 'Hierarchical knowledge structures and the canon: A preference for judgments', in F. Christie, and J. Martin (eds), *Language, Knowledge and Pedagogy: Functional Linguistic and Sociological Perspectives*. London: Continuum.

Chapter 8 is an expanded version of: Maton, K. (2009), 'Invisible tribunals: Progress and knowledge-building in the humanities', in P. Singh, A. Sadovnik and S. Semel (eds), *Toolkits, Translation Devices, Conceptual Tyrannies: Essays on Basil Bernstein's Sociology of Knowledge*. New York: Peter Lang.

References

Ahier, J., Beck, J. and Moore, R. (2003), *Graduate Citizens? Issues of Citizenship and Higher Education*. London: Routledge/Falmer.

Alexander, J. C. (1995), *Fin de Siècle Social Theory: Relativism, Reduction and the Problem of Reason*. London: Verso.

Apple, M. (1975), *Ideology and Curriculum*. London: Routledge & Kegan Paul.

Archer, M. (1990), 'Resisting the revival of relativism', in M. Albrow and E. King (eds), *Globalisation, Knowledge and Society*. London: Sage.

—(1995), *Realist Social Theory: The Morphogenetic Approach*. Cambridge: Cambridge University Press.

Archer, M., Bhaskar, R., Collier, A., Lawson, T. and Norrie, A. (eds) (1998), *Critical Realism: Essential Readings*. London: Routledge.

Arnold, M. (1960), *Culture and Anarchy*. Cambridge: Cambridge University Press.

Baggini, J. (2002), 'Death of an idea'. *Prospect*, September, 10.

Bates, I., Bloomer, M., Hodkinson, P. and Yeomans, D. (1998), 'Progressivism and the GNVQ: Context, ideology and practice'. *Journal of Education and Work*, 112, 109–26.

Beck, J. (1998), *Morality and Citizenship in Education*. London: Cassell.

—(1999), 'Makeover or takeover? The strange death of educational autonomy in neo-liberal England'. *British Journal of Sociology of Education*, 20, (2), 223–38.

Beck, J., Jenks, C., Keddie, N. and Young, M. (eds) (1977), *Worlds Apart: Readings for a Sociology of Education*. London: Collier Macmillan.

Beck, J. and Young, M. (2005), 'The assault on the professions and the restructuring of academic and professional identities: A Bernsteinian analysis'. *British Journal of Sociology of Education*, 26, (2), 183–97.

Beer, G. (1989), *Arguing with the Past*. London: Routledge.

Benjamin, W. (1919–22/1996), 'Goethe's elective affinities', in M. Bullock and M. W. Jennings (eds), *Selected Writings, Vol. 1*. Cambridge: Harvard University Press.

Benson, O. and Stangroom, J. (2006), *Why Truth Matters*. London: Continuum Books.

Berlin, I. (2000), *Three Critics of the Enlightenment: Vico, Hammann, Herder*. Princeton: Princeton University Press.

Bernstein, B. (1971a), 'On the classification and framing of educational knowledge', in M. F. D. Young (ed.), *Knowledge and Control: New Directions for the Sociology of Education*. London: Collier Macmillan.

—(1971b), *Class, Codes and Control, Volume I: Theoretical Studies Towards a Sociology of Language*. London: Routledge & Kegan Paul.

—(1975), *Class, Codes and Control, Volume III: Towards a Theory of Educational Transmissions*. London: Routledge & Kegan Paul.

—(1977), *Class, Codes and Control Volume III: Towards a Theory of Educational Transmissions* (2nd edn). London: Routledge & Kegan Paul.

—(1990), *Class, Codes and Control, Volume IV: The Structuring of Pedagogic Discourse*. London: Routledge.

—(1996), *Pedagogy, Symbolic Control and Identity: Theory, Research, Critique*. London: Taylor & Francis.

—(1997), 'Official knowledge and pedagogic identities: The politics of recontextualising', in I. Nilsson and L. Lundahl (eds), *Teachers, Curriculum and Policy: Critical Perspectives in Educational Research*. Umea, Sweden: Umea University.

—(1999), 'Vertical and horizontal discourse: An essay'. *British Journal of Sociology of Education*, 20, (2), 157–73.

—(2000), *Pedagogy, Symbolic Control and Identity: Theory, Research and Critique* (2nd edn). Oxford: Rowman & Littlefield.

Bernstein, B. and Solomon, J. (1999), 'Pedagogy, identity and the construction of a theory of symbolic control: Basil Bernstein questioned by Joseph Solomon'. *British Journal of Sociology of Education*, 20, (2), 265–79.

Bhaskar, R. (1975), *A Realist Theory of Science*. London: Verso.

—(1979), *The Possibility of Naturalism: A Philosophical Critique of the Contemporary Human Sciences*. Hemel Hempstead: Harvester Wheatsheaf.

—(1998), *The Possibility of Naturalism: A Philosophical Critique of the Contemporary Human Sciences* (3rd edn). London: Routledge.

Bloom, A. (1987), *The Closing of the American Mind*. New York: Simon & Schuster.

Bloom, H. (1973), *Anxiety of Influence*. Oxford, Oxford University Press.

—(1996), *The Western Canon: The Books and School of the Ages*. London: Macmillan.

Bloomer, M. (1998), 'They tell you what to do and then they let you get on with it': The illusion of progressivism in GNVQ'. *Journal of Education and Work*, 11, (2), 167–86.

Blundell, V., Shepherd, J. and Taylor, I. (eds) (1993), *Relocating Cultural Studies: Developments in Theory and Research*. London: Routledge.

Bohman, J. (1991), *New Philosophy of Social Science*. Cambridge: Polity Press.

Bourdieu, P. (1984), *Distinction: A Social Critique of the Judgement of Taste*. London: Routledge & Kegan Paul.

—(1988), *Homo Academicus*. Cambridge: Polity Press.

—(1993), *The Field of Cultural Production: Essays on Art and Literature*. Cambridge: Polity.

Bourdieu, P. and Passeron, J-C. (1977), *Reproduction in Education, Society and Culture*. London: Sage Publications.

Bourdieu, P. and Wacquant, L. J. D. (1992), *An Invitation to Reflexive Sociology*. Cambridge: Polity Press.

Brantlinger, P. (1990), *Crusoe's Footprints: Cultural studies in Britain and America*. London: Routledge.

Bridges, D. (2000), 'Back to the future: The higher education curriculum in the 21st century'. *Cambridge Journal of Education*, 30, (1), 37–56.

Brown, J. (2001), *Who Rules in Science? An Opinionated Guide to the Wars*. Cambridge, MA: Harvard University Press.

Brunsdon, C. (1996), 'A thief in the night: Stories of feminism in the 1970s at CCCS', in D. Morley and K-H. Chen (eds), *Stuart Hall*. London: Routledge.

Burton, L. (1964), 'Film study at a college of art'. *Screen Education*, 26, 34–43.

Canaan, J. E. and Epstein, D. (eds) (1997), *A Question of Discipline: Pedagogy, Power and the Teaching of Cultural Studies*. Boulder, CO: Westview.

Carby, H. (1982), 'White women listen: Black feminism and the boundaries of sisterhood', in CCCS (1982) *The Empire Strikes Back*. London: Hutchinson.

Carey, J. (2005), *What Good Are the Arts?* London: Faber.

Carvalho, L., Dong, A. and Maton, K. (2009, in press) 'Legitimating design: A sociology of knowledge account of the field'. *Design Studies*.

Castells, M. (1996, 1997, 1998), *The Information Age: Economy, Society and Culture* (Volumes I, II & III). Oxford: Blackwells.

CCCS (Centre for Contemporary Cultural Studies) (1964–81), *Annual Reports*. Birmingham: CCCS.

—(1968), *Fourth Report, 1966–1967*. Birmingham: CCCS.

—(1982), *The Empire Strikes Back: Race and Racism in 70s Britain*. London: Hutchinson.

Cleary, M., Flynn, R. and Thomasson, S. (2006), *Employability Skills. From Framework to Practice. An Introductory Guide for Trainers and Assessors*. Canberra: Department of Education, Science and Training.

Collier, A. (1997), 'Unhewn demonstrations'. *Radical Philosophy*, 81, 22–6.

—(1998), 'Stratified explanation and Marx's conception of history', in M. Archer, R. Bhaskar, A. Collier, T. Lawson and A. Norrie (eds), *Critical Realism: Essential Readings*. London: Routledge.

Collins, R. (2000), *The Sociology of Philosophies: A Global Theory of Intellectual Change*. Cambridge, MA: Harvard University Press.

Community Services and Health Industry Skills Council (2005), *CHC02 Community Services Training Package Volume 3 of 4 National Competency Standards*. Melbourne: Australian Training Products Ltd.

Dawe, A. (1970), 'The two sociologies'. *British Journal of Sociology*, 21, (2), 208–18.

Dearing, R. (1996), *Qualifications for 16–19 Year Olds*. London: Qualifications and Curriculum Authority.

Delamont, S. (1997), Fuzzy borders and the fifth moment: Methodological issues facing the sociology of education'. *British Journal of Sociology of Education*, 18, (4), 601–06.

Delanty, G. (2001), *Challenging Knowledge: The University in the Knowledge Society*. Milton Keynes: Open University Press.

Demaine, J. (1981), *Contemporary Theories in the Sociology of Education*. London: Macmillan Press.

Denby, D. (1996), *The Great Books*. New York: Simon & Schuster.

Department of Education Science and Training (2005), *Training Package Development Handbook, October*. Canberra: DEST.

Department for Education and Employment (DfEE) (1998), *The Learning Age: A Renaissance for a New Britain*. London: Department for Education and Employment.

—(1999), *Learning to Succeed*. London: Department for Education and Employment.

Derrida, J. (1976), *Of Grammatology*. Baltimore, MD: Johns Hopkins University Press.

Doherty, C. (2008), 'Student subsidy of the internationalized curriculum: Knowing, voicing and producing the Other'. *Pedagogy, Culture and Society*, 16, (3), 269–88.

Dowling, P. (1994), 'Discursive saturation and school mathematics texts: A strand from a language of description', in P. Ernest (ed.), *Mathematics, Education and Philosophy: An International Perspective*. London: Falmer.

Driver, R. (1982), *Pupil as Scientist*. Bletchley: Open University Press.

Durkheim, E. (1956), *Education and Sociology*. New York: Free Press.

—(1967), *The Elementary Forms of Religious Life*. New York: The Free Press.

—(1977), *The Evolution of Educational Thought: Lectures on the Formation and Development of Secondary Education in France*. London: Routledge.

—(1983), *Pragmatism and Sociology*. Cambridge: Cambridge University Press.

Durkheim, E. and Mauss, M. (1967), *Primitive Classifications*. Chicago: University of Chicago Press.

Dworkin, R. (1993), *Life's Dominion*. London: Harper Collins.

Eliot, T. S. (1980), 'Tradition and individual talent', in *Selected Essays* (2nd edn). London: Faber.

Epstein, D. (1997), 'The voice of authority: On lecturing in cultural studies', in J. E. Canaan and D. Epstein (eds), *A Question of Discipline*. Boulder, CO: Westview.

Fay, B. (1996), *Contemporary Philosophy of Social Science*. Oxford: Blackwell.

Filmer, P., Philipson, M., Silverman, D. and Walsh, D. (1972), *New Directions in Sociological Theory*. London: Collier Macmillan.

Floud, J. and Halsey, A. H. (1958), 'The sociology of education: A trend report and bibliography'. *Current Sociology*, 3, (3), 66.

Frankfurt, H. G. (2005), *On Bullshit*. Princeton: Princeton University Press.

Freebody, P., Maton, K. and Martin, J. (2008), 'Talk, text and knowledge in cumulative, integrated learning: A response to "intellectual challenge"'. *Australian Journal of Language and Literacy*, 31, 188–201.

Furedi, F. (2004), *Where Have All the Intellectuals Gone?: Confronting Twenty-First Century Philistinism*. London: Continuum.

Fuss, D. (1990), *Essentially Speaking: Feminism, Nature & Difference*. London: Routledge.

—(1995), *Identification Papers*. London: Routledge.

Gellner, E. (1974), 'The new idealism', in A. Giddens (ed.), *Positivism and Sociology*. London: Heinemann.

—(1992a), *Postmodernism, Reason and Religion*. London: Routledge.

—(1992b), *Reason and Culture*. Oxford: Blackwell.

Gibbons, M., Limoges, C., Nowotny, H. Schwartzman, S. Scott, P. and Trow, M. (1994), *The New Production of Knowledge*. London: Sage.

Gibbons, M., Nowotny, H. and Hand-Scott, P. (2000), *Rethinking Science: Knowledge Production in an Age of Uncertainties*. Cambridge: Polity Press.

Gilbert, S. M. (1985), 'What do feminist critics want? A postcard from the volcano', in E. Showalter (ed.), *The New Feminist Criticism: Essays on Women, Literature, and Theory*. London: Pantheon.

Giroux, H. (1983), *Theory and Resistance in Education: Towards a Pedagogy for the Opposition*. New York: Bergin and Garvey.

Goozee, G. (2001), *The Development of TAFE in Australia* (3rd edn). Adelaide: National Centre for Vocational Education Research.

Gorbutt, D. (1972), 'Education as the control of knowledge: The new sociology of education', *Education for Teaching*, 89, 3–12.

Gould, J. (1977), *The Attack on Higher Education: Marxist and Radical Penetration*. London: Institute for the Study of Conflict.

Grace, G. R. (1995), *School Leadership: Beyond Education Management. An Essay in Policy and Scholarship*. London: Falmer.

Graff, G. (1992), *Beyond the Culture Wars: How Teaching the Conflicts can Revitalize American Education*. New York: W. W. Norton & Company.

Gray, A. (1997), 'Learning from experience: Cultural studies and feminism', in J. McGuigan (ed.), *Cultural Methodologies*. London: Sage.

Griffin, A. (1997), 'Knowledge under attack: Consumption, diversity and the need for values', in R. Barnett and A. Griffin (eds), *The End of Knowledge in Higher Education*. London: Cassell.

Griffith, R. (2000), *National Curriculum: National Disaster*. London: Falmer.

Haack, S. (1998), *Confessions of a Passionate Moderate*. Chicago: Chicago University Press.

Hacking, I. (1999), *The Social Construction of What?* Boston: Harvard University Press.

Hall, S. (1964), 'Liberal studies', in P. Whannel and P. Harcourt (eds), *Film Teaching*. London: BFI.

—(1971), 'The Centre – history and intellectual development'. *CCCS Sixth Report, 1969–1971*, 1–6.

—(1990), 'The emergence of cultural studies and the crisis of the humanities'. *October*, 53, 11–23.

—(1992), 'Cultural studies and its theoretical legacies', in L. Grossberg, C. Nelson and P. A. Treichler (eds), *Cultural Studies*. London: Routledge.

Hall, S. and Whannel, P. (1964), *The Popular Arts*. London: Hutchinson.

Hammersley, M. (1995), *The Politics of Social Research*. London: Falmer.

Hammersley, M. and Gomm, R. (1997), 'Bias in social research', *Sociological Research Online*, 2, (1), http://www.socresonline.org.uk/socresonline/2/1/2.html.

Harcourt, P. (1964), 'Towards higher education'. *Screen Education*, 26, (September to October), 21–30.

Harding, S. (1991), *Whose Science? Whose Knowledge?* Ithaca, NY: Cornell University Press.

Harker, R. and May, S. A. (1993), 'Code and habitus: Comparing the accounts of Bernstein and Bourdieu'. *British Journal of Sociology of Education*, 14, (2), 169–78.

Harre, R. and Krausz, M. (1996), *Varieties of Relativism*. Oxford: Blackwell.

Harris, D. (1992), *From Class Struggle to the Politics of Pleasure: The Effects of Gramscianism on Cultural Studies*. London: Routledge.

Hartley, D. (1997), *Re-Schooling Society*. London: Falmer Press.

Hartsock, N. (1990), 'Foucault on power: A theory for women?', in L. Nicholson (ed.), *Feminism/Postmodernism*. New York: Routledge.

Hatcher, R. (1998), 'Class differentiation in education: Rational choices?'. *British Journal of Sociology of Education*, 19, (1), 5–24.

Hickox, M. (1995), 'The English middle class debate'. *British Journal of Sociology*, 46, (2), 311–24.

Hickox, M. and Moore, R. (1994), 'Vocationalism and educational change'. *Curriculum Journal*, 5, 277–89.

—(1995), 'Liberal-humanist education: The vocationalist challenge'. *Curriculum Studies*, 3, 45–59.

Hirsch, E. D. (1987), *Cultural Literacy: What Every American Needs to Know*. New York: Random House.

Hirst, P. H. (1967), 'The logical and psychological aspects of teaching a subject', in R. S. Peters (ed.), *The Concept of Education*. London: Routledge & Kegan Paul.

Hirst, P. and Peters, R. (1970), *The Logic of Education*. London: Routledge & Kegan Paul.

Hoggart, R. (1957), *The Uses of Literacy*. London: Chatto & Windus.

—(1966), 'Literature and society', *American Scholar*, Spring, 277–89.

—(1982), *An English Temper*. London: Chatto & Windus.

—(1995), *The Way We Live Now*. London: Chatto & Windus.

Hoggart. R. and Williams, R. (1960), 'Working class attitudes', *New Left Review*, 1, (January to February), 26–30.

Hoskyns, K. W. (1993), 'Education and the genesis of disciplinarity: The unexpected reversal', in E. Messer-Davidow, D. Shumway and D. Sylvan (eds), *Knowledges: Historical and Critical Studies in Disciplinarity*. Charlottesville: University of Virginia Press.

Huggins, D. (1996), *The Big Kiss*. London: Picador.

Hughes, R. (1993), *Culture of Complaint*. Oxford: Oxford University Press.

Jenks, C. (1977), *Rationality, Education and the Social Organization of Knowledge: Papers for a Reflexive Sociology of Education*. London: Routledge & Kegan Paul.

Johnson, R. (1983), 'What is cultural studies anyway?'. *CCCS Stencilled Occasional Paper*, 74.

—(1997), 'Teaching without guarantees: Cultural studies, pedagogy and identity', in J. E. Canaan and D. Epstein (eds), *A Question of Discipline*. Boulder, Colorado: Westview.

Jones, L. and Moore, R. (1995), 'Appropriating competence: The competency movement, the New Right and the 'culture change' project'. *British Journal of Education & Work*, 8, (2), 78–92.

Kant, I. (1790/1951), *Critique of Judgment*. New York: Hafner.

Keddie, N. (1971), 'Classroom knowledge', in M. Young (ed.), *Knowledge and Control: New Directions for the Sociology of Education*. London: Collier Macmillan.

Keddie, N. (ed.) (1973), *Tinker, Tailor . . ., The Myth of Cultural Deprivation*. London: Penguin.

Kenny, M. (1995), *The First New Left: British Intellectuals after Stalin*. London: Lawrence & Wishart.

Kernan, A. (1990), *The Death of Literature*. London: Yale University Press.

Kermode, F. (1983), *The Classic*. London: Harvard University Press.

King, J. (1970), 'The typology of universities'. *Higher Education Review*, 2, (3), 52–61.

Kitses, J. (1964), 'Screen education and social studies'. *Screen Education*, 22, (January to February), 19–27.

Knight, R. (1962), 'Film and television study in a training college'. *Screen Education*, (March to April), 7–18.

Knorr-Cetina, K. (1999), *Epistemic Cultures: How The Sciences Make Knowledge*. Cambridge MA: Harvard University Press.

Kuhn, T. S. (1970), *The Structure of Scientific Revolutions.* Chicago: University of Chicago Press.

Ladwig, J. (1995), 'The genesis of groups in the sociology of school knowledge', in W. Pink and G. Noblit (eds), *Continuity and Contradiction: The Futures of the Sociology of Education.* Cresskill, NJ: Hampton Press.

Lamont, A. and Maton, K. (2008), 'Choosing music: Exploratory studies into the low uptake of music GCSE'. *British Journal of Music Education,* 25, (3), 267–82.

Layton, D. (1984), *Interpreters of Science: A History of the Association for Science Education.* London: Murray; Association for Science Education.

Lopez, J. and Potter, G. (eds) (2001), *After Postmodernism: An Introduction to Critical Realism.* London: Athlone.

Lorde, A. (1984), *Sister Outsider.* Trumansburg, NY: Crossing Press.

Lukes, S. (1975), *Emile Durkheim – His Life and Work: A Historical and Critical Study.* London: Peregrine.

Luntley, M. (1995), *Reason, Truth and Self: The Postmodern Reconditioned.* London: Routledge.

McEwan, I. (2006), 'A parallel tradition'. *The Guardian Saturday Review,* 1 April, p. 4.

McGuigan, J. (ed.) (1997), *Cultural Methodologies.* London: Sage.

McNeil, M. (1997), 'It ain't like any other teaching': Some versions of teaching cultural studies', in J. E. Canaan and D. Epstein (eds), *A Question of Discipline.* Boulder, Colorado: Westview.

McRobbie, A. (1994), *Post-modernism and Popular Culture.* London: Routledge.

McRobbie, A. (ed.) (1997), *Back To Reality? Social Experience and Cultural Studies.* Manchester: Manchester University Press.

Mainds, R. (1965), 'Sixth form'. *Screen Education Yearbook 1965,* 99–102.

Markus, G. (2003), 'The paradoxical unity of culture: The Arts and the Sciences'. *Thesis Eleven,* 75, 7–24.

Mathieson, M. and Bernbaum, G. (1988), 'The British disease: A British Tradition'. *British Journal of Educational Research,* xxvi, (2), 126–75.

Maton, K. (2000), 'Recovering pedagogic discourse: A Bernsteinian approach to the sociology of educational knowledge'. *Linguistics & Education,* 11, (1), 79–98.

—(2002), 'Popes, Kings and cultural studies: Placing the commitment to non-disciplinarity in historical context', in S. Herbrechter (ed.), *Cultural Studies: Interdisciplinarity and Translation.* Amsterdam: Rodopi.

—(2005), 'A question of autonomy: Bourdieu's field approach and policy in higher education'. *Journal of Education Policy,* 20, (6), 687–704.

—(2007), 'Knowledge-knower structures in intellectual and educational fields', in F. Christie, and J. Martin (eds), *Language, Knowledge and Pedagogy.* London: Continuum.

—(2008), 'Grammars of sociology'. *Proceedings of the Fifth International Basil Bernstein Symposium.* Cardiff: Cardiff University, 9–12 July.

—(2009a), 'Cumulative and segmented learning: Exploring the role of curriculum structures in knowledge-building'. *British Journal of Sociology of Education,* 30, (1), 43–57.

—(2009b) 'Invisible tribunals: Progress and knowledge-building in the humanities', in Singh, P., Sadovnik, A. and Semel, S. (eds), *Toolkits, Translation Devices,*

Conceptual Tyrannies: Essays on Basil Bernstein's Sociology of Knowledge. New York: Peter Lang.

—(2009c), *Knowledge and Knowers.* London: Routledge.

Mendick, H. (2006), 'Review Symposium of Moore (2004)'. *British Journal of Sociology of Education,* 27, (1),117–23.

Merton, R. K. (1973), *The Sociology of Science: Theoretical and Empirical Investigations.* Chicago: University of Chicago Press.

Mills, C. (1998), 'Alternative epistemologies', in L. A. Alcoff (ed.), *Epistemology: The Big Questions.* Oxford: Blackwell.

Milner, A. (1994), *Contemporary Cultural Theory.* London: UCL Press.

Moore, R. (1996a), 'Back to the future: The problem of change and possibilities of advance in the sociology of education'. *British Journal of Sociology of Education,* 17, (2), 145–62.

—(1996b), 'Extended review: Richard Hoggart, "The Way We Live Now"'. *British Journal of Sociology of Education,* 17, (4), 521–30.

—(2000), 'For knowledge: Tradition, progressivism and progress in education – reconstructing the curriculum debate'. *Cambridge Journal of Education,* 30, (1), 17–36.

—(2004), *Education and Society: Issues and Explanations in the Sociology of Education.* Cambridge: Polity Press.

—(2009), *Towards the Sociology of Truth.* London: Continuum.

Moore, R. and Maton, K. (2001), 'Founding the sociology of knowledge: Basil Bernstein, intellectual fields and the epistemic device', in A. Morais, I. Neves, B. Davies and H. Daniels (eds), *Towards a Sociology of Pedagogy: The Contribution of Basil Bernstein to Research.* New York: Peter Lang.

Moore, R. and Muller, J. (2002), 'The growth of knowledge and the discursive gap'. *British Journal of Sociology of Education,* 23, (4), 627–37.

Morley, D. (1992), *Television, Audiences and Cultural Studies.* London: Routledge.

Morrissey, L. (2005), 'The canon brawl: Arguments over the canon', in L. Morrissey (ed.), *Debating the Canon.* New York: Palgrave Macmillan.

Muller, J. (2000), *Reclaiming Knowledge. Social Theory, Curriculum and Education Policy.* London: Routledge Falmer.

—(2007), 'On splitting hairs: Hierarchy, knowledge and the school curriculum', in F. Christie and J. Martin (eds), *Language, Knowledge and Pedagogy.* London: Continuum.

Muller, J. and Taylor, N. (1995), 'Schooling and everyday life: Knowledges sacred and profane'. *Social Epistemology,* 9, 257–75.

Murdock, G. (1997), 'Thin descriptions: Questions of method in cultural analysis', in J. McGuigan (ed.), *Cultural Methodologies.* London: Sage.

Nash, R. (2005), 'The cognitive habitus: Its place in a realist account of inequality/ difference'. *British Journal of Sociology of Education,* 26, 5.

National Committee of Inquiry into Higher Education (1997), *Higher Education in the Learning Society.* London: NICIHE.

National Union of Teachers (1960), *Popular Culture and Personal Responsibility: Verbatim Report.* London: NUT.

Newman, J. and Clarke, J. (1994), 'Going about our business? The managerialization of the public services', in J. Clarke, A. Cochrane and E. McLaughlin (eds), *Managing Social Policy.* London: Sage.

Newsom Report [Central Advisory Council for Education (England)] (1963), *Half Our Future*. London: HMSO

Niiniluoto, I. (2002), *Critical Scientific Realism*. Oxford: Oxford University Press.

Norris, C. (1997a), *Against Relativism*. London: Blackwell.

—(1997b), *New Idols of the Cave: On the Limits of Anti-Realism*. Manchester: Manchester University Press.

Nozaki, Y. (2006), 'Riding tensions critically: Ideology, power/knowledge, and curriculum making', in L. Weiss, C. McCarthy and G. Dimitriadis (eds), *Ideology, Curriculum and the New Sociology of Education*. New York and London: Routledge.

O'Halloran, K. L. (2007), 'Mathematical and scientific knowledge: A systemic functional multimodal grammatical approach', in F. Christie and J. Martin (eds), *Language, Knowledge and Pedagogy*. London: Continuum Press.

Olssen, M. (1997), 'Radical constructivism and its failings: Anti-realism and individualism'. *Journal of Educational Studies*, 14, 275–95.

Osborne, P. (1997), 'Friendly fire: The hoaxing of Social Text'. *Radical Philosophy*, 81, 54–6.

Papineau, D. (ed.) (1996), *The Philosophy of Science*. Oxford: Oxford University Press.

Penrose, R. (2006), *The Road to Reality: A Complete Guide to the Laws of the Universe*. London: Vintage.

Pickering, M. (1997), *History, Experience and Cultural Studies*. London: Macmillan.

Pollert, A. (1996), 'Gender and class revisited; or, the poverty of "patriarchy"'. *Sociology*, 30, (4), 639–59.

Popper, K. (1983), *Objective Knowledge: An Evolutionary Approach*. Oxford: Claredon Press.

—(1994), *The Myth of the Framework*. London: Routledge.

Priestley, M. (2002), 'Global discourses and national reconstruction: The impact of globalization on curriculum policy'. *The Curriculum Journal*, 13, (1), 121–38.

Pring, R. (1972), 'Knowledge out of control'. *Education for Teaching*, 89.

Qualifications and Curriculum Authority (1999), *Curriculum Guidance for 2000: Implementing the Changes to Post 16 Qualifications*. London: QCA.

Readings, B. (1996), *The University in Ruins*. Cambridge, MA: Harvard University Press.

Ross, T. (2000), *The Making of the English Literary Canon: From the Middle Ages to the Late Eighteenth Century*. Montreal: McGill-Queen's University Press.

Royal Society of Arts (1998), *Redefining Schooling: A Challenge to a Closed Society*. London: RSA.

Sayer, A. (2000), *Realism and Social Science*. London: Sage.

Schmaus, W. (1994), *Durkheim's Philosophy of Science and the Sociology of Knowledge*. Chicago: University of Chicago Press.

Schofield, K. and McDonald, R. (2004), *Moving On . . . Report of the High Level Review of Training Packages*. Brisbane: Australian National Training Authority.

Scott, J. (1994), 'The evidence of experience', in J. Chandler et al. (eds), *Questions of Evidence: Proof, Practice and Persuasion Across the Disciplines*. Chicago, IL: Chicago University Press.

Scott, P. (ed.) (2000), *Higher Education Reformed*. London: Falmer Press.

Scruton, R. (1991), 'The myth of cultural relativism', in R. Moore and J. Ozga (eds), *Curriculum Policy*. Oxford: Pergamon/OU.

Shapin, S. (1994), *A Social History of Truth: Civility and Science in 17th Century England.* Chicago: University of Chicago Press.

Shay, S. (2008), 'Beyond social constructivist perspectives on assessment: The centring of knowledge'. *Teaching in Higher Education,* 13, (5), 595–605.

Showalter, E. (1977), *A Literature of Their Own.* Princeton, NJ.: Princeton University Press.

—(1989), 'A criticism of our own: Autonomy and assimilation in Afro-American and feminist literary theory', in R. Cohen (ed.), *The Future of Literary Theory.* London: Routledge.

Siegel, H. (1997), *Rationality Redeemed?* London: Routledge.

Singh, P. (1998), *School Knowledge and Cultural Relevance.* Griffith University: mimeo.

Smith, E. and Keating, J. (2003), *From Training Reform to Training Packages.* Tuggerah: Social Science Press.

Sokal, A. (1998), *Intellectual Impostures: Postmodern Philosophers' Abuse of Science.* London: Profile Books.

Spivak, C. G. (1990), *The Postcolonial Critic: Interviews, Strategies, Dialogues.* London: Routledge.

Steele, T. (1997), *The Emergence of Cultural Studies: Cultural Politics, Adult Education and the English Question.* London: Lawrence & Wishart.

Stone, M. (1981), *The Education of the Black Child in Britain.* London: Fontana.

Stone, R. L. (ed.) (1989), *Essays on The Closing of the American Mind.* Chicago: Chicago Press Review.

Street, B. (1984), *Literacy in Theory and Practice.* Cambridge: Cambridge University Press.

Taylor, C. (1992), *Ethics of Authenticity.* Cambridge, MA: Harvard University Press.

Thompson, E. P. (1963), *The Making of the English Working Class.* Harmondsworth: Penguin.

Thornton, S. and Gelder, K. (eds) (1996), *The Subcultures Reader.* London: Routledge.

Tight, M. (1996), 'University typologies re-examined'. *Higher Education Review,* 29, (1), 57–77.

Toulmin, S. (1996), 'Knowledge as shared procedures', in Y. Engestrom, R. Mietennen and R. Punamaki (eds), *Perspectives on Activity Theory.* Cambridge: Cambridge University Press.

Turner, G. (1990), *British Cultural Studies: An Introduction.* London: Unwin Hyman.

Turner, R. H. (1971), 'Sponsored and contest mobility and the school system', in E. Hopper (ed.), *Readings in the Theory of Educational Systems.* London: Hutchinson.

University of Birmingham (1964–74), *Report of the Vice-Chancellor and Principal for the Calendar Year.* Birmingham: University of Birmingham.

—(1975–89), *Annual Reports and Accounts.* Birmingham: University of Birmingham.

Usher, R. and Edwards, R. (1994), *Postmodernism and Education.* London: Routledge.

von Hallberg, R. (1984a), 'Introduction', in R. von Hallberg (1984b), *Canons.* Chicago: University of Chicago Press.

von Hallberg, R. (ed.) (1984b), *Canons.* Chicago: University of Chicago Press.

Ward, S. (1996), *Reconfiguring Truth: Post-Modernism, Science Studies and the Search for a New Model of Knowledge.* New York: Rowman & Littlefield.

—(1997), 'Being objective about objectivity: The ironies of standpoint epistemological critiques of science'. *Sociology*, 31, (4), 773–91.

Watson, J. G. (1977), 'Letter to the Editor: Cultural studies and English studies'. *Times Higher Education Supplement*, 29 July 1977, (301), 5.

Warburton, N. (2004), 'Is art sacred?', in B. Rogers (ed.), *Is Nothing Sacred?* Abingdon, Oxfordshire: Routledge.

Weiss, L., McCarthy, C. and Dimitriades, G. (eds) (2006), *Ideology, Curriculum and the New Sociology of Education: Revisiting the Work of Michael Apple.* New York and London: Routledge.

Wellens, J. (1970), 'The anti-intellectual tradition in the west', in P. Musgrave (ed.), *Sociology, History and Education.* London: Methuen.

West, D. (1996), *An Introduction to Continental Philosophy.* Oxford: Polity Press.

Wexler, P. (1997), *Social Research in Education: Ethnography of Being.* University of Rochester: mimeo.

Wheelahan, L. and Moodie, G. (2005), 'Separate post-compulsory education sectors within a liberal market economy: Interesting models generated by the Australian anomaly', in J. Gallacher and M. Osborne (eds), *A Contested Landscape: International Perspectives on Diversity in Mass Higher Education.* Leicester: NIACE.

Wheen, F. (2004), *How Mumbo-Jumbo Conquered the World.* London: Harper Perennial.

Whitley, R. (2000), *The Intellectual and Social Organisation of the Sciences.* Oxford: Oxford University Press.

Whitty, G. and Young, M. (1976), *Explorations in the Politics of School Knowledge.* Driffield, Yorks: Nafferton Books.

Williams, B. (2002), *Truth and Truthfulness: An Essay in Genealogy.* Princeton: Princeton University Press.

Williams, C. (2005), 'The discursive construction of the 'competent' learner-worker: From Key Competencies to "employability skills"', *Studies in Continuing Education*, 27, (1), 33–49.

Williams, R. (1958), *Culture and Society: 1780–1950.* Harmondsworth: Penguin.

—(1961), *The Long Revolution.* London: Chatto and Windus.

—(1968), 'Different sides of the wall'. *The Guardian*, 26 September.

—(1989), *The Politics of Modernism: Against the New Conformists.* London: Verso.

Willis, P. (1977), *Learning to Labour: How Working-Class Kids Get Working-Class Jobs.* London: Saxon House.

Wolpe, A. (1998), '"Where angels fear to tread": Assessment of feminism in South Africa', in J. Mouton and J. Muller (eds), *Theory and Method in South African Social Research.* Pretoria: Human Sciences Research Council.

Women's Studies Group, CCCS (1978), *Women Take Issue: Aspects of Women's Subordination.* London: Hutchinson.

Woodhead, C. (2001), 'Blair and Blunkett have not delivered. The children have been betrayed'. Telegraph online 1 March 2001. http://www.telegraph.co.uk.

Wright, H. K. (1998), 'Dare we de-centre Birmingham? Troubling the "origin" and trajectories of cultural studies'. *European Journal of Cultural Studies*, 1, (1), 33–56.

Young, M. F. D. (ed.) (1971), *Knowledge and Control: New Directions for the Sociology of Education.* London: Collier Macmillan.

Young, M. F. D. (1976), 'Commonsense categories and curriculum thought', in R. Dale, G. Esland and M. Macdonald (eds), *Schooling and Capitalism.* London: Routledge & Kegan Paul/Open University Press.

—(1998), *The Curriculum of the Future: From the 'New Sociology of Education' to a Critical Theory of Learning.* London: Falmer Press.

—(1999), 'Knowledge, learning and the curriculum of the future'. *British Educational Research Journal,* 25, (4), 463–77.

—(2000a), 'Bringing knowledge back in: A curriculum for lifelong learning', in A. Hodgson (ed.), *Policies, Politics and the Future of Lifelong Learning.* London: Kogan Page.

—(2000b), 'Rescuing the sociology of knowledge from the extremes of voice discourse: Towards a new theoretical basis for the sociology of the curriculum'. *British Journal of Sociology of Education,* 21, (4), 523–36.

—(2003), 'Durkheim, Vygotsky and the curriculum of the future'. *London Review of Education,* 1, (2), 100–17.

—(2006), 'Review of Weiss et al. (ed.) (2006)'. *London Review of Education* 4, (3), 306–08.

—(2008), *Bringing Knowledge Back In: From Social Constructivism to Social Realism.* London: Routledge.

Young, M. F. D. and Whitty, G. (eds) (1977), *Society, State and Schooling.* Brighton: Falmer Press.

Ziman, J. (2000), *Real Science.* Cambridge: Cambridge University Press.

Index